CURRENT ISSUES IN HUMAN RIGHTS AND INTERNATIONAL RELATIONS

PAPERS FROM THE CLEMENS NATHAN RESEARCH CENTRE

CURRENT ISSUES IN HUMAN RIGHTS AND INTERNATIONAL RELATIONS

PAPERS FROM THE CLEMENS NATHAN RESEARCH CENTRE

Clemens N. Nathan
Editor

MARTINUS NIJHOFF PUBLISHERS

Leiden • Boston
2010

Printed on acid-free paper

ISBN 978-90-04-17985-1

Koninklijke Brill NV incorporates the imprints Brill, Hotei Publishing, IDC Publishers, Martinus Nijhoff Publishers and VSP.

http://www.brill.nl

Cover picture from a series of photographs of an art work by Miri Greenson: "Memory, Contemplation and Hope" (mirigreenson@yahoo.com)

Typeset by AETS (aetsonline@gmail.com)

PRINTED AND BOUND IN THE NETHERLANDS

Table of Contents

Part II: Foreign Policy and Human Rights

Part III: International Development and Human Rights

Part IV: Public Lectures on Conflict

Introduction

The Clemens Nathan Research Centre (CNRC), an organisation dedicated to the promotion of international human rights, began life as the research arm of the Consultative Council of Jewish Organisations (CCJO), a human rights NGO with consultative status at the United Nations, founded in 1946 by the Nobel Prize Laureate René Cassin. The constituent organisations of the CCJO are currently the Anglo-Jewish Association and the Alliance israélite universelle.

In recent times, the CNRC has operated more independently. It is named after its Chairman, Clemens N. Nathan. Its Director of Research is Alan Stephens. Since its establishment in 2004, the CNRC has initiated a number of innovative programmes, including a long-term research project, in collaboration with the International Bar Association (IBA) and the Raoul Wallenberg Institute, Lund University, Sweden, to formulate rules of conduct for human rights fact-finding missions. This project reached an important milestone on 1 June 2009, with the inauguration, in London, of the Guidelines on International Human Rights Fact-Finding Visits and Reports (The Lund-London Guidelines; see: www.factfindingguidelines.org).

Since February 2005, the CNRC has organised seven ground-breaking and widely-acclaimed conferences: in Lund on Fact-Finding (with the Raoul Wallenberg Institute and the IBA), in The Hague on Reparations for the Victims of Human Rights Abuses (with REDRESS and with the support of the Hague Academic Coalition),[1] in Chester on Reparations and Prosthetics, and in London on Religion and Human Rights (with the Commonwealth Institute, University of London),[2] Terrorism and Human Rights, Foreign Policy and

[1] Carla Ferstman, Mariana Goetz and Alan Stephens (eds.), *Reparations for Victims of Genocide, War Crimes and Crimes Against Humanity. Systems in Place and Systems in the Making* (Leiden & Boston, Martinus Nijhoff Publishers 2009).

[2] Nazila Ghanea, Alan Stephens and Raphael Walden (eds.), *Does God Believe in Human Rights? Essays on Religion and Human Rights* (Leiden & Boston, Martinus Nijhoff Publishers 2007).

Human Rights and Freedom of the Media and Human Rights, the last three having been held at Arundel House, the premises of the International Institute of Strategic Studies. The keynote speakers at the these conferences included Richard Harries, then Bishop of Oxford; Lord Guthrie, former Chief of the Defence Staff of the United Kingdom; Sir Jeremy Greenstock, former UK Ambassador to the United Nations; and Andrew Puddephat, Director of Global Partners and Associates. The Centre's forthcoming events include a conference on Health and Human Rights.

The CNRC also organises periodic René Cassin Memorial Lectures. Lecturers have included Professor Bertrand Ramcharan, former acting UN High Commissioner for Human Rights (lecture held at Chatham House, London) and M. Robert Badinter, former Minister of Justice of France (lecture held at the Law Society, London).

Prior to the Centre's establishment, similar projects had been part of the range of activities undertaken directly by the CCJO, which was founded to encourage recognition of human rights for all and for the protection of Jews from persecution throughout the world. A younger members' group, CCJO-René Cassin, has recently been formed to encourage young people in the fields in which CCJO operates. Through its constituent organisations, the CCJO played a central role from the beginning of the negotiations for the rights of surviving victims of the Nazi Holocaust to receive reparation and restitution. In the 1970s, it lent its weight to the campaign to highlight the plight of the persecuted Jews of the Soviet bloc. The CCJO was particularly concerned with the situation of former slave workers, victims of the Nazi regime, who had not received compensation. It is now following closely the development of UN guidelines on reparations, restitution and compensation that will underlie the right of all victims of international human rights violations to recourse to justice for the evils they have suffered.

The CCJO has been an active supporter of efforts to increase the effectiveness of the UN's human rights treaties and institutional mechanisms. From the 1940s to the 1970s, it was involved in the creation of the United Nations human rights instruments that form the basis of UN human rights protection work. The CCJO keeps a watching brief on some international human rights problems and developments and took a particular interest in the establishment of the International Criminal Court. CCJO briefings have been presented to various international bodies on subjects ranging from the conflicts in former Yugoslavia to problems relating to laws dealing with the migration of workers.

CCJO representatives were active at the Durban Conference on Racism, at conferences on counter-terrorism in Israel and at meetings and conferences on anti-Semitism held by the Organisation for Security and Cooperation in Europe (OSCE). The CCJO has sponsored a collection of essays on Racism and Human Rights and a work by Professor Anne Bayefsky entitled *How to Complain to the UN Human Rights Treaty System*.[3]

The activities of both the Clemens Nathan Research Centre and the CCJO have benefited from the very generous support of the Shoresh Charitable Trust.

The CNRC is now pleased to present this collection of papers, selected and edited by its Chairman in order to make available to a wider public the excellent materials prepared within the context of its conferences and other activities.

[3] Anne F. Bayefsky (ed.), *How to Complain to the UN Human Rights Treaty System* (Leiden, Kluwer Law International 2002).

Part I:
Terrorism and Human Rights

Terrorism:
How Dangerous is the Threat?

General the Lord Guthrie of Craigiebank*

Terrorism has been around since the dawn of history. It has not just been invented. In the twentieth century, terrorism was a familiar phenomenon. Many countries suffered: France, Northern Ireland, the United Kingdom, Spain, India, Pakistan, the Middle and Near East and Russia. The list goes on and on. Some countries were more fortunate than others and have had less of a terrorist problem. Until recently, the United States could be numbered among them.

Although terrorism has always been with us, there is still no common agreement on how to define a terrorist. Politicians, the military and the United Nations cannot agree. There is a well-known saying, an unhelpful one but one that has some truth in it, that one man's terrorist is another man's freedom fighter. Palestinians who take their own lives when killing others are described by some as heroes going on martyrdom operations and by others as evil suicide bombers. It was only a short time ago that many US citizens advocated and funded the cause of the IRA, which was killing British soldiers and civilians. I am not going to attempt to give you a definition but have some sympathy with the judge who said he could not define pornography but knew what it was when he saw it. The paradox of terrorism and violence is that most of us both condemn it and condone it. Violence is widely abhorred, yet frequently employed.

Are we now, since 9/11 in New York, really living in a different world? Are the Russians really living in a different world because of Chechen terrorists? Is the world at war with terrorism? There is a serious divergence of opinion. Many do not accept the idea of a 'war'. They believe good policing, good intelligence, justice, human rights and good governance solve terrorism.

---

* General the Lord Guthrie of Craigiebank, GCB, LVO, OBE.

Many fear that the United States is engaging in an endless war and became engaged without considering all the possible consequences. The Americans use the term war more freely than we do. They talk about a 'war on drugs', a 'war on poverty'; neither of which incidentally look like being won.

I do not think we should be surprised that attitudes are different. What happened in New York created an urgency and a reaction that were not replicated elsewhere, where it was felt in the recent past that terrorism could be managed with democratic measures. Moreover, the rhetoric of the United States – 'axis of evil', 'crusade', 'smoke them out', 'kick butt' and the very term 'war' itself – was less than helpful. Understandably, many governments in Europe and elsewhere were also anxious not to stir up or frighten their own Muslim populations, who needed to be calmed down rather than excited.

These differences do not help, but I do believe we need a new and more international approach. I speak as someone who spent a surprisingly large part of his forty-four years as an army officer on active anti-terrorist operations in different parts of the world – in Malaysia, Cyprus, East and West Africa, the South Pacific, the Yemen, Oman and Northern Ireland. Unlike some of today's terrorists, none of those I was operating against, though some were Islamic, wished to die for their cause like some Muslims do today. I was never confronted by a suicide bomber.

We may not be at *war*, but much of today's terrorism is, in some ways, *different* to what we knew; and I suggest we should have faced up to this some time ago. The signs were there *well before* 9/11. But the Twin Towers brutally brought home to us what the problem was. Al-Qaeda and Osama bin Laden were known about in the 1980s. They committed atrocities, but governments were very coy about doing anything about it, such as spending money, cooperating internationally with intelligence and defining threats or even discussing the problem, and having a common approach to terrorism. They hoped the problem would go away; at the very least it would be another government's problem, not theirs. How often did the United States or the United Kingdom discuss al-Qaeda with Russia, or *vice versa*? How often did we share intelligence? I was very struck how, when I retired, my Russian opposite number told me that he felt that the British should wake up to the threat of Islamic terrorism and that we had Islamic terrorists living in England plotting against Russia. Russia, I think, was more aware of the threats than we were; but when I asked General Krasnin, my opposite number, for evidence of terrorists living in the United Kingdom, none was produced.

Today, several developments have made societies more vulnerable. Modern civilisation, with its highly developed technology, has certainly made our lives more efficient, comfortable and easy, but many of our vital systems such as air, road and rail travel, information systems and energy are easy targets to attack and disrupt, which would lead to catastrophe. Sophisticated states, societies and businesses are easy to damage.

We also see technology helping the terrorist in other ways. Weapons of mass destruction, which used to be expensive and unwieldy, are now small, light and cheap to manufacture. A terrorist who hijacks a high-tech aircraft can also find himself flying a devastating weapon for little more than the price of an airline ticket, as the Twin Towers illustrated.

The information revolution has provided an inexpensive means of communication to ill-intentioned groups and individuals. Once, such communications were so expensive that only governments, the military, the police and multinational companies could afford them. Today, terrorists in London, New York, Bali, Afghanistan and Moscow can cheaply hold a conference call. Plotting, research, exchanging information and planning are now easier for the terrorist than they ever were. Terrorists do not have to meet before they carry out an operation.

Another difference of terrorism today, a new trend, is *what* motivates terrorists. In the mid-twentieth century, most terrorists tended to have relatively well-defined political objectives, such as liberation from colonial rule, the righting of perceived or real social and ethnic grievances and the release of political prisoners. Sometimes governments supported and controlled terrorists, often covertly supporting terrorism in other countries. Towards the end of the century, radical groups grew up on the fringes of several religions. Most numerous were the thousands of young Muslim men who went to fight against the Soviet occupation of Afghanistan. Many were recruited to organisations with an extreme view of the religious obligation of *jihad*. Terrorism has become more brutal and indiscriminate. This is reinforced for some terrorists (though by no means all or even a majority) by promises of rewards in another world. At the touch of a button a young suicide bomber can be transported to eternal paradise.

Terrorist organisations have changed. For example, al-Qaeda's network of 10,000 people with loosely affiliated cells in some sixty countries gives it a scale well beyond anything we have seen before. The emphasis here is on loosely affiliated: slum dwellers in Cairo, second generation Pakistanis in the United Kingdom, Afghan *mujahedin*, Muslim fanatics in the United States, Chechens and Algerian and Moroccan immigrants in France have little in common – except a roughly similar ideology. They certainly do not have a chain of command as we know it. Terrorists can now operate both internationally and cross-border. Because terrorists are now loosely affiliated, less structured and less hierarchical, their networks are much harder to penetrate.

We now have two new aspects of terrorism – the first technological, the second ideological – that have increased our difficulties in dealing with terrorism.

Today, we have terrorists who embrace globalisation. Because of 9/11 and the unprecedented scale of al-Qaeda and their affiliates, the current focus is on terrorism associated with Islamic extremists. But we should not forget that every large group of people has some members who deviate from the norm and that some of them are bent on destruction and creating catastrophe.

For example, the worst case of terrorism in the United States before 9/11 was perpetrated by Timothy McVeigh in Oklahoma. He killed 168 people and injured 600. He was a purely home-grown, anti-US-government fanatic. In addition, the Japanese cult that released sarin gas in the Tokyo subway system in 1995 – leading to thousands being hospitalised – had nothing to do with Islam, like Timothy McVeigh. There are many more examples of non-Islamic terrorism. Islamic terrorism may be what currently preoccupies much of the world, but the threat can be multifaceted and we would be unwise to forget this. What about the anti-abortionists in the United States who have killed doctors who work in abortion clinics, or even the animal rights fanatics who kill those who carry out experiments on animals? They are terrorists.

Today, a pathological individual can – alone or with very little help form others – kill thousands. It is not inconceivable that, in the future, such an individual could kill millions. In the past, when pathological killers murdered vast numbers – people like Hitler and Stalin – they could only do so with the apparatus of a state behind them.

Lethality has been increasing. The 9/11 attack cost thousands of lives. Beslan cost hundreds. These attacks did not involve weapons of mass destruction. Much of the new terrorism is not like the 1970s' terrorism of the IRA in the United Kingdom, ETA in Spain or the Red Brigades in Germany and Italy. The what you might call 'business as usual' attitude towards curbing terrorism is not enough. Although I do not believe that we should overemphasise the threat, it must be faced head-on. The risk of a dirty 'radiological' bomb is increasing. In 1996, there were eight incidents of smuggling radioactive materials suitable for such a device. In 2003, there were fifty-one. We know that al-Qaeda wants to acquire radiological materials, but we should not overemphasise the risk. It is extremely difficult to make such devices, and there are other ways to terrorise that are cheaper. We know that they exist today because they have already been used.

What should we be doing to tackle terrorism? Can we succeed? We need to ask ourselves whether we have the will. It may be impossible to eliminate all terrorist incidents, but if we can reduce their number, their frequency and their lethality our societies will greatly benefit. I do not believe that we will ever be able to stop every terrorist, but we should be able to find an acceptable level. We must not regard the situation as too difficult and inevitable.

Many would disagree with me about even talking about an acceptable level. I was certainly very much criticised by the British prime minister, Margaret Thatcher, when, as chief of the defence staff, I told her we could not eliminate every terrorist in Northern Ireland but should be able to reach an acceptable level of violence.

Can we develop a strategy to tackle terrorism? There are several factors that need to be considered in this regard.

First of all, terrorism cannot be solved unilaterally. Multinational cooperation is essential, as terrorism is everybody's burden. Some countries – I believe mistakenly – wish to avoid the budgetary burden of military and civil measures or providing assistance. Even more dangerous is the temptation to think that by appeasing terrorists, paying them off, a country can avoid trouble for itself. This is very unlikely to be a solution in the long term. Saudi Arabia, for example, has been accused of paying al-Qaeda not to attack them.

Secondly, there is inevitable tension between the need for security measures and the need to protect freedoms. Issues of national security can never justify abandoning the rule of law. But neither can the law be so interpreted as to frustrate legitimate measures designed to protect the public against terrorism. I believe that it is absolutely right to consider changing our laws because of recent developments and new threats. I recognise that this is an extremely difficult area in which to reach agreement. It goes without saying that our liberties are of the greatest importance to the nation, but so are the lives of innocent people. It seems to me that what the British government proposed regarding the detention of terror suspects, and I speak as a crossbench peer who spends more time criticising the government over defence and security than supporting it, was thoroughly sensible. It recognised people's concerns. The proposed 90-day detention period was not like internment in Northern Ireland, and those who suggested it were either ignorant or disingenuous. Every seven days, the police would have to argue before a high court judge why they needed to detain a suspect. The burden of proof was on the police. Surely, high court judges are capable of ensuring procedures are fair. The government also added a sunset clause to alleviate fears of unnecessarily prolonging the legislation.

Terrorist organisations are now far more sophisticated and international than they were before. Investigations are complicated and often involve searching for evidence in other countries. The trail could lead to Pakistan, Indonesia or the Philippines – and needs to be followed if outrages in our own or other countries are to be prevented.

I think the government and police deserved our support on the issue of 90-day detention. The hysterical and shrill protests of some, including certain law lords, was misplaced, and our country now faces a greater risk than necessary. To say that we are being propelled towards a police state seems to me to be complete nonsense.

Illegal measures such as torture very rarely assist in counter-terrorist operations. Very occasionally they may help in the short term, but hardly ever in the long term. Torture is almost bound to make matters far worse. It brutalises the torturers and rots the soul, adding to those who sympathise with the terrorist. The example of French army in Algeria is very illustrative in this regard. Torture should never be condoned or excused, and those who carry out torture must be pursued and severely punished.

Thirdly, every effort must be made to suppress the financing of terrorist acts. This is a hugely important area. It involves governments, banks, financial institutions and regulators and forms an international challenge. So far, the international community has failed to achieve much success.

Fourthly, the military certainly has an important part to play – a part only it can play. However, civil measures are also very important, perhaps more so than military measures. The police, judges, drafters of constitutions, prison officers and others all play a crucial role. This is what we call 'soft' power, as opposed to 'hard' power. Having spent forty-four years in the army, I am sure that conflict is easier than conflict resolution, which is almost always more expensive than the conflict itself and goes on for longer. The aim should be to combine hard power (military power) and soft power (civil measures) in the correct manner, and that is a very difficult balance to achieve.

Intelligence also has to be more widely shared. This is not as easily done as it sounds. Sources have to be protected. It would be foolish to share intelligence with certain countries where many people openly or secretly sympathise with the terrorists. But we do need to assess long-term threats together and share both strategic and tactical intelligence whenever we can. This can be costly. Huge sums of money have been spent on technical intelligence, particularly by the United States. However, in my view, not enough has been spent on human intelligence: spies, agents and friends.

In the past, the United States – particularly the administrations of President Carter and President Clinton – appears to have been rather squeamish about agents and human intelligence gathering. One reason for this was that they had been embarrassed by the criminal activities of some of their agents. But if you want to find out about nasty, evil people – terrorists – you probably need to send nasty people to penetrate their networks and mix with them. Agents and spies take many years to develop and at the time of 9/11 we had very few.

We also need to actually understand why a terrorist is a terrorist and why he follows a certain leader before we can develop a coherent approach.

For example, why does Osama bin Laden have so many followers? Whether we like it or not, he is a hero to many Muslims. Why is he such an attractive leader? I believe that there are several reasons for this. He is a fine-looking man. This matters, because he looks the part. He speaks beautiful Arabic. He is articulate and advocates his beliefs well. He has a simple message he repeats again and again. In addition, he understands Arab history. Most Arabs have an interest in history. I have rarely heard an Arab dismiss the past as though it did not matter. You do hear history being dismissed in Europe and the United States as having little relevance to the future. Osama bin Laden plays on the Arab interest in history and has talked about how the once all-powerful and civilised Islamic world has been humiliated since the fall of the Ottoman Empire eighty years ago. Bin Laden has often spoken about this. Many Arabs do feel humiliated and their shame is crucial for us to understand.

Osama bin Laden is also unusual in that he has actually shared the same dangers as his followers. He has been in the mountains of Afghanistan and been bombed by US planes. He has taken the same risks, and he has given his wealth to the cause. He came from an immensely rich family, and he himself sponsored al-Qaeda. He is no longer immensely rich. All these things make him charismatic and an icon for tens of thousands of Muslims worldwide.

In Kano, a Muslim town in Nigeria, of one hundred boys born in the government hospital in one week, seventy-two were given the name Osama.

Bin Laden has a very simple message: remove from the region the despotic Arab rulers and their evil supporters, the United States and its allies. Having such a simple message is important. It must be easy to understand if it is to be effective.

I find it alarming that world there are many people in the Muslim who still believe that al-Qaeda will prevail. They say, first, that al-Qaeda is resolute and totally committed to its cause. Is the United States? What do they really believe in? What are Americans passionate about and willing to die for? Many of them – and I am not talking about uneducated Arabs – are certain the United States will abandon Iraq. They are convinced the United States always does leave when the going gets tough. They cite Beirut, Somalia and, of course, Vietnam. They also say the United States will abandon its allies. Certainly many Pakistanis feel that they will be abandoned. They say they were abandoned before by the United States after the Soviet Union left Afghanistan and they were no longer useful. The fact that the United States did not stand by the Kurds or the Marsh Arabs after they had been encouraged to revolt against Saddam Hussein and were brutally suppressed is well remembered. It is depressing that this is the perception of many people in the Muslim world. Whatever we think, it matters what they think.

We also need to develop a common approach towards proliferation. Weapons of mass destruction are not science fiction. They have been used. Although difficult, it is not inconceivable for a terrorist to make a nuclear weapon if he can get his hands on the necessary nuclear materials. These could be procured. They are not all in safe hands. Nuclear fissile material is certainly not impossible to find. Today, the suicide bomber is armed with explosives; tomorrow, if the opportunity arises, he could be armed with much more deadly nuclear, chemical or biological devices.

Next, what can be done about failed or failing states? Failed states are fertile breeding grounds for terrorists; it is in our interests to coordinate our efforts to help them. Helping is, of course, not only about funding and aid. It is much more. Every failed state is different. Some require firmness, some encouragement. But if the ultimate goal is good governance, dignity and human rights, the more the international community can adopt a common approach the better. We need to identify states before they fail.

Lastly, religion and conflict are ancient partners that remain inextricably linked. Many wars and conflicts in human history were supported by at least one religious institution. But if religion sometimes supports war or conflict, it is important to remember that religion usually also forms the basis of antiwar and peace movements. The trouble with the current situation is that good, civilised men and women from different religions can achieve dialogue and understanding, but that they have no influence whatsoever on the extremists who come from the fringes of their own religion and are intent on destruction.

and the West, along with moderate Muslims throughout the world, is up against extremists, some of whom believe in death and regard the innocent people they kill as a passport to paradise. They represent a radically new danger. I believe that perhaps the greatest downside of the war in Iraq today is that many moderate Muslims have become sympathetic to the extremists. I firmly believe that, in the long term, moderate Muslims are far better equipped to handle Muslim extremists than anybody else. The war has made it harder for this to happen.

In my view, terrorism can never be excused or condoned. We are faced with a long and gruelling struggle against terrorists, many of whom have a passion for their cause and have no doubt they will prevail. Whether one was for or against US and British actions in Iraq, the support should now be unequivocal. Too many people in the world would like to see the United States humiliated further and fail. If this happens, terrorists around the world – not just Muslim terrorists – and their sympathisers will be energised, and the forces of tolerance and progress will be on the run.

The threat is very serious, but it is crucial that we maintain a sense of perspective. The terrorists are certainly not having it all their own way. They have suffered serious reverses. In many areas, they have been weakened and their operatives killed or captured. The security services have done well and thwarted numerous attacks. We owe them much in the United Kingdom. However, we must not drop our guard, as terrorists only need to get lucky once. We need to hold our nerve and not falter. Do we really have the will to prevail?

Future Tasks for Security Agencies in the Fight Against Terrorism

Anthony Glees*

I believe that we are at war – a war against terror. It is a different sort of war from the wars we have previously fought, against an enemy who is different in some ways – but not every way – from the sorts of enemies that the liberal democracies faced in the twentieth century.

I very much hope that one day the key problems posed by this war will be solved. I am not sure they will be solved, but in the short term we have to take short-term measures to deal with what I believe is a new war. This paper argues that there are four big tasks for the security agencies in the fight against terrorism in the future.

The first of these tasks is to think of ways to help the security and intelligence agencies, and also the British public, to understand the nature of the threat we face. I will argue that the UK agencies did not always properly understand that threat prior to 9/11. In order that they may do so properly today, I believe that that the government should establish what I would call, for want of a better term, a 'national institute of intelligence excellence'. My argument is that the importance of having excellent intelligence on which the UK security and intelligence community can act is so great that it cannot simply be left to the people who are charged with collecting and analysing intelligence to decide what they should be doing and how they should be doing it. I believe that a national institute of intelligence excellence should exist to add a new dimension to the UK security and intelligence community and introduce fresh thinking into how it goes about its duties.

The second task for the future is to carry out a proper, dispassionate and objective public audit of Britain's intelligence and security successes and

* Professor Anthony Glees, Director of the Centre for Intelligence and Security Studies, Brunel University.

failures. I believe that the relevant statutory body – the Security and Intelligence Committee of Parliamentarians – is not sufficiently skilled for what has become a vitally important job.

The third task for the future is for the experts in the field to continually *remind* the public of the nature of the security threat. It is in the nature of human beings that they do not wish to dwell on the unpleasant things in their life. However, people need to be reminded, since public opinion is rightly deemed to be very important in our democracy. I have been very shocked by some of the things that were said in the UK parliament during the debate on anti-terrorism and by parliamentarians on radio and television and in newspapers. Memories can be very short where difficult and unpleasant matters are involved.

The fourth future task for the agencies is to begin work now on a series of much smaller tasks. I have listed several of tasks below.

That is the scope of the argument presented in this paper. These are all specifically targeted tasks that address the future issues facing us in our search for security, bearing in mind that some long-term political solution may or may not be found that would allow us to take a step back. It would be wonderful if this were the case, but I do not believe it will be.

Academics have historically played a remarkable role in the development of British intelligence and security agencies, particularly during their 'finest hour' in the Second World War. The great intelligence successes of the United Kingdom at that time may in large part be attributed to the fact that the agencies pulled into the community first-rate minds from academia. Bletchley Park is the obvious example, but it is by no means the only example of the ways in which academics have contributed to national security. They can and should do so today.

Academic skills and talents are also ways of adding value to the analysis of intelligence. It appears that the UK security services, including MI5, for example, are going to have to double the number of officers that they are recruiting. Academics may need to be brought in to make sure these people are properly trained. Indeed, academics may also be needed to advise on recruitment issues that exist when any institution is to be doubled in size. At the moment, the UK intelligence services tend to recruit people a bit like a modelling agency tends to recruit models. It goes for people with self-evident talents, who present straightaway the qualities of potential self-starting intelligence officers, with the necessary personal and analytical skills – just as a particularly pretty face and body are the prime requirements for a model. Perhaps, however, this is not the best way to recruit intelligence officers.

Perhaps the intelligence and security agencies should recruit individuals in the same way as the armed forces do, that is to say, by selecting people whom they believe they can train and turn into the final product that they need and want. Natural talent is, of course, always part of any recruitment activity. But good skills training is just as important – arguably even more important – because those who seem to have most potential and promise in their early or mid-twenties may turn out to be disappointments ten years later. Perhaps the UK intelligence and security agencies have recruited too many high-flyers and not enough people who simply want to be trained to be good detectives, which is what the basis of first-rate intelligence and security work must always be.

This is one good reason why academic experts should be entitled to make an input into this secret world. Another is that academics can alert the intelligence and security authorities to the continuous need to question the constraints under which they operate. Academics, as outsiders, can see the things to which the insiders have become blind. During the past thirty years, I have been struck by the extent to which agencies have moved from being *impervious* to democratic pressures to being almost too *porous* to real and imagined democratic pressures. If one examines the attitude, for example, of the legal profession or many media commentators towards the intelligence and security agencies (including the police) and observes what they say about them, it appears that that the security and intelligence agencies too often become highly nervous. Indeed, they frequently give the impression of being cowed, wrong-footed in public and placed on the defensive. I do not believe that this is a very good place for the security and intelligence agencies to be, especially at a time like this.

This brings us back to the so-called national institute of intelligence excellence, which may be defined as a safe forum where security, intelligence and even ordinary police officers can meet with academics, journalists, lawyers and others to discuss the major intelligence and security issues of the day. Why have an institute rather than one or two specific experts? It is true that the latter idea has been mooted and that it has also been realised. In my view, our society sets too much store in including in our governance just one or two pundits rather than a much larger, and more representative, number. An analogy is provided by those criminal and medical trials in which huge weight is placed on the testimony of one particular expert, only for it to be seen as biased and ultimately worthless. That is why I am *not* suggesting 'punditry'. Instead, I am suggesting that a hundred flowers should bloom. One or two pundits can only queer the pitch, relishing the power they possess and forgetting their duty to be scientific and objective at all times.

At the moment, in intelligence, security and elsewhere, too much weight is placed on too few. Pundits do not always get things right. One pundit in this field is Crispin Black. He is rightly seen as one of the United Kingdom's foremost intelligence and security experts, a man with actual practical experience as an intelligence analyst, who is widely consulted in the media and listened to with care and attention. He wrote in *The Guardian* on 7 April 2004 that British intelligence was doing very well in the campaign against Islamist terror. 'In many ways,' he said, 'the news is good'. He pointed to the success of the computer programme code-named Echelon, which is able to sniff through millions of messages a day for hints of terrorist communications. In April 2004, he gave an assurance that the UK security community had a good sense of how Islamist terrorists planned and mounted their attacks, and concluded, 'We already have one *inestimable* advantage in our battle against these terrorists – we know where to look.'

However, fifteen months later, it emerged that he was quite wrong. We *did not* know where to look. We *did not* know where to look in our own *communities* for people who were prepared to kill themselves and as many other people as they could get.

It is not only pundits that get things wrong and claim that things are alright when in fact the reverse is the case. This is also something that one finds in parts of the media from time to time. One example of this is a BBC Radio 4 programme that was never broadcast. It was a pilot for a new series that, on this occasion, took the form of an address by a noted professor of international law from the London School of Economics to a panel (including the present author) on whether there was a new and dangerous terror threat to Britain following 9/11. Recording was arranged for 30 June 2005.

The professor did not believe there was any need for new anti-terrorist legislation in Britain, because there was nothing to suggest that we were dealing with any new kind of terrorist threat from Islamist extremists. It seems to me that the context in which his remarks were to be understood was the famous statement of Lord Hoffmann, who said on 16 December 2004 in respect of the government's policy of detaining suspected terrorists who were not UK nationals and did not wish to return to their country of origin: 'There is no state of public emergency threatening the life of the British nation. The *real* threat to the life of this nation comes not from terrorism but from laws such as these.' While it is the case that the judgment that Lord Hoffmann helped to construct had touched on the European Convention on Human Rights and whether the government's plans conflicted with it, he was not simply making a legal assessment (which is what he was meant to be doing) but also making a political one (which he should not be doing). It is not for a judge, even one in the House of Lords, to say to an elected government that its *political* evaluation of the future terrorist threat to Britain is wrong and, indeed, that its proposed laws are the real threat to British democracy.

Apparently building on this argument, the law professor from London declared repeatedly that no special laws were necessary. In effect, his case was there was no new terrorist threat facing Britain. Any so-called terrorists should be treated, he explained, simply as straightforward criminals, because that was what they were. I strongly disagreed with his argument, as did others, including the distinguished legal expert Joshua Rozenberg and security expert Dr Sandra Bell from the Royal United Services Institute, where the programme was being recorded. We all argued that it was not a question of whether but of when an Islamist terror attack would take place on mainland Britain.

At the end of the debate, the audience was asked to vote on whether they believed what the law professor or what the panellists, who disagreed with him, had said. I believe that four to one they voted with the law professor, on the grounds that there was no a terrorist threat. In particular, they appeared to have accepted the argument that, because the prime minister had used intelligence about weapons of mass destruction in Iraq to justify a war and there had been none, there was no reason to believe him now when he said intelligence suggested there would be a terror attack.

The reason that this programme was never broadcast is that, between the recording and the proposed broadcast date, London had come under attack. The BBC eventually decided to redo the programme with a different panel and allow the professor the benefit of hindsight in staking out his interesting claims.

Let me turn very briefly to a programme that *was* broadcast. This was a programme shown on BBC2 in October 2004 called *The Power of Nightmares*, made by a man called Adam Curtis, who was quoted as saying: 'The perceived threat of Islamist terrorism is a politically driven fantasy. Al-Qaeda is an illusion.' The programme went on in this vein and relied on a number of people to support this line of argument. The director of the International Centre for Security Analysis at King's College, London, was quoted as saying: 'The reality of al-Qaeda's threat to the West has been essentially one-off'. There has been *one* incident in the developed world. Apart from that there is no real evidence these groups are connected in any way.' The aforementioned Crispin Black, who was also on the programme, said: 'There's no need to get worried about any of this. We think there is a bit of a gulf between the terrorists' ambitions and their ability to pull it off.' The people of London and

Britain discovered to their great cost in July 2005 that these pundits were utterly mistaken.

An institute of national intelligence excellence might thus operate as a counterweight to dangerous and foolish ideas, however well-intentioned they may be and however reasonable it is not to wish to alarm people. The United Kingdom and British intelligence need a strong counterweight to those who seek to influence the public debate either because they pronounce on matters about which they clearly know little or because they use their high position as law lords to make statements that we reserve for our political representatives in parliament.

The third task for the future is that academics should provide the public and the agencies with a proper evaluation of the strengths and weaknesses of British intelligence without fear or favour. Again, I would argue that only academics can do this. Everybody else has a vested interest. In particular, I believe that we need to examine the whole issue of Iraqi weapons of mass destruction a little more closely. As long as you have very senior politicians, like the Right Honourable Claire Short MP, putting forward the argument that you cannot believe what the government says about intelligence issues because it got it wrong on weapons of mass destruction, I believe it is essential that this issue is looked at with care and caution. Clearly, even after the 7/7 and 21/7 attacks on London, we should be wary of what the government says about intelligence-derived assessments.

The truth is that all the evidence we have today, most importantly from Lord Hutton and Lord Butler, shows beyond any doubt that Mr Blair did not invent the intelligence about WMD as was initially alleged by the BBC's *Today* programme and is repeatedly claimed by journalists and academics even today. The intelligence about WMD may have been scant, but it was definitely genuine. *That* was the problem. The intelligence agencies got it wrong – and what they were required to pass to the government was fairly standard intelligence work. They should not have got it wrong, but they did. The consequences of their failure have been enormous.

We therefore need to look objectively at past successes and failures in the same way. I would argue that the two London attacks represent a failure of British intelligence. However, it could also be argued that British intelligence gets many things right and that little could be done to prevent the London attacks without pre-emptive intelligence. My response as an academic who claims a limited expertise in this field is simply: these people are charged with *getting* pre-emptive intelligence. If they are not getting it, that is a failure that needs to be addressed.

The fourth task for the future consists of a number of mini-tasks.

One of these mini-tasks is to help the security and intelligence agencies define the targets for their operations. This is an area where I believe there is a greater willingness on the part of the security and intelligence agencies to listen to what people outside their particular loop may be saying about what the agencies should be keeping their eyes on.

For example, together with Chris Pope, I wrote a report about the security threat posed by British universities and colleges. This report is based on hard evidence, much of that hard evidence researched with great diligence by Chris Pope. We expected to be attacked by the extremist groups we looked at – the Animal Liberation Front, neo-Nazi groups and various Islamist groups recruiting on UK university campuses – even as we wrote our report. What we did not expect was that the most virulent reaction to our findings came from a small number of university vice-chancellors who attacked us both publicly and privately. They were not keen to acknowledge that their campuses may be becoming a real security problem for the United Kingdom.

In our report, we made a number of suggestions about what universities could do. Some people were surprised that these things were not already being done. For example, we suggested that universities and colleges offer places only to people who have proof of identity. This might seem logical, but the universities and colleges did not think so. We suggested that universities abolish the clearing process, which is used by universities to fill their places indiscriminately. We suggested that universities be required to submit the names of all overseas students they accept for vetting before arranging the paperwork to give them visas. The figures are absolutely amazing.

In 2003-2004, some 17,000 overseas students were given visas to study at British universities and colleges but did not even bother to register. That is not to say that those 17,000 people were all extremists, but it does show that universities are careless regarding the identity of persons to whom they offer places. If I were a terrorist wishing to come to Britain to recruit and manage an operation, I would do so under the guise of a graduate student at a British university.

The next task that I propose is that the security service MI5 should once again be formally instructed to operate against subversion. In 1992, MI5 took a policy decision – of all the United Kingdom's secret agencies, MI5 is really the only one that is allowed to have its own policy – to no longer operate against subversion. They continued to operate against terrorism, but my argument is that subversion precedes terrorism. Operating against subversion is therefore a much more effective way of dealing with the problem of extremist recruitment. After all, if you wait until subversion has turned into terrorism, it is too late. You are reacting rather than being proactive.

The next measure is to invest far more time and resources into the intelligence debriefings of Islamist detainees currently held by the government. A lot of evidence exists that there is wide-scale recruitment by people in prisons, and the crossover point between an ordinary criminal – such as Richard Reid, the so-called 'shoe bomber' – and Islamist terror is very clear. Similarly, I believe that there should be much more investigation of imams, the priests who come to speak at various institutions – prisons, universities and so forth. We have very little idea who many of these people are. They are often given visas and are then not carefully monitored.

To conclude, the purpose of this paper is to provide some specific policy proposals that should be enacted now to prepare for the future. It is not to criticise the very good work that is being done and has been done since 9/11. I believe the security agencies when they say that they have already foiled a number of plots since July 2005. I also believe that the outreach measures of the security service, in particular, and the Special Branch are excellent, especially those towards the Muslim community. What is absolutely vital is to realise that most Britons of the Muslim faith want to enjoy exactly the same sort of security from the threats of terrorism and extremism as Britons of Christian or Jewish or any other faith. It is a form of racism to believe that a strong line against Islamist extremism and terrorism is 'anti-Muslim' – that because a person has a particular faith he or she may automatically adopt what a few extremists erroneously claim as what this faith demands. Muslim mothers and fathers are no different from any other mothers and fathers: they want their children to be safe. They do not want them, on the whole, to be recruited by extremist organisations.

The tasks that I have outlined are meant to be manageable tasks. They do not offer any prospect of solving what may be the underlying political problems of terrorism, but I believe that they do enable us to take off our jackets, roll up our shirtsleeves and get on with the job.

Legal Measures Against Terrorism

Françoise Hampson*

The focus of this paper is not specifically on international law, but more on domestic law. It considers how we should decide what *should* and what *should not* be in the law and how we should balance two 'goods' – human security, which is a good, and human rights and fundamental freedoms, which also constitute a good.

In this context, I would identify three key elements. First, we are only talking about reducing risk. You cannot eliminate risk, and nobody should pretend that you can. Secondly, law is only one of the tools available. The law can do certain things. It cannot do other things that are not the appropriate subject of law. It is particularly important that the law is not used as a substitute for policy. We are very good at that, both domestically and internationally: 'Let's be *seen* to be doing something, so let's pass a piece of legislation. We don't know what to do about Yugoslavia, so let's create an international criminal tribunal.' There is a very real risk that the law may be used inappropriately. Thirdly, we need to learn from experience.

Based on experience in Northern Ireland and in other situations in which British forces and British personnel have been involved, and also on the basis of the Israeli experience, it is important to stress the incredible importance for any effective fight against terrorism of intelligence, particularly human intelligence.

It is extremely important to obtain the support of, or at least avoid alienating, the community from which the fighters come. Having the support of Ulster Protestants is not much use if most of the attacks are in fact directed against you by the Catholics – and not just Catholics, but a particular *group* of Northern Ireland Catholics. One needs the support of the relevant community and must positively avoid alienating it.

---

* Professor Françoise Hampson, Human Rights Centre, University of Essex; member of the UN Sub-Commission for the Promotion and Protection of Human Rights.

Based on experience, one also needs scrupulous adherence to the rules on the part of one's own agencies. The killing of Jean Charles de Menezes by police at a London tube station in July 2005 was a tragic accident, but it certainly did not help; neither did the timing.

In a document that has been made available on the Home Office website, the Metropolitan police argues that Northern Ireland is not relevant because there the IRA sought to avoid civilian casualties. Apart from attacks like Enniskillen, which did not seem to be an avoidance of civilian casualties, I accept this general point. In addition, they tended to give warnings and were not generally volunteering to be suicide bombers. I accept that these are significant differences from the situation that we are facing at present, but the point that I wish to make is that the lessons to be learnt in Northern Ireland remain valid even in this context, because they are about the importance of intelligence and support. They *are not* lessons about civilian casualties or the real risk of manipulation of the situation by the state, such as in Russia since 9/11.

Before 9/11, Russia was dealing harshly with Chechen freedom fighters, and Europe was making a great noise about human rights violations. Since 9/11, however, it is seen as a terrorist problem, so Western Europe does little or nothing about it.

There is one final point in relation to the context, and that is the question of hypocrisy and inconsistency. Since the West actually armed Osama Bin Laden twenty years ago, it looks slightly odd that we now treat him as the world's number one villain. If what we are saying is 'our terrorist good, their terrorist bad', we are not going to be able to tackle the problem as a criminal law problem. For that reason, I define 'terrorist' in a very particular way.

A terrorist attack is an attack against civilians, the foreseeable effect of which is to provoke terror in other civilians, and which is normally carried out for political or 'religious' gain. In other words, this does *not* include attacks against the armed forces. Such attacks may well be criminal, for example if they occur within the state to which the armed forces, but they are *not* terrorist attacks, and I do not believe that it is helpful to regard them as such attacks. This is a bit tough on the armed forces, but they have got other ways of defending themselves.

Against this background, I want to turn to the principal issue, namely: what is the law for and what can it do?

In this context, the law defines what is criminal. It does not define what is wrong or who should be disapproved of. It defines what is criminal – in other words, who one can lock up – and it defines the powers of the police and the rules of due process, including rules of evidence. This gives rise to three points.

First, law should be seen as a bottom line. Just because something is legally possible does not mean that it is a good idea or that it should be used in every case. For example, just because *may* be able to detain someone for five years does not mean that they will do it to *everyone*. They will only do it to a limited number. I am convinced that this is true. I do not believe that such powers would lead to some form of widespread, arbitrary detention. It might be arbitrary, but it would not be widespread.

However, the lessons of history also make it absolutely clear that there is a tendency for any new power given to the state to leak into other areas. It is meant to be used only in very defined circumstances, but the authorities end up using it in a much wider range of circumstances. This is illustrated by Israel's use of tactics or interrogation methods that were not supposed to constitute torture and by some of the measures that were adopted by the United Kingdom in Northern Ireland.

There is a solution to this problem, which is to assume that one cannot in general do X but to provide very precise criteria for when one can. Instead of saying that one can lock up people for ninety days, one says: one cannot lock up people for more than *x* days, unless... I believe that this way of dealing with the problem will possibly avoid some of the risk of abuse.

What criteria need to be applied when looking at law in the area of counter-terrorism? I suggest that there should be three. The first is a fairly obvious one: necessity. An existing right or freedom should not be restricted simply because it is convenient to do so, but only because it is necessary and no lesser alternative will meet the need. The means adopted actually do need to relate to the difficulty. If locking up people for ninety days makes you feel good but actually contributes in no way at all to reducing the risk then it is not necessary. One does need to see a relationship of cause and effect between the measure taken and the reduction in the threat.

The second criterion is the importance of safeguards. Where there is a departure from the normal rule, it should be necessary to put in place some form of safeguard. For example, if people are allowed to be detained for longer than normal, the government should make sure they are given access to a lawyer and to their own doctor, and if access to a lawyer is denied for any reason this should be judicially reviewable. That is the kind of safeguard that can be put in place, and it tries to avoid the risk of abuse.

The third criterion is that no measure should be adopted that makes the situation worse or increases the risk. What does this mean in practice? The first thing that needs to be looked at is creating new crimes. There is no problem with creating new crimes, on the condition that they do not relate to something that is already covered. For example, instead of introducing a new crime of glorification of terrorism – with all the problems this raises with regard to attempting to rewrite history and presumably closing every university history department in the country – what is wrong with the current crime of inciting murder? Failure to use this implies that there is something wrong with the crime of incitement to murder. In my view, therefore, glorification of terrorism, even if you add intent, does not satisfy the necessity test. We already have a perfectly good law that we are not using, and in the process we are undermining it.

A further objection to creating the crime of glorifying terrorism is that it necessitates a definition of terrorism and, as already noted, the authorities were unable to decide whether or not the ANC, for example, was a terrorist organisation. I think that a particularly useful concept with regard to new rules is the one relating to acts preparatory to terrorism. I believe that this will actually offer the police many advantages when it comes to charging people with crimes.

If a crime is being created, it has to obey the rules for creating crimes. That is to say, there has to be a clearly defined act, and the mental element must also be defined. The less precise the act – such as the rather vague 'acts preparatory to the commission of terrorism' – the higher the threshold of the mental element – intent or recklessness – should be. In contrast, if you can be very precise about the act, you can afford to lower the mental threshold.

The next issue is the question of rules of evidence. It may be that we need special rules for certain crimes. In other words, the current rules for normal crimes can be kept, but special rules for special crimes should be introduced, together with the relevant safeguards. For example, certain states have special rules of evidence when it comes to drug crimes, enabling persons to give evidence behind a screen so that they can be cross-examined but not seen and, thus, not identified. Another possibility – but one would have to show a much greater need to justify this – is the law that exists in some continental European states according to which evidence can be given in writing, including question and answer sessions, because it is believed to be too dangerous even to provide it from behind a screen.

The law thus allows the creation of special rules for special crimes. An obvious example in this context is the question of the use of intercept evidence, which is routinely used in civil law jurisdictions and common law jurisdictions such as Australia. Why should the British police and the British courts be the only institutions that appear to be incapable of using intercept evidence? This does not mean giving them *carte blanche*. Measures need to be taken to protect the identity of sources and so on, but is the use of intercept evidence not better than locking up the potentially innocent for ninety days?

On addition, if we have not used intercept evidence, how can we say that the other measures are necessary?

The next point concerns actual police powers. The first question here is an odd issue that has arisen specifically in the United Kingdom about the relationship between questioning and charging. The current rule is that once a person is charged they can no longer be questioned. It is conceivable that this needs to be reconsidered, at least with regard to terrorist offences, so that it will be possible to carry on questioning a person even after they have been charged.

One solution that has been suggested is to use a holding charge. This means charging a person with something minor while investigating another crime. However, this may not be practicable in some circumstances, and it is only useful in cases where both crimes have *actually* been committed and the question is who committed them.

If the issue is crimes that *might* have been committed, then it is difficult to see how holding charges can be used. This leads to the tricky question of detention. Clearly, if a person is charged with a serious crime, he or she can be detained, although we may need to look at the rules on questioning in such cases. However, if a person is charged with a minor crime, he or she would normally expect to get bail. It might be necessary to take another look at situations in which a person is charged with a minor crime but is being also investigated for a more serious one, as that might be a ground on which bail could be refused. This is something that is worth looking at.

Then, of course, there is the question how long a person can be detained without any charge at all. It is important to remember that there are two different situations. One is where the crime *has* been committed and the question is whether the person in question committed it. The second situation, which is much more complicated, is the one in which no crime has been committed, but where there might be grounds for locking somebody up, for example, simply because of the mosque he attends or because of people who were in the mosque at the same time. In this context, it is important to remember the case of Lotfi Raissi, an Algerian national lawfully resident in the United Kingdom, whose extradition was sought by the United States because his time at an American flying school had overlapped with some of the people involved in 9/11. The magistrates kept giving the United States more time to produce evidence, but it never produced a shred of evidence. Nevertheless, Raissi claims that his life has been destroyed, because although he is still resident in the United Kingdom and can lawfully remain here nobody will employ him.

This is a situation in which there was apparently no evidence. It was considered important that there was no evidence. Is the position within the United Kingdom different now? In cases where a crime has not yet occurred, but the authorities fear that it might, it is extremely difficult to identify what the threshold should be. However, if there is no evidence that the person in question has actually done anything sinister, I believe that the authorities should exercise caution before they start thinking in terms of locking him or her up.

Finally, what about the role of judges? Judges are clearly there to apply the will of parliament. That includes counter-terrorist legislation and the Human Rights Act. The judiciary are also there to secure accountability of the executive, including the police.

The case law on the European Convention on Human Rights, which UK judges have to take into account, is not rigid. It allows a remarkable degree of flexibility, even without the need to derogate. It is permissible to have different rules of evidence for different crimes and to create special categories of crimes. Countries are expected to put in place safeguards when they intrude on the normally acceptable provisions, but there is flexibility in the system. When it comes to the views of the European Court of Human Rights on pre-charge detention, the case law regarding Northern Ireland suggests that seven days is lawful on condition that there are adequate safeguards.

In a case against Turkey, the Court found that fourteen days was excessive, not least because there were no safeguards in place. This concerned incommunicado detention without the right to see a lawyer or a doctor. The view of the Court was that the exigencies of the situation did not require fourteen days. If the government can prove that the exigencies require whatever period it has imposed, it will satisfy the Court, but it cannot simply impose such a period. It has to show the need and the fact that the problem actually requires this measure.

In my view, if the government cannot show that it has tried lesser alternatives that have not worked, I do not see how it can justify something as draconian as a 90-day detention period.

A final function of the courts is to listen to the public, but not simply to do whatever the public wants. For a start, the public needs to be better informed than it is at present. It needs to know that protection cannot be guaranteed and that even a 90-day detention period does not mean that there will be no more terrorist attacks. It also needs to be made aware that some measures might make the situation worse. For example, in this kind of situation, where the risk comes largely from one community, it is inevitable that the people most likely to be detained will come from that community. It is going to look discriminatory, even though it may well not be discriminatory.

In these circumstances, there is a risk that certain measures could make the situation worse, and the public needs to understand this. It needs to know that is the government needs the support of the Muslim community in order to take effective measures against those members of the community that are determined to kill civilians.

The public also needs to be reminded that power designed for exceptional circumstances has the tendency to leak into other areas unless it is very carefully controlled. One of the reasons the public debate is so uninformed and unsophisticated is because of the pressure that the public puts on government to be seen to be doing something. As in the case of Northern Ireland, this is one of the factors that led to convictions that later had to be overturned. The public ends up putting so much pressure on the police, for example, that they simply arrest someone, put him on trial, get him to serve a sentence and, in some cases, allow him die in prison.

The public must understand that the government needs the room to identify what needs to be done and then do it and that it does not need to be harangued into taking measures that may not serve the intended purpose. I believe that the public has a certain responsibility here, as does the media. At the moment, I believe that the quality of the debate, as reflected in the newspapers, in particular, is really letting the public and the government down. I hope that some of the concerns that have been raised in this paper provide some food for thought.

Freedom of Religion or Belief in the 'Age of Terror': Muslims as the Prime Victims of Religiously-Motivated Terrorism

Sara Khan*

Freedom of thought, conscience and religion[1] is a complicated freedom. Since the beginning of the current human rights era, this freedom has found itself to be the topic of much contention with many differing views on what specific elements it represents and how or even why it should be protected. Some consider religion to be a hindrance for human rights, especially for those most vulnerable in society, while others argue that religion not only encompasses human rights but provides greater depth to human rights theory by also considering duties and responsibilities of individuals in ensuring that human rights are enforced.

It is clear, however, that much weakness exists in its protection and that it has in fact been neglected or even considered to be of lesser value in comparison to other freedoms. Lerner considers religious human rights as a 'neglected chapter ... of observance and respect for human rights'.[2] John Noonan refers to religious freedom as 'the neglected stepchild of the human rights movement'.[3] Nearly eight years on from the terrorist attacks on 11 September 2001 in the United States, these statements have even greater resonance today. Many authors have debated whether human rights have become a casualty of our post-9/11 world. One of those human rights is indeed freedom of religion

* Sara Kahn, Human Rights Activist.

[1] Hereinafter, I will be using the shorter phrase 'freedom of religion or belief'.

[2] N. Lerner, 'Religion, Beliefs and International Human Rights' (Maryknoll NY, Orbis Books 2000) p. 39.

[3] John Noonan, quoted in W. Cole Durham, 'Perspectives on Religious Liberty: A Comparative Framework', in J.D. Van Der Vyver and J. Witte Jr. (eds.), *Religious Human Rights in Global Perspectives* (The Hague, Martinus Nijhoff Publishers 1996).

or belief. With a lack of a binding convention in international human rights law and in the post-9/11 world of counter-terrorism measures with much suspicion focused on certain religious communities, what we see today is the slow erosion and the undermining of certain aspects of religious freedom, justified for the sake of national and international security.

In this paper, I will firstly focus on what standing freedom of religion or belief has in international human rights law. I will then highlight some key issues that are relevant to freedom of religion or belief, which will put into context how counter-terrorism measures after 9/11 have weakened the very concept of this freedom. Throughout the paper, I will concentrate on Western-European countries and, in particular, on Muslims, being the set of believers that have suffered the most consequences post-9/11.

1. Freedom of Religion or Belief in International Human Rights Law

Living in today's globalised, diverse world, freedom of religion or belief is considered to be one of the most important freedoms of the contemporary human rights era for a number of different reasons. Some refer to its importance in terms of preventing persecution, torture and conflicts as witnessed by history. Others view the value of religious freedom as being essential in today's diverse world in helping to produce a functioning pluralist society.[4] It is considered to be one of the 'foundations of a democratic society'[5] and is vital in its protection, as religion shapes the identity of millions of people across the world. More importantly, however, 'freedom of religion or belief is an essential and independent component of treating human beings as autonomous persons deserving of dignity and respect'.[6] Freedom of religion or belief also respects those with beliefs such as atheism, agnosticism and others. Religion or belief does not have an agreed international definition and has been defined so broadly as to include the above-mentioned forms of belief, new religions and others.

Freedom of religion or belief exists in all major international and regional treaties. It is found in Article 18 of the Universal Declaration of Human Rights:

---

[4] P. Edge, 'Current Problems in Article 9 of the ECHR', 42 *Juridical Review* (1996).

[5] *Kokkinakis* v. *Greece,* Application No. 14307/88 [1993] *ECHR* 20 (25 May 1993) para. 13.

[6] C. Evans, 'Freedom of Religion under the European Convention on Human Rights' (Oxford University Press 2001) p. 29.

'Everyone has the right to freedom of thought, conscience and religion; this right includes freedom to change his religion or belief, and freedom, either alone or in community with others and in public or private, to manifest his religion or belief in teaching, practice, worship and observance.' Similar wording can be found in Article 9 of the European Convention on Human Rights, Article 12 of the American Convention on Human Rights, Article 8 of the African Charter and Article 18 of the International Covenant on Civil and Political Rights (ICCPR). Article 4 of the ICCPR also specifically prohibits derogations that involve 'discrimination solely on the grounds of race, colour, sex, language, religion or social origin.' Furthermore, the ICCPR in Article 26 requires states parties to ensure that their laws 'guarantee to all persons effective protection against discrimination', and in Article 20 to prohibit 'any advocacy of national, racial or religious hatred that constitute incitement to discrimination, hostility or violence.'

The general formulation of freedom of religion or belief in most treaties makes clear that everyone has the right to freedom of thought, conscience and religion. This is an absolute right that cannot be limited at all, nor can it be derogated from during times of emergency, including for reasons of national security. However, the second aspect of freedom of religion or belief focuses on manifesting one's faith either alone or in community with others, in public and in private, in worship, teaching, practice and observance. This aspect is subject to limitations, but only in the interests of public safety, morals, health or for the protection of the rights and freedoms of others. The European Convention on Human Rights also mentions that limitations can only be applied 'where necessary in a democratic society'.

The UN Human Rights Committee, in discussing what these limitations are, states that they are to be 'strictly interpreted: restrictions are not allowed on grounds not specified there ... even [for] national security. Limitations may be applied only for those purposes for which they were prescribed and must be directly related and proportionate to the specific need...'. The Committee also mentions that the limitations must not be 'imposed for discriminatory purposes or applied in a discriminatory manner'.[7]

The 1981 UN Declaration on the Elimination of all Forms of Intolerance and Discrimination Based on Religion or Belief took nearly nineteen years to draft but is considered to be a weak instrument, firstly for being no more than a non-binding declaration and, secondly, and more importantly, for not having a

[7] HRC General Comment 22: The Right to Freedom of Thought, Conscience and Religion (Art. 18): 30/07/93, CCPR/C/21/Rev.1/Add.4.

monitoring machinery. This in itself, though, does not completely negate any kind of monitoring of religious freedom. The monitoring machinery exists in a narrow sense, firstly, in the form of other treaty bodies such as the Committee on the Elimination of all Forms of Racial Discrimination (CERD), the ICCPR's Human Rights Committee (HRC), the Committee on the Elimination of all Forms of Discrimination Against Women (CEDAW) and the Committee on the Rights of the Child (CRC). However, there is little consistency, and committees such as CERD have caused confusion in relation to how they see their role towards religion. CERD has looked at ethnic minorities with a religious dimension and has even expressed concern over reported cases of Islamophobia,[8] but its role is still limited in relation to religion. Secondly there are regional human rights courts such as the European Court of Human Rights, which seeks to protect Article 9, but many, such as Carolyn Evans, have criticised the narrow remit of the European Court in relation to Article 9 cases. Thirdly, whereas the 1981 Declaration has no monitoring machinery, the UN Commission on Human Rights has mandated a Special Rapporteur on freedom of religion or belief to promote the declaration since 1986. Though under-resourced, the Special Rapporteur carries out visits to many countries, prepares detailed annual reports and responds to initiatives by the United Nations and NGOs.

Based on the above, it is therefore not surprising that international human rights law is considered to be tokenistic when it comes to freedom of religion or belief.

2. Current Social Trends Relevant to Freedom of Religion or Belief

Before reviewing the impact that 9/11 had on freedom of religion or belief, it is important to consider briefly some key social phenomena that help to contextualise the actual effect of post-9/11 measures.

Firstly, in the twentieth century, many European countries underwent a strong secularisation process, not only in the political landscape but also in social attitudes in general. Secularisation by its very nature considers religion to be less important or even 'backwards' and no longer relevant in the modern world. Secular attitudes enforce the belief that religion should be limited to the private sphere and should not have a role in the public sphere. In their

---

[8] Concluding Observations of CERD: United Kingdom of Great Britain and Northern Ireland, CERD/C/63/CO/11, 63rd Session of CERD, 4-22 August 2003.

World Report on Freedom of Religion or Belief, Boyle and Sheen suggest that 'the idea that religion belongs only to the private sphere is meaningless to the vast bulk of believers of all religions in the world.'[9] This is understandable, as many of the major religions do not have a demarcation between the public and the private. There is a widespread belief that religion has brought inhumanity and superstition to Europe and that it forms an obstacle to science, freedom and the progression of mankind. Many Dutch people, for example, believe Islam represents 'dogmatic religious authoritarianism and unquestioning collectivity',[10] which the Netherlands strongly opposed in its efforts to secure a division between church and state.

To secularists, modernity is synonymous with secularism, which represents the ideal model for Europe. With Europe becoming increasingly secular in its outlook, many have questioned how comfortably secularism and religion can sit together. General hostility towards religion has led to secularism. Part of the secularisation process has contributed to the discussion on the worthiness of religion itself. Followers of a religion can legitimately be subjected to mockery and ridicule.[11] The publication of cartoons of the Prophet Mohammed in *Jyllands-Posten*, which caused a furore in Denmark and beyond, was defended on the basis of freedom of expression. In fact, the cartoons were considered by many to be 'just another episode of European racism disguised as high moral principle'.[12] Free expression and religious freedom have clashed – and will most likely continue to clash – in the future, but such an example indicates that, as Europe becomes ever more secular, it fails to understand or even appreciate the importance of religion to those who hold such values dearly. 'The West has clearly demonstrated once more that a secularised society simply has no room for the very concept of the holy.'[13]

Weller argues that, in recent times, religion began to emerge as a marker of individual and community identity for a significant number of people.[14] By

---

9 K. Boyle and J. Sheen (eds.), *Freedom of Religion and Belief: A World Report* (London, Routledge 1997) p. 10.

10 M. Valenta, 'Facing up to Islam in the Netherlands', open Democracy News Analysis, 9 February 2006, available at: <http://www.opendemocracy.net>.

11 T. Madood, 'The Liberal Dilemma: Integration or Vilification?', open Democracy News Analysis, 8 February 2006, available at: <http://www.opendemocracy.net>.

12 S. Sayyid, 'Old Europe, New World', open Democracy News Analysis, 15 February 2006, available at: <http://www.opendemocracy.net>.

13 M. Hofman., 'Sliding towards the Clash', *EMEL Magazine* (March 2006) p. 44.

14 P. Weller, 'The Dynamics and Dimensions of Religious Discrimination: Findings and Analysis from the UK', in N. Ghanea (ed.), *The Challenges of Religious Discrimina-*

the end of the twentieth century, a shift had emerged from identity being talked of mainly in racial or ethnic terms to religion as a major factor in the public sphere. For example, the United Kingdom's Home Office Citizenship Survey (2001) indicated that for Muslims religion is a more important aspect of identity than ethnicity and is second only to family.[15] It could therefore only be expected that friction would develop between secularism and religion in today's world.

Secondly, during the 1960s and 1970s, immigration and an ever-increasing number of asylum applications, mainly from Muslim countries, caused great unease and tension in many European countries. With religious symbols becoming ever more visible in the form of mosques and headscarves, many questioned the cultural and religious beliefs of such immigrants. Right-wing political parties exploited the 'fear' that was already rising in society. In the Netherlands, for example, Pim Fortuyn said that Islam 'was backwards', that it was responsible for 'diluting Dutch liberal values' and that it treated women and homosexuals as second class citizens, something unacceptable according to today's Western values. Muslims have allegedly brought an alien culture that is at odds with Western heritage. In a recent Pew Global Study, the Netherlands was criticised for being the most anti-Islamic country in the West, with 51% of the population viewing Islam unfavourably, followed by 47% of Germans.[16] A survey conducted in 2003 in Germany indicated that negative stereotypes against Muslims were on the rise among all groups in society. Of those interviewed, 46% partly or fully agreed that 'Islam is a backward religion' and 27% agreed with the statement that 'immigration to Germany should be forbidden for Muslims'.[17] A survey carried out in September 2004 indicated that 93% of Germans associated the word 'Islam' with 'oppression of women' and 83% with 'terrorism'.[18]

After the London bombings of 7 July 2005, the British National Party (BNP), which originally focused on race and ethnicity as its main campaign target, began to focus on Islam with even greater ferocity. Two days after the

---

tion at the Dawn of the New Millennium (The Hague, Martinus Nijhoff Publishers 2004) p. 61.

15 Open Society Institute, 'Muslims in the UK: Policies for Engaged Citizens', EU Monitoring and Advocacy Program (2005).

16 See *supra* n. 9.

17 International Helsinki Federation for Human Rights, 'Intolerance and Discrimination against Muslims in the EU' (March 2005) p. 76.

18 DPA, 'Germans have negative views of Islam', 16 September 2004, available at: <http://www.expatica.com>.

terror attack, for example, the BNP used a photograph of the blown up bus with the caption: 'Maybe it's time to start listening to the BNP'.[19]

Finally, with the Cold War well and truly over, Samuel Huntington's 'clash of civilisations' theory predicted that religion would be the predominant factor in modern conflicts, with Islam generally being a big contributory factor. Many felt that these predictions were substantiated by the September 11 attacks and that 'Islamic' terrorism was the next greatest threat to modern civilisation.

The connecting theme of these three phenomena is religion, in particular Islam. As the attacks on the World Trade Center were committed 'in the name of Islam', it was not surprising that Muslims underwent and are still experiencing a period of vulnerability, hatred and portrayal as a suspect community. This undoubtedly calls into question the strength of freedom of religion or belief.

3. Counter-Terrorism Measures and Religious Discrimination Post-9/11

The 'war on terror', as declared by George W. Bush after 9/11, highlighted the reality that this 'war' was also wide enough to include those who stood against the values of freedom, democracy and human rights. At the same time that its remit widened, however, the war was also defined very narrowly as targeting 'Islamic' terrorism and Muslim countries rather than terrorism in general. The irony behind such a war was that the counter-terrorism measures adopted by many countries were sacrificing many freedoms and human rights, including freedom of religion or belief, with the repercussions being felt by Muslims in particular.

Immediately after the terrorist attacks in the United States on September 11, thousands of Muslim, Middle Eastern and South Asian men were detained by the FBI and the police and held secretly and indefinitely without charge.[20] Many of those detained were eventually released or deported. Muslims and Arabs suffered humiliation at airports by undergoing special security checks.[21]

---

19 European Monitoring Centre on Racism and Xenophobia, 'The Impact of 7 July 2005 London Bomb Attacks on Muslim Communities in the EU' (November 2005) p. 27.

20 International Helsinki Federation for Human Rights, 'Anti-terrorism Measures, Security and Human Rights' (April 2003) p. 108.

21 L. Cainkar, 'The Impact of the September 11 attacks and their aftermath on Arab and Muslim communities in the United States', *GSC Quarterly* (Summer/Fall 2004).

Indeed, many Muslims from the United Kingdom, when travelling to the United States, also experienced such humiliation, most prominently Yusuf Islam[22] and the late Zaki Badawi,[23] individuals well respected by both Muslims and non-Muslims alike. Such targeting of people was not based on highly classified intelligence – far from it. Individuals were targeted because of their association with a faith or their country of birth – in most cases Muslim countries. Such individuals were targeted for having a recognisable Muslim name or happening to 'look' Muslim. As Louise Cainkar states: '… Muslims or more specifically non-US-born Muslim males from Asia, the Middle East and North Africa are a security risk for the United States. This assumption lies at the foundation of many Bush administration programmes including ones which affect Muslims who are US citizens … including wire-tapping and undercover activities to a number of mosques.'[24]

Religious profiling of Muslims was common in the United States, the United Kingdom and other EU countries. In the United States, it was clear that such profiling was occurring, and the then Attorney General, John Ashcroft, stated that such 'special registration' was 'not new' and was based on nationality.[25] Yet it was quite clear that religious profiling was in fact occurring. Surveillance of mosques and Muslim neighbourhoods, random questioning of Muslim men and targeting and freezing assets of Islamic charities[26] indicated that being Muslim and being associated with the religion of Islam was the number one factor that would make an individual more likely to be targeted and suspected.

Germany, in carrying out similar tactics, weakened its privacy laws to carry out nationwide computer profiling of men of Muslim faith or Arab descent. Thousands of Muslims had their personal data screened because their profiles matched certain basic criteria, foremost of which was an affiliation with Islam.[27]

In the United Kingdom, Home Office minister Hazel Blears stated that Muslims should accept the 'reality' that they were more likely to be stopped

---

22 'Detained Cat Stevens heading home', CNN, 22 September 2004, available at: <http://www.cnn.com/2004/US/09/22/plane.diverted.stevens>.

23 'UK Muslim Leader barred from US', BBC News, 15 July 2005, available at: <http://news.bbc.co.uk/1/hi/world/americas/4684489.stm>.

24 See *supra* n. 19.

25 Ibid.

26 S. Mathur, 'Surviving the dragnet: "special interest" detainees in the US after 9/11', 47(3) *Race & Class* (2006) p. 32.

27 See *supra* n. 18.

and searched than others.[28] At the same time, however, the Association of Police Authorities' *Know Your Rights* leaflet stated that one should not be stopped or searched based on race, religion, the way one looked or dressed and so forth.[29] After the London bombings in July 2005, Ian Johnston, the chief constable of the British Transport Police, declared that his officers would not be stopping 'little old white ladies'. 'It is going to be disproportionate when it comes to ethnic groups.'[30]

The Anti-Terrorism, Crime and Security Act 2001 was brought in after the US terror attacks. In 2002-2003, the Home Office revealed a 300% increase in stops of Asians. Of those who were stopped, nearly 70,000 had committed no offence whatsoever. With only 1.18% of cases actually resulting in arrests, it became obvious that the low arrest rate and the large number of people stopped and searched indicated that these powers were being used widely and arbitrarily with little effect.[31] Such statistics demonstrate that it is Muslims who are being stereotypically targeted. Those that had been arrested on suspicion were not arrested for reasons of greater security but intimidation and surveillance of the 'suspect community'.[32] That suspect community, of course, happens to be a religious community, and it is clear that it is the religious aspect of the community that is the pretext for being targeted.

This religious profiling, occurring as part of counter-terrorism operations, violates the very concept of freedom of religion or belief and the principle that an individual should not be discriminated against on the basis of his or her religion. A similar conclusion was reached by a number of members of the then European Commission on Human Rights in the case of *Tsavachidis* v. *Greece*.[33] These members argued that the systematic surveillance by the secret police of people based on their religion violated the right to hold a belief.[34] The case never reached the European Court of Human Rights itself due to a

---

28 Source: <http://www.irr.org.uk/2006/january/ha000025.html>.

29 Available at: <http://www.apa.police.uk/APA/Features/Stop+and+search>.

30 'Using Intelligence', *The Guardian*, Leader, 3 August 2005, available at: <http://www.guardian.co.uk/attackonlondon/comment/story/0,,1541523,00.html>.

31 Source: <http://www.statewatch.org/news/2004/jan/13UK-stop-and-search-targets-Muslim-communities.htm>.

32 See *supra* n. 21, at p. 33

33 *Tsavachidis* v. *Greece*, Application No. 28802/95, ECHR, 4 may 1997, unreported.

34 The Commission did rule, however, that there had been no violation of the right to freedom of religion secured in Article 9 (nine votes to eight), with the majority agreeing that such surveillance amounted to a breach of the right to privacy (Article 8, Section2).

friendly settlement, but it shows how religious profiling can be considered a violation of freedom of religion by the state when it targets individuals on the basis of their religion. It is hard to say whether the European Court of Human Rights would ever reach such a conclusion. However, its case law indicates that decisions made by the Court with respect to Article 9 cases are unfortunately usually overridden by the consideration of other articles. Article 9, Section 2, receives some attention, but sometimes to the detriment of the right to actually hold a religion or belief.[35]

A number of reports have been published on the treatment of Muslims in the aftermath of 9/11. The European Monitoring Centre on Racism and Xenophobia reported that Muslims have suffered increased hostility and physical attacks since September 11.[36] The International Helsinki Federation for Human Rights published an in-depth report on intolerance and discrimination faced by Muslims in the EU since 9/11. Aaron Rhodes, Executive Director of the IHF, states that 'Muslim minorities in the EU have experienced growing distrust and hostility … pre-existing patterns of prejudice and discrimination have been reinforced and Muslims have increasingly felt they are stigmatised *because of their beliefs*.'[37] Such hostility and discrimination included stereotypical media reports portraying Muslims as an enemy within and a 'fifth column' (imagery that has historically been used to describe Roman Catholics and Jews), verbal and physical assaults and discrimination against Muslims in terms of housing, employment and access to services. Many EU countries have also controversially opposed the wearing of headscarves and *jilbaab* in schools and public buildings, have opposed private Muslim schools, the practice of ritual slaughter and the opening and building of mosques.[38] Five weeks after the London bombings, the Metropolitan Police recorded a sharp rise in faith hate crimes as compared to the same period in 2004, with the majority of attacks directed at British Muslims. Crimes motivated by religious hatred had increased by nearly 600% in London since the 7 July bombings.[39]

After the 7/7 bombings in London, the United Kingdom proposed its fourth counter-terrorist measure in five years with the Prevention of Terrorism Act 2005. Tony Blair controversially announced that 'the rules of the

[35] See *supra* n. 6, at p. 200.

[36] European Monitoring Centre on Racism and Xenophobia, 'Summary Report on Islamophobia in the EU after September 11th', Allen and Nielsen (2002).

[37] See *supra* n. 15.

[38] Ibid.

[39] Source: <http://www.politics.co.uk/domestic-policy/faith-hate-crimes-increases-$14016741.htm>.

game had changed'. Rules and rights that for centuries had been part of British law were now being done away with. Some of the new laws that the Labour government wanted to introduce included proscribing Muslim organisations like Hizb ut-Tahrir (HT)[40] and creating new powers to close down places of worship that were suspected of being breeding grounds for terrorism. It was clear that Prime Minister Blair was referring specifically to mosques, but after much lobbying the government temporarily decided not to pursue this proposal. However, it still wanted to ban HT, a group that, while religious and political in nature, did not actually advocate violence. Many of its views were considered extreme by the Muslim community itself,[41] but this alone was not a sufficient justification for banning it. The British National Party, which many believe is a party that advocates racial and religious hatred and extremism but is disguised as a political party in a suit and tie, would not be affected by the new proposals. Since both may be considered 'extreme' organisations, it can only be that, as HT is of a religious nature, it has been targeted for religious reasons. As a consequence of so-called religiously motivated terrorism,[42] the United Kingdom, by focusing on Muslim organisations and Muslims in general, like many other states, seems to be confirming that Muslims are indeed considered more likely to become terrorists. Religious freedom has been a casualty in the 'war on terror', a 'war' that has clearly made security the primary objective at the expense of human rights.

4. Religious as opposed to Ethnic or Racial Discrimination

Having touched on the sharp rise of hostility, targeting and discrimination faced by Muslims since 9/11, it is important to analyse whether Muslims are being targeted for ethnic or religious reasons. Muslims, unlike Jews or Sikhs, do not have a particular ethnic background. Throughout the world, Muslims

---

40 A political religious organisation that calls for a worldwide Islamic caliphate but does not advocate violence. Mainstream Muslims consider HT to be an extreme Muslim organisation that does not have a significant following in the United Kingdom or other parts of Europe.

41 Many of the mainstream British Muslim organisations, such as the MCB and other bodies, have rejected HT's extreme views. This view is generally shared by the majority of British Muslim citizens.

42 Many argue that religious terrorism as currently witnessed around the world is not due solely to religion but also to a number of different factors such as political and even socioeconomic issues.

encompass all shades of colour and race, and many reject being placed in either a racial or ethnic category. The concept of a 'Muslim identity' in the United Kingdom, for example, began to emerge during the late 1980s due to a number of different high-profile factors. Salman Rushdie's *The Satanic Verses* caused previously passive Muslims to congregate on religious rather than ethnic grounds. Other issues included the lack of legal protection from religious discrimination for Muslims, whereas Sikhs and Jews, despite being religious communities, were protected by racial discrimination legislation because they are both considered to be a race. With ethnic cleansing of Muslims in Kosovo and Bosnia in the mid-1990s, Muslims gathered around their religious identity with even greater conviction. As noted previously, many Muslims felt that their primary marker of identity was religion, and in 'a very short space of time "Muslim" [had] become a key political minority identity, acknowledged by Right and Left, bigots and the open-minded, the media and the government.'[43] Counter-terrorism measures as documented above have only further increased the reality of a Muslim religious identity. This religious identity is now widely accepted by society in general and is strongly propagated by Muslims themselves. Regardless of this, many continue to place Muslims in racial categories that do not do justice to the reality of a religious community. A religious aspect combined with ethnicity makes it harder to distinguish whether people are experiencing hate crimes for reasons of religiosity or ethnicity.[44] Even the United Nations is sometimes guilty of such action. In one of its recent news bulletins, for example, it stated that racism and racial discrimination was on the rise around the world and included Islamophobia as a form of racial discrimination rather than religious discrimination.[45] In the United Kingdom, the category of faith hate crimes only emerged relatively recently. Prior to this, anti-Muslim crime would have been classified under racial hate crimes, which clearly did not provide a true reflection of the reality of religiously motivated hate crimes.

Madood states that 'it is difficult to gauge to what extent contemporary British Islamophobia is "religious" and to what extent "racial"'.[46] This is true,

[43] T. Madood, 'The Place of Muslims in British Secular Multiculturalism', in N, Ghanea (ed.), *The Challenges of Religious Discrimination at the Dawn of the New Millennium* (The Hague, Martinus Nijhoff Publishers 2004) p. 234.

[44] See *supra* n. 18, at p. 123.

[45] 'Racism and racial discrimination on the rise around the world, UN Expert Warns', 7 March 2006, available at: <http://www.un.org/apps/news/story.asp?NewsID=17718&Cr=racis&Cr1>.

[46] See *supra* n. 40, at p. 242.

but the counter-terrorism measures and data on hostility and discrimination towards Muslims do imply that it is more for religious reasons. For example, white English women identifiable as Muslim solely by their headscarves have also been victimised. The executive director of the International Helsinki Federation for Human Rights, Aaron Rhodes, also believes that Muslims are being stigmatised 'because of their beliefs'. Individuals exploit the religious background of the 9/11 attacks and other terrorist attacks as an excuse for attacking and abusing the Muslim community.[47] It therefore has to be acknowledged that the discrimination and targeting faced by Muslims are more likely to be for religious reasons than ethnic ones. This is what Muslims themselves believe. A survey conducted in March 2004 in the United Kingdom showed that 64% of Muslims believed that anti-terrorism laws were being used unfairly against the Muslim community.[48] Eighty per cent said they had experienced discrimination because of their faith.[49]

The overall picture of religious discrimination faced by Muslims ranges from counter-terrorism measures driven by religious profiling after 9/11 and the lack of legal protection of religious minorities against religious discrimination to the high levels of immigration and asylum in European countries, where questions of assimilation and integration are raised. When these factors are compounded by the strong foothold of secularism in European society, which considers religion 'backwards', it is obvious that the picture of freedom of religion or belief is not very pretty, especially for Muslims. In Denmark and Italy, for example, the post-9/11 xenophobic backlash was clearly intertwined with an upsurge in anti-immigration and anti-Islamic rhetoric due to the political elite in those countries.[50] In the Netherlands, Muslim citizens have been called on to abandon or reinvent religious practices that are perceived as conservative. Such abuse constitutes an attack on the *forum internum* of freedom of religion or belief; an attack on the very fundamental and absolute law that everyone has the right to freedom of religion or belief. The absolute and non-derogable nature of this freedom suddenly becomes irrelevant, whereas, being non-derogable, it should actually apply more strongly in times of hostility towards religious minorities. Religious communities face the double misfortune of not obtaining much protection from the concept of collective rights, as current international human rights law and theory have a strong

47 See *supra* n. 17, at p. 3.

48 See *supra* n. 15, at p. 18.

49 Ibid., at p. 19.

50 See *supra* n. 18, at p. 123.

individualistic outlook, with protection offered mainly on an individual basis rather than for communities. This lack of legal protection is particularly relevant to religious communities that, by their very nature, congregate on a community level.

5. Conclusion

'From a human rights perspective, the terrorism of September 11 was caused in large part by the hijacking of a religion… Islam was not a cause of the terrorism, it was a victim, and it is now in danger of becoming a scapegoat as well.'[51]

One of the biggest challenges facing freedom of religion or belief relates to the implications of religiously motivated terrorism: firstly, the fact that certain forms of terrorism are driven by religious reasons and, secondly, the effect that this has on those religious communities that belong to the same religion as the group carrying out terrorist attacks in the name of their religion. Religious communities are the ones that suffer in almost every aspect. Like any other individual, they too have become victims of terror attacks (for example, many Muslims were killed in the 9/11 and 7/7 attacks). Secondly, they are more likely to be discriminated against in counter-terrorism measures as a result of the use of religious profiling methods that violate freedom of religion or belief. Thirdly, the religious community is likely to face hostility, stereotyping, hatred and violence from many different parts of society, such as media, the general public, employers and the academic sector and even government. In its current form, freedom of religion or belief is unable to deal adequately with these violations, yet it needs to be applicable to such challenges in order to be relevant in today's world. The United Nations, states and international and regional courts, as well as equality bodies,[52] have all played a role in undervaluing religious freedom. They need to give it the greater relevance it deserves. Otherwise, as Noonan observes, religious freedom will continue to be the neglected stepchild of the human rights movement, which, in this current globalised world, is no longer an option.

---

[51] J. Shattuck, 'Religion, Rights, and Terrorism', 16 *Harvard Human Rights Journal* (2003) p. 188.

[52] 'The UK's Commission for Racial Equality (CRE)', in *The Future of Multi-Ethnic Britain – The Parekh Report* (1999) Part 2, Chapter 17, stating that, since the CRE is itself a secular body, it is likely to have neglected religious discrimination and hatred.

International Law and the 'War on Terror'

David Kretzmer*

1. INTRODUCTION

Terror threatens society in many ways. The obvious danger is to human life and personal security. A different danger lies in the way society reacts to terror. The abominable attacks of 9/11 in the United States and 7/7 in the United Kingdom have created an atmosphere of fear in which many people are prepared to support harsh measures suggested by their governments, even if such measures are incompatible with standards of international law. Abandoning commitment to the rule of law and international standards of human rights will not advance the struggle against terror. It will, however, endanger the very values of our democratic society that are threatened by terror itself.

In this paper, I shall present the general picture of international law as it relates to the struggle against terrorism. I shall not be discussing specific anti-terror conventions or other instruments, but shall concentrate on general principles of international human rights law and international humanitarian law. My object is to show that international law makes allowance for effective measures against terror, without endangering the rights of the vast majority of members of society who have no connection whatsoever with it.

Before embarking on the discussion it is important to state what is meant by terror. As is well known, it has proved to be exceedingly difficult to reach an agreed international definition. The constraints have been political, rather than conceptual. Some states have opposed a definition that would include acts (such as terrorist attacks in Israel) that they support politically. Their argument that acts by groups fighting against colonial domination and foreign occupation should not be regarded as terrorist acts totally ignores the

* Professor David Kretzmer, Hebrew University of Jerusalem; former member of the UN Human Rights Committee.

essential distinction between ends and means that is fundamental in both international human rights law and international humanitarian law. Both these legal regimes rest on the assumption that no matter how legitimate your ends may be, there are limits to the means that may legitimately be employed to achieve them.

The political constraints in reaching a legal definition of terror in international law came to the fore recently when the Legal Committee of the General Assembly failed to reach agreement on a draft comprehensive convention against all forms of terrorism. Despite these constraints, it is widely accepted in academic circles that terror consists of intentional acts of violence against civilians, the aim of which is to spread fear among the population for political, religious or ideological purposes.[1] Under this definition, which will be accepted here, the legitimacy of those purposes is totally irrelevant. Even if one sympathises with a national liberation movement, intentional violence against civilians carried out by members of that movement, or on its behalf, are acts of terror. This has been recognised by implication in a recent resolution of the United Nations Security Council. While not defining terror, this resolution explicitly condemns 'all acts of terrorism irrespective of their motivation' (UNSC resolution 1624 of 14 September 2005). One may also cite the statement of Judge Rosalyn Higgins, in her separate opinion in the Advisory Opinion of the International Court of Justice on the *Legal Consequences of the Construction of a Wall in the Occupied Palestinian Territory*, that 'the protection of civilians remains an intransgressible obligation of humanitarian law' that binds all parties in a conflict, including those fighting against occupation.[2] Common Article 3 of the Geneva Conventions, which binds all parties in all armed conflicts, prohibits violence to life and person against persons taking no active part in the hostilities 'at any time and in any place whatsoever'.

2. 'THE WAR ON TERROR'

International law makes a clear distinction between situations of armed conflict and other situations. In the former situation, the law of armed conflict,

---

1 For an academic discussion of the definition of terror, see Teichman, 'How to Define Terrorism', 64 *Philosophy* (1989) p. 505; Primoratz, 'What is Terrorism?' 7 *J. of Applied Philosophy* (1990) p. 129; Gearty (ed.), *Terrorism* (Dartmouth 1996).

2 See International Court of Justice, *Legal Consequences of the Construction of a Wall in the Occupied Palestinian Territory*, Advisory Opinion (9 July 2004), 43 *ILM* 1009 (2004), Separate Opinion of Judge Higgins, 43 *ILM* at 1058, para. 19.

or international humanitarian law (IHL), as it is now generally called, comes into play. In the latter situation, this body of law has no application and a state is bound by its international human rights obligations and other obligations in international law.

From a legal point of view, then, whether we are talking about a situation of armed conflict (the term now used instead of war) has important implications. First and foremost among these is the distinction between categories of persons: combatants and non-combatants or civilians. In an armed conflict, it is lawful to target combatants of the enemy (unless they are *hors de combat*), even if they do not immediately threaten the adversary's forces, and it is prohibited to attack civilians, unless they are taking a direct part in hostilities. In international armed conflicts, combatants captured by the enemy are entitled to prisoner-of-war status and may be held until hostilities end; civilians who are not charged with criminal offences may not be interned unless such internment is absolutely necessary for the security of the detaining state. Finally, in international armed conflicts, combatants are not subject to criminal liability for fighting according to the laws of war; civilians do not enjoy the privilege to fight and may be prosecuted for doing so.

While use of the term 'war on terror' is a rhetorical device, similar to talk of the 'war on drugs' or the 'war on poverty', use of the term may have serious implications. If we are talking about a 'war', or an 'armed conflict', then maybe it is legal to target suspected terrorists rather than arresting them and trying them before a court of law. Maybe persons regarded as combatants (whether 'lawful' or 'unlawful' combatants) may be detained until the end of hostilities (whenever that may be in the 'war on terror'). It is therefore important to clarify whether we are indeed talking about a war or not.

From a legal point of view, there can be no doubt that there is no such thing as a 'war on terror'. International law recognises two types of armed conflict: international armed conflicts between states and non-international armed conflicts, which involve protracted violence between the forces of a state and organised armed groups (and sometimes between different armed groups). In both cases, we have a conflict between defined entities (states and/or organised armed groups); not a struggle against a phenomenon such as terror, no matter how serious and pernicious it may be.

It is worthwhile for a moment to dwell on the logic behind this distinction. Given the privilege in war to kill combatants, it is essential for us to know who these combatants are and thus distinguish them from civilians, who enjoy immunity from being the object of attack. In international armed conflicts, the answer is clear: members of the armed forces and of armed groups belonging to the state that fulfil certain requirements are combatants; all others are non-combatants or civilians. In non-international armed conflicts, the position is somewhat more complicated as there is no recognised status of combatants, and consequently no definition thereof. Nevertheless, it would seem that members of the armed forces of the state involved and members of the organised armed groups who take an active part in hostilities are combatants, or fighters, as some would prefer to call them. Only they may be attacked.

There is some debate over the question whether there can be an armed conflict between a state and a transnational or international armed group that does not operate mainly in the territory of that state. The main international instruments dealing with non-international armed conflicts (Common Article 3 of the 1949 Geneva Conventions and Additional Protocol II to those Conventions) both refer to conflicts taking place within the territory of a state. But even those (like the present writer) who have argued that there may be a non-international conflict between a state and a transnational organised armed group accept that such a conflict is between the state and active members of the armed group and that it is not an armed conflict with 'terror'.

In conclusion, from a legal point of view, even if there is an armed conflict between – say – the United States and al-Qaeda, there cannot be a 'war on terror'. This misnomer should be avoided.

3. International Law and Terror: Fundamental Principles

The approach of international law to counter-terrorist measures by states is based on the following general principles:

A. Duty to respect and ensure rights

International human rights conventions impose a dual obligation on states. The International Covenant on Civil and Political Rights obligates states parties both to *respect* and to *ensure* the rights of individuals in their territory and subject to their jurisdiction. The European Convention on Fundamental Rights and Freedoms refers to the duty to *secure* the rights recognised therein. Hence, states have an obligation not only to avoid acts that harm the rights of individuals; they also have an obligation to take positive action to protect the rights of persons subject to their jurisdiction against harm to their rights by others. Thus states are obligated under international human rights law to adopt measures to protect persons subject to their jurisdiction against acts of terror that threaten their rights to life and to personal security.

The duty under international law to protect against acts of terror was emphasised in Security Council Resolution 1373, adopted on 28 September 2001. In that Resolution, the Security Council decided, *inter alia,* that all states shall 'take the necessary steps to prevent the commission of terrorist acts, including by provision of early warning to other States by exchange of information'. Similarly, the Committee of Ministers of the Council of Europe, in its 'Guidelines on Human Rights and the Fight Against Terrorism', reaffirmed the 'imperative duty of States to protect their populations against possible terrorist acts'.[3]

B. *Means of fulfilling that obligation are never unlimited*

While it should never be forgotten that the *human rights obligations* of a state include the obligation to take measures to protect persons against terrorist acts, in the choice of measures it has to consider its obligation to respect the human rights of those likely to be affected by the measures, especially innocent individuals who are uninvolved in terror. There is an unfortunate tendency among people who favour stronger measures to protect the public against terror to present the issue as one of a conflict between the rights of perpetrators and those of victims. Nothing could be further from the truth. While perpetrators of terrorist acts still retain many rights (such as the right not to be tortured or subjected to cruel, inhuman or degrading treatment or punishment and the right to a fair trial), the main fear of placing unlimited powers in the hands of states carrying out the 'war on terror' is that many of the victims of the measures will not be perpetrators at all. They will be persons suspected of involvement who turn out to be ordinary citizens who have no connection whatsoever to terrorism.

The duty to make sure that all counter-terrorist measures are consistent with the state's other obligations under international law was emphasised in a recent Security Council resolution on terrorism. In resolution 1624, the Security Council stresses that states must ensure that any measures taken to implement the Council's demands for action against terrorism 'comply with all of their obligations under international law, in particular international human rights law, refugee law, and humanitarian law'. The recent Council of Europe Convention on the Prevention of Terrorism, adopted in Warsaw in May 2005, also reaffirms 'that all measures taken to prevent or suppress terrorist offences have to respect the rule of law and democratic values, human rights

[3] See Guidelines of the Council of Ministers, 804/4.3/11 July 2002.

and fundamental freedoms as well as the other provisions of international law, including, where applicable, international humanitarian law'.

C. *Types of limitations: between IHL and human rights law*

What limitations are placed on states in their choice of measures to combat terrorism? It all depends on which of two models of law applies in the given situation. If we are talking about an armed conflict situation – such as the situation in Iraq, in which there have at some times been daily indiscriminate attacks on civilians – the primary model will be that of international humanitarian law, although some of the norms of international human rights law may apply too. If we are not talking of an armed conflict situation, the limitations are those contained in international human rights law. The differences between these two legal regimes will be explained below.

D. *There are no gaps – all persons are covered*

All persons are covered by one (and sometimes both) of the above legal regimes. There are no gaps in the legal situation, which would leave certain classes of individuals unprotected and subject to the unfettered discretion of the military or civilian authorities of a state. Some experts do indeed claim that international humanitarian law does not cover conflicts between a state and transnational armed groups acting outside its territory. However, that view does not leave suspected members of such groups as unprotected 'outlaws'. Suspected terrorists will be covered by some of the human rights obligations of the state concerned, including its obligation not to arbitrarily deprive persons of their right to life, not to torture them and not to subject them to arbitrary detention.

In this context, it must be mentioned that the European Court of Human Rights has on occasion given a narrow interpretation to the sphere of application of the European Convention on Human Rights, thus allowing for cases in which acts of a state party that harm the rights of individuals are not covered by the Convention.[4] However, the Human Rights Committee, which monitors the ICCPR, to which over 150 states are party, has taken a wider view that would not allow, for instance, for cases of intentional deprivation of the life of

---

[4] See *Bankovic* v. *Belgium and Others* (2001) 11 BHRC 435, in which the Court held that the civilians killed in the NATO bombing of a television station in Belgrade during the Kosovo campaign were not in the jurisdiction of the states parties to the European Convention.

a person by state authorities that were not covered by that state's obligations.[5] Furthermore, it would seem that customary rules of international law cover all individuals against arbitrary deprivation of their right to life and of certain other rights, even if no particular human rights treaty is applicable. The right not to be tortured is recognised as part of *ius cogens*, that is, law that binds all states and may not be abrogated or modified by treaties. The duty to respect this right binds state authorities, wherever they operate.

4. TWO MODELS OF LAW: DIFFERENCES

As mentioned above, international law recognises two different legal regimes: one that applies only in situations of armed conflict and one that applies in all other situations. These regimes are based on different philosophies. The object of international humanitarian law is to limit the use of force that may be used in an armed conflict, so as to spare those who do not, or no longer, directly take part in hostilities, and to ensure that the force used does not exceed what is necessary to achieve the aim of the conflict: weakening the military potential of the enemy. This legal regime recognises that armed conflict is essentially a conflict between groups: two or more states, or a state and an organised armed group. It rests on distinctions between categories of persons: enemy combatants and civilians. An enemy combatant may be killed not because he or she personally threatens the lives of the adversary's population, but because the group to which he or she belongs (the armed forces of the enemy) does so. Even a civilian who strongly supports the war efforts of his country may not be targeted, because civilians are not permitted to fight and therefore do not threaten the adversary.

The human rights regime, on the other hand, rests on the rights of every individual, irrespective of the group to which he or she belongs. The rights to life, liberty and due process of an individual who does not harm the rights of others may not be curtailed merely because he or she belongs to a particular group. There must be individual cause for any action against a specific person. This emphasis on the equal value of all individuals is the fundamental premise of human rights law, which, in the words of the preamble to the Universal Declaration of Human Rights, flows from 'recognition of the inher-

[5] See the Committee's views in Communication No. 52/1979, *Lopez Burgos* v. *Uruguay*, CCPR/C/OP/1 at 88 (1984). See also Meron, 'Extraterritoriality of Human Rights Treaties', 89 *AJIL* (1995) p. 78; Fitzpatrick, 'Speaking Law to Power: The War Against Terrorism and Human Rights', 14 *EJIL* (2003) p. 241.

ent dignity and of the equal and inalienable rights of all members of the human family'.

Human rights law adopts a law-enforcement model that rests on a number of principles. For present purposes, the main principles are:

(a) No person may intentionally be deprived of his or her life unless it is absolutely necessary to use lethal force against him or her in strictly restricted circumstances, such as the case when he or she presents an imminent danger to the lives of others.
(b) Every person is presumed innocent, and, if suspected of involvement in criminal activities, including threats to the lives of others, he or she must be apprehended and treated with due process of law.
(c) All individuals enjoy equal protection of the law.

In the next section I shall elaborate on these principles and the types of limitations on rights permitted by the system.

5. International Human Rights Law: What Limitations on Rights?

Under the human rights regime, every human being possesses certain basic rights merely by virtue of his or her humanity. Most of these rights are not afforded absolute protection and may be limited when necessary for the protection of the rights of others or of certain social values, such as public order and security. It is important to stress, however, that not all rights are limitable. A few rights are given absolute protection. They may not be restricted even if it is claimed that such restriction is necessary to protect others. The main right that enjoys this 'absolute' status is the right not to be tortured. Under international law, torture (defined in the UN Convention Against Torture as the causing of severe pain or suffering, physical or mental, by the authorities of a state for purposes such as obtaining information or punishing persons) is prohibited in all circumstances. No exceptional circumstances, such as war or public emergency, may be used to justify torture. The right to be free from torture binds states not only to refrain from employing or condoning torture in their own jurisdiction, but also to refrain from deporting, extraditing, expelling or returning a person to a state where there are substantial grounds for believing that that person would be in danger of being subjected to torture.

The right not to be subject to torture is an exception (albeit an extremely important one) to the general principle that rights may be limited in certain circumstances. However, the fact that a right may be limited never grants unfettered discretion to the authorities to decide on the nature of the limitations. The power to limit rights does not include the power to abrogate them or abolish them.

Limitations on rights must comply with certain requirements:

(a) They must be *prescribed by law* and not decided upon according to the unregulated discretion of the authorities.
(b) They must be aimed to serve a *proper purpose*, such as state security or protection of the rights of others.
(c) They must be *necessary* to achieve that purpose. This implies that every restriction on a right must meet a test of *proportionality*: it should have a rational connection to the protection of the given purpose; it should be the least restrictive measure available to achieve the purpose; and the damage caused by the restriction should not outweigh the benefit to the purpose to be served.
(d) They must not be *discriminatory*.
(e) There must be a *fair procedure* including the real possibility of contesting the legality of the restriction in a court of law and obtaining an effective remedy if the restriction is unlawful.

6. International Humanitarian Law: What Limitations?

Even if we are dealing with an armed conflict situation, such as the one in Iraq, there are clear limitations on the means that may be used by parties in the conflict, whatever the justice of their cause. The main limitation has been mentioned above: it is strictly prohibited to make civilians the object of an attack. This is not the only limitation.

Torture in all its forms is absolutely prohibited not only under human rights law but under international humanitarian law too. No person may be subjected to arbitrary detention. With the possible exception of persons recognised as prisoners-of-war, all detained persons shall be afforded the opportunity for review of the legality of their detention and should be allowed to contest their detention before a judicial body. Detained persons must all be treated with respect for their human dignity and may not be subjected to any forms of cruel, inhuman or degrading treatment or punishment. Detainees must be registered and held in recognised places of detention and shall be entitled to visits by the International Committee of the Red Cross. Persons must never be discriminated against solely on the basis of their race, religion, ethnic group or similar status. Persons charged with criminal offences must be afforded a fair trial before a properly constituted and competent military or civilian court. Nobody may be charged with a criminal offence in respect to any act that did not constitute a criminal offence, under domestic or international law, when it was committed; nor may a convicted person be subject to a heavier penalty than the penalty applicable when the crime was committed. It is forbidden to take hostages and to use people as human shields. Collective punishment is not permitted.

7. States of Emergency

Many politicians and security personnel have advanced the argument that the constraints of domestic and international human rights norms hamper the authorities in their primary duty of protecting people against terrorist attacks. Proponents of harsher counter-terrorist measures sometimes claim that the norms of international human rights law prevent effective action against terrorism and, at best, that the system should be revised or, at worst, that it should simply be ignored.

If the existing regime of human rights protection did indeed prevent governments from taking effective measure to protect their populations against terror, one would have had to give serious consideration to proposals for reform of the regime, so as to cater to the demands of counter-terrorist measures. However, there is little justification for the argument that the present regime places an unacceptable burden on states wishing to counter terrorism.

As seen above, most rights protected under human rights law may be limited, when necessary, to protect the rights of others, such as their rights to life and to personal security, when they are threatened by terrorism. In most cases, it is possible to employ counter-terrorist measures that will meet the requirements for legitimate limitations on existing rights. Thus, for example, to the extent that the gathering of information may require invasion of privacy, security authorities may be given legal authority to use methods such as wire-tapping and other forms of surveillance when necessary and subject to adequate controls.

International law recognises that there may be extreme circumstances in which measures that meet normally permissible limitations may be inadequate to deal with the dangers facing society and that special measures are required. It therefore allows states to derogate from certain of their human rights obligations when a state of emergency exists.

While recognising that emergency situations may require emergency powers, international lawyers were justifiably wary lest such powers be abused, especially by regimes that employ the rhetoric and powers of emergencies to protect themselves against their own people, rather than protecting society itself from internal or external dangers. They were therefore careful, in drawing up human rights conventions, to place defined limits on the power of a state to resort to emergency measures.

In order for a state to employ emergency measures, there must indeed be a real emergency. Such an emergency exists according to international law only where there is a threat to the life of the nation and the relevant organ of government has made an official proclamation of an emergency. The demand that the situation justifying proclamation of a state of emergency is serious enough to threaten the very life of the nation rests on the notion that, unless this threshold is reached, the state should be able to meet its duties to protect its residents' rights by using normal limitation clauses. Only when this becomes impossible, because of the scale or intensity of the concrete dangers to society, may it be said that there exists a threat to the life of the nation. The prime example is the case of war, in which a country is attacked from outside, or an internal armed conflict, in which the violence reaches a high level and intensity.

Do terrorist attacks justify the proclamation of a state of emergency? Not necessarily. All depends on the scale and intensity of those attacks and the capability of the state to defend itself by normal means. A number of states have dealt with fairly harsh situations of terror without resorting to emergency powers. There may, however, be cases in which the dangers of terror are great enough to justify a decision that the life of the nation is threatened and that a proclamation of emergency is required.

After 9/11, the British government proclaimed a state of emergency and informed the Council of Europe of its decision to do so under the European Convention on Human Rights and the Secretary-General of the United Nations of its decision to do so under the International Covenant of Civil and Political Rights. In the *Belmarsh* case,[6] which related to special emergency legislation, the majority of Law Lords did not take issue with this proclamation, although they found the legislation itself discriminatory. Lord Hoffman, on the other hand, opined that the conditions were not such as to threaten the life of the nation and that the proclamation of the state of emergency was not

[6] *A.* v. *Secretary of State for the Home Department* [2004] UKHL 56.

justified. After the 7/7 bombings in London, Lord Hoffman was criticised for his view. The critics assumed that these bombings had vindicated the emergency proclamation. These critics forget, however, that the justification cited by the British government for the state of emergency, which would allow them to introduce special measures, was the need to deal with aliens who posed a security risk and could not be deported. All the perpetrators of the 7/7 bombings were, it would seem, British citizens. The critics have not explained how the state of emergency would in any way have allowed the authorities to adopt measures relating to such citizens that they could not have adopted under normal legislation.

Even if a state of emergency is proclaimed, the state does not acquire *carte blanche* to place restrictions on rights.[7] In the first place, there are certain rights from which a state may not derogate even in a state of emergency. Among these are freedom from torture and cruel, inhuman or degrading treatment or punishment. A state may not torture persons even if it argues that this is required because of the threat to the life of the nation. Secondly, even if we are talking about rights that are subject to derogation, such derogation is allowed only if strictly required by the exigencies of the situation. The state must show why the specific derogation is required and why the danger it wishes to contain cannot be contained through normal means. In the recent debate in the British parliament on the prime minister's proposal to change the law so as to allow persons to be held in detention without charge for up to ninety days, the legal argument raised against the proposal was that such a long period was not strictly required by the exigencies of the situation. In the end, parliament agreed to a period of twenty-eight days.

Finally, no state may use its power to derogate from human rights provisions in order to escape from its other obligations under international law. The most relevant obligations in emergency situations are the state's obligations under international humanitarian law (IHL). This branch of international law, which only applies, as we have seen, in armed conflict situations, takes into account issues of military necessity and security in its substantive rules. It is built for classic emergency situations (wars) and may not be derogated from. Unless a specific norm allows for questions of military necessity to be considered – and many of the norms of IHL do – a state may not plead military necessity as a defence against violation of the norms of IHL.

---

[7] For a detailed description of the rules relating to states of emergency in international law, see Human Rights Committee, General Comment No. 29, CCPR/C/21?rev.1/Add11.

8. Conclusions

States have an obligation to take effective measures to protect persons subject to their jurisdiction from terror. However, in doing so, they must be mindful of the danger that counter-terrorist measures will be incompatible with the very values threatened by terror itself.

International law provides a framework for counter--terrorist measures both in situations of armed conflict and in other situations. This framework allows for counter-terrorist measures that place limits on certain rights, without destroying those rights themselves. In extreme circumstances, further emergency measures may be legitimate, but these are never unlimited. While the threat of modern-day terror may require us to devise new and original methods of defeating terror, these methods must be compatible with the principles of international law. This presents a serious challenge to countries faced with terror, but it is a challenge that can be met and is well worth meeting. As the former Secretary-General of the United Nations, Kofi Annan, stated in his statement to a conference on fighting terrorism:

> Upholding human rights is not at odds with battling terrorism: on the contrary, the moral vision of human rights – the deep respect for the dignity of each person – is among our most powerful weapons against it.[8]

---

[8] Statement of UN Secretary-General Annan to conference on 'Fighting Terrorism for Humanity: A Conference on the Roots of Evil' (New York, 22 September 2003).

Tactical Victory and Defeat in a War Against Terror

Aryeh Nusbacher*

In the South African war of 1899-1904, the British army was shocked by the indecent tactics used by its enemies, the Boers – the Dutch farmers in two of South Africa's states. Shocked, because they used irregular cavalry tactics. They used machine guns – British-built machine guns – to tremendous effect against the British army. They did not wear uniforms – they wore their own clothes. They could easily present themselves as innocent members of the public – neutral, pro-British – without any trouble at all. The British were outraged. Their tactics at the time were absolutely unsuited to dealing with the enemy in the South African war. Britain could not cope with what the Boers were doing. Afterwards, Ernest Swinton (later a professor of the history of war at Oxford University) and others led a reform of tactics which resulted in a much more 'modern' approach to tactics.

In a similar vein, we are currently faced with systematic menacing, maiming and murdering of the innocent in order to inspire terror and thereby achieve a policy aim. We are outraged, frustrated and repulsed by this, but we must find ways of reforming our approach to tactics that can take into account the reality of fighting a war against terror. Armed forces have, largely uncharacteristically, run away from the task – uncharacteristically, because there is a tremendous amount of funding attached to the task, as the security service discovered by reaching forward, seizing the task of defending the country from terrorism and finding itself financially enhanced. Armed forces, with a few exceptions, notably in Israel, have disclaimed responsibility for fighting a war against terror. The defence of the realm against this most imminent danger becomes homeland security. It is given to intelligence officers (those whose job it is to collect, analyse and disseminate intelligence),

* Dr Aryeh Nusbacher, Senior Lecturer, Sandhurst.

not those whose job it is to confront the state's enemies with force. One result of this has been that the priorities attached to fighting terrorism in much of the West are those of intelligence agencies rather than those of the armed forces.

This is not to denigrate intelligence agencies. It is just not their purpose. Their culture is not designed for confronting armed force. One result of this is that the discipline that the study of war has lent to wise armies over many years is, to some extent, absent. In analysing the Vietnam War in a very problematic but interesting book called *On Strategy*, the American colonel David Hapworth says that the 'root of the American difficulties in Vietnam was that they did not have a clear policy, did not have clear strategy and therefore tactical action in Vietnam was not especially likely to result in achieving victory. If victory had been achieved, it would have been serendipitous – brute force applied without reason.' I would suggest that as we look for tactics, the application of the currency of war, of fighting and destruction to achieving a strategic aim, we rapidly find that we do not have clear strategic aims in this war against terror.

If we are still fighting the global war against terror, we are fighting what is more or less a declared war, but we are fighting it, depending on what country you look at, with a variety of strategies and non-strategies.

Are we trying to make everyone in the world who would adopt terrorist tactics choose other tactics? Is this struggle against terrorism like the struggle the United States led against piracy – which was a tactic for state policy and making money – in the early nineteenth century? Is it like the British struggle against the slave trade in the early and mid-nineteenth century? Are we just offended by the tactic and therefore seek to direct people to choose other violent tactics that we find more acceptable? Do we seek to push the terrorist into guerrilla war so that we can embrace the struggle with the terrorist on terms more favourable perhaps to ourselves, more suitable to our view of right and wrong?

We are not really fighting a war against terror. We do not really abominate the terrorist so much as the idea that the terrorist might blow up somebody we think ought not to have been blown up. We are not fighting an offensive war against terror in which, in the big picture, we must seek out those who practice terror wherever they may be and make them stop. If we were, UK Foreign and Commonwealth Office spokesmen would not announce that they were restricting discussions with Hamas to members of the Hamas political wing who had been elected to office in the West Bank. For years, in order to enable governments to talk to terrorists they said they were not talking to, they invented the idea of the 'political wing'. I am sure that everyone at

Hamas was very amused by the idea that the FCO representatives would only talk to members of Hamas's political wing.

Perhaps our strategic aim, to which all of our tactics must be targeted, is to support, where possible, American opposition to the application of terrorism worldwide. Perhaps the United States really is opposed to the application of terror worldwide, and, although Europe may not be, it will claim to support the United States' efforts to extirpate terrorism while actually just look after itself. Maybe that is our strategic aim. Maybe our strategic aim is just to make sure that we are not blown up – a fundamentally defensive aim. Indeed, that accords much more with the tactics that we see all over the world. That is certainly the most durable potential strategic aim.

How do we do it? Models abound, but there are a couple of key ones. The military model is assumed by almost everyone who discusses it to be repressive by nature.

Examples include the British army's arrival in Northern Ireland, in the late 1960s and early 1970s, where a Roman Catholic population that had previously been welcoming to the British army found that having their linen cupboards searched by squaddies with dirty boots and bayonets and having the helicopter hovering over the house by night was uncongenial.

The military model of repressive counter-terrorism assumes that soldiers are not intelligent enough to apply tactics to a strategic aim in a sensitive manner. for the West has therefore opted for another model: the criminal justice model, sometimes referred to as the 'enhanced criminal justice model'. We have indeed made the pursuit of criminal justice an end in itself with respect to dealing with terrorism, to the extent that we may perhaps be putting our ideas of criminal justice at risk.

Abraham Lincoln suspended *habeas corpus* during the American Civil War for two periods, in 1861 and 1862, in order to enable him and his people to lock up those who opposed the war. For that, he was roundly criticised.

We are now talking about suspending *habeas corpus* and various equivalent steps. We are talking about suspending and changing our criminal justice system purely to deal with terrorism – make permanent changes to make terrorism a special crime. Indeed, it negates a lot of the value of treating a terrorist as an ordinary criminal, of pretending the terrorist is an ordinary criminal, when we invent crimes that he has committed. When we seek to apply criminal sanctions designed to deter, punish, rehabilitate and achieve justice for victims and families, I wonder whether we expect a terrorist who is dealt with by the criminal justice system will go to prison and learn a trade, become a better person, pay his or her debt to society and return to the practice of paediatrics or engineering as a new person whom we can live with, or whether we are admitting that this is not really what we expect our criminal justice system to do anyway.

How do we achieve victory at the tactical level? How do we *exploit* that victory to achieve our strategic aims? How do we recognise defeat when we find it and how do we cope with it?

We have to address these four questions by seeking achievements that do not entail slaughtering our enemies in their hundreds or thousands but which disrupt their activities so that they cannot achieve their aims.

We have weak strategic aims, but if we seek to disrupt our enemies' aims and prevent them from achieving their aims, then at least our tactical activity is not nugatory. Capturing actual or potential terrorists, controlling an enemy resource, enables us to achieve the public relations victory of giving somebody a platform in a courtroom where he can make speeches about us. It also creates a whole new opportunity for hostage taking.

We have only recently started to incarcerate members of groups who have violent friends. How long is it before the 2010 equivalent of 1970s-style airline hijacking begins again? Capturing the terrorist may have value, but not for the sake of capturing terrorists. It has value only if it disrupts terrorist networks, makes it difficult for them to achieve their aims and enables us to achieve the victory of continuing to run our democracies as we believe they ought to be run.

Killing terrorists is another option. But if we kill somebody who is prepared to die anyway – it is just a question of how many people he is able to kill in the process – we are not necessarily achieving an aim. If we are going to kill, we have to kill *advisedly*. We have to kill in a way that achieves our aims. This is a bizarre and harsh thing to say, but killing is not remarkable in time of war.

We were willing to kill a few thousand Serb civilians in the course of pursuing our aims in the Kosovo war. We have to be willing to kill people we think are terrorists as though they were fighting a conventional war. It is difficult to say and it is difficult to do, but it must not be done indiscriminately. It must not be done as killing for the sake of killing, because we have learned in the twentieth century that wholesale attrition is inappropriate in any sort of war, whether in a war against terrorism or a war against absolutism.

We must identify enemy centres of gravity, not just personalities or high-profile terrorists. We must identify enemy centres of gravity which, if hit by tactical action, will cause the enemy to be disrupted, and this is especially difficult. How much more difficult is it to learn how to accept tactical defeat and turn it into success at the strategic level? of the West has been attacked several times in recent years, and we struggle to deal with it in a way that enables us to successfully prosecute a war against the enemy. We must respond to successful enemy tactical action by taking the initiative and disrupting the enemy. This requires a very different attitude than that adopted, for example, by the intelligence agencies, to which those we must destroy are assets.

Broadly speaking, we need clear strategic aims in order to start thinking about what we need to do tactically to fight this war properly. If we are not prepared to do so, we must be prepared, as Spain was, to concede strategic defeat in the war against terrorism – to put up our hands and say: we will not participate, we will do what our enemies say they want us to do – and stop pretending to fight a war that we do not have the resources to fight to win.

Muslims and the Aftermath of 7 July 2005: Revisiting Minority Rights in the United Kingdom

Javaid Rehman*

1. INTRODUCTION

Islam and Islamic legal principles have become the focus of world attention. Critics of Islam argue that Islam *per se* is an aggressive religion advocating recourse to violence, terrorism and destruction.[1] In order to reinforce their prejudices against Islam, they point to a lack of constitutionalism, abuse of power, political manipulation and violations of fundamental human rights in many Islamic states.[2] In legal literature as well as societal discourses, identifying

* Professor Javaid Rehman, Brunel University.

1 'Many horrific acts have been, and continue to be carried out in the name of Islam, just as they have been in the name of Christianity. But unlike Islam, Christianity does not justify the use of all forms of violence. Islam does.' P. Sookhdeo, 'A Religion that sanctions violence', *Daily Telegraph* (17 September 2001) p. 22. For a detailed consideration of the issues, see J. Rehman, *Islamic State Practices, International Law and the Threat from Terrorism: A Critique of the 'Clash of Civilizations' in the New World Order* (Oxford, Hart Publishing 2005).

2 Amongst the extensive literature on Islam and human rights protection, see, A.A. An-Na'im, *Toward an Islamic Reformation: Civil Liberties, Human Rights and International Law* (Syracuse NY, Syracuse University Press 1990); F.M. Denny, *An Introduction to Islam* (New York, Macmillan Pub. Co. 1994); A.E. Mayer, *Islam and Human Rights: Tradition and Politics*, 2nd edn. (Boulder, Westview Press 1995); C.G. Weeramantry, *Islamic Jurisprudence: An International Perspective* (London, Macmillan Press 1988); R. Landau, *Islam and the Arabs* (London, George Allen and Unwin Ltd. 1958); M.A. Baderin, *International Human Rights and Islamic Law* (Oxford, Oxford University Press 2003); R. Afshari, 'An Essay on Islamic Cultural Relativism in the Discourse of Human Rights', 16 *Human Rights Quarterly* (1994) p. 235; P.J. Riga, 'Islamic Law and Moder-

Islam with terrorism is not uncommon.[3] In an environment of immense sensitivity, any discussion on the contemporary position of Muslims is enormously controversial. The overall objective of the present paper is to examine critically the position of Muslim minorities within the United Kingdom. It considers a number of issues and concerns encountered by the Muslim minorities both historically and post 7 July 2005. The paper is divided into six sections. After these introductory remarks, section two presents a historical overview of Muslim minorities in the United Kingdom. Section three examines the practices and policies of successive British governments and the factors that have led to disenchantment, discrimination and aggravation. Sections four and five focus specifically upon the implications of the 11 September 2001 and 7 July 2005 bombings respectively. The final section, section six, provides a number of concluding observations.

2. Historical Overview of Muslim Minorities in the United Kingdom

The Muslims of the United Kingdom represent a diverse group – an assortment of various races, nationalities and traditions. Their migratory and location patterns have also been varied, with some of the earliest, more settled immigration having taken place over 150 years ago.[4] These earlier, albeit limited, settlements took place in the cities of Liverpool, Cardiff, Manchester, South Shields and the East End of London.[5] From the early part of the nineteenth century up until the end of the Second World War (1945) there were very limited, often uncoordinated, waves of Muslim settlements. It was only from the late 1940s to the early 1960s that increasing demands for labour prompted significant large-scale migration of workers to the United Kingdom.[6]

---

nity: Conflict and Evolution', 36 *American Journal of Jurisprudence* (1991) p. 103; J. Entelis, 'International Human Rights: Islam's Friend or Foe? Algeria as an Example of the Compatibility of International Human Rights regarding Women's Equality and Islamic Law', 20 *Fordham International Law Journal* (1997) p. 1251; S.S. Ali, *Gender and Human Rights in Islam and International Law: Equal Before Allah, Unequal Before Man?* (The Hague, Kluwer Law International 2000).

3 H. Ansari, *Muslims in Britain* (London, Minority Rights Group 2002) p. 6.

4 Ibid.

5 Ibid.

6 This was a pattern followed in the larger economies of Western Europe. See S. Knights, 'Religious Symbols in the School: Freedom of Religion, Minorities and Education', 5 *European Human Right Law Review* (2005) p. 499 at p. 501.

This class of economic migrants hailed principally from Commonwealth countries such as India and Pakistan. They were unskilled workers with little or no education. Upon arrival, these Muslim migrants faced issues of joblessness and, more significantly, alarmingly high levels of racism and social exclusion. The successive restrictive legislation in the shape of the Commonwealth Immigrants Act 1962,[7] the Commonwealth Immigrants Act 1968[8] and the Immigration Act 1971[9] respectively curtailed the growth of migrants, while at the same time raising genuine concerns about race relations in the United Kingdom. Indeed, elements contained within the 1971 Act became the subject of criticism and legislative action for supporting certain communities and groups at the expense of others.[10] Successful challenges were launched against the United Kingdom before the European human rights institutions. Bradley and Ewing make the valid point that:

> The elaborate concept of patriality was subject to much criticism. Foremost was the criticism that patriality did not extend to persons who, like the East African Asians, were citizens of a Commonwealth country but had no country to which they might go other than the United Kingdom. For this reason the United Kingdom government could not ratify the fourth protocol to the European Convention on Human Rights, which declares that 'no one shall be denied the right to enter the territory of which he is a national'. Patriality was also criticized for including citizens of other Commonwealth countries at least one of whose parents had been born in the United Kingdom; this rule favoured those of British origin from countries such as Australia, Canada and New Zealand, exposing the 1971 Act to the charge that it was racially motivated.[11]

---

7 The Act was aimed at restricting immigration from South Asia and the Caribbean. It subjected all Commonwealth citizens to immigration control, save those who were British citizens and those holding British passports. See A.W. Bradley and K.D. Ewing, *Constitutional and Administrative Law*, 13th edn. (London, Longman 2003) p. 433.

8 The 1968 Act was meant to restrict large-scale immigration from Kenya. The operation of the Act provided for further limitations of entry for non-resident British passport holders. For details, see I.A. Macdonald and F. Webber, *Immigration Law and Practice in the United Kingdom* (London, LexisNexis Butterworths 2005); A. Dummett and A. Nicol, *Subjects, Citizens, Aliens and Others* (London, Weidenfeld & Nicolson 1990).

9 See D. Feldman, *Civil Liberties and Human Rights in England and Wales*, 2nd edn. (Oxford, Oxford University Press 2002) p. 479.

10 See *East African Asians* v. *UK*, 3 EHRR 76 (1973); *Abdulalziz, Cabales and Balkandali* v. *UK*, 7 EHRR 471 (1985).

11 Bradley and Ewing, *supra* n. 7, at p. 435.

The migrant Muslim community remained an isolated segment of the wider British society, unable and unwilling to integrate into the mainstream of majority ethos. Typical of a beleaguered minority group, these settlers tended to establish their own associations, with their social activities being confined to religious institutions such as the mosques. In a society challenging the prevailing social and moral values, this generation of Muslims felt vulnerable and exposed; conservatism and religious orthodoxy were adhered to rigidly and staunchly. A conscious decision to become permanently settled within the United Kingdom provoked substantial challenges of integration and assimilation – these challenges have probably been more acute for the first generation of Muslims who were born and raised in the British society while at the same time feeling pressured to maintain a religious and cultural identity.

The 2001 United Kingdom National Census introduced for the first time tabulation based on religious denomination. According to the census, there are 1.6 million Muslims in the United Kingdom, a figure that in 2006 equated to approximately 2 million.[12] UK Muslims hail principally from an Asian ethnic background (73%), with over a million coming from Pakistan, Bangladesh or India.[13] In 2001, 43% were Pakistanis, 16% Bangladeshi, 8% Indian and 6% of other Asian ethnic background. A further 8% of Muslims have Black African origins. Forty-six per cent of Muslims currently living in the United Kingdom were born there, while 18% were born in Pakistan, 9% in Bangladesh, 9% in Africa and 3% in Turkey. British Muslims also have the youngest age profile of all faith groups in the country, with the 2001 census confirming that one-third of all Muslims were under the age of sixteen. The average age of Muslims in contemporary Britain is twenty-eight. Although primarily an urban population, Muslims have tended to concentrate in larger urban cities, with over 40% residing in Greater London. There are other concentrations in Scotland, Glasgow and Yorkshire. Over the past two decades, there has been a drop in migrant worker settlement from Pakistan and Bangladesh, though significant secondary migration has taken place through family and marriage resettlement. There has also been a noticeable increase in the number of asylum seekers and refugees entering the United Kingdom

---

[12] UK 2001 National Census, Religion in Britain, available at: <http://www.statistics.gov.uk/cci/nugget.asp?id=293>.

[13] UK 2001 National Census, Ethnicity and Religion, available at: <http://www.statistics.gov.uk/cci/nugget.asp?id=395>.

from countries and regions with large Muslim populations, such as the former Yugoslavia, Afghanistan and the Middle East.

In recent times, the Muslim minorities in the United Kingdom have become relatively well-established, with a noticeable improvement in their socioeconomic and educational standards. British Muslims are represented in many walks of life. A survey conducted in 2002 estimated that there are as may as 5,000 Muslim millionaires in the United Kingdom.[14] Despite this notable improvement in the living and educational standards of the first generation of these migrants, on the whole, British Muslims continue to suffer from 'unemployment, poor working conditions, poverty, poor and overcrowded housing, poor health, and low educational qualifications'.[15] A majority of the Muslim population is likely to be living in rented, often substandard accommodation. More than two-thirds of the entire Muslim women population remains economically inactive, the highest number in any faith group. Muslim men continue to be least likely to obtain managerial and professional jobs and predominate in low-skilled vocations. On average, Muslim households continue to have a larger proportion of members and there is greater evidence of child poverty and domestic violence.

3. Concerns and Grievances

The Muslim minorities of the United Kingdom have a range of concerns and grievances. Many of these are a consequence of neglect and ostracism on the part of successive British administrations, while others emanate from substantial cultural, religious and ethical differences between Muslim minorities and the majority of the British population. The many significant areas of concern include the absence of a comprehensive legislative framework to prevent religious discrimination and protect religious sentiments, inadequate protection from blasphemy laws and other forms of exclusion and discrimination. For British Muslims, a matter of substantial disquiet is the failure of law to protect individuals from discrimination based on religious grounds.[16] In the historic development of discrimination laws in Britain, a particular emphasis

14 '5000 Muslims Make Millions', *The Guardian* (1 February 2002).

15 Ansari, *supra* n. 3, at p. 9.

16 See P. Thornberry, 'Rights of Minorities', in D. Harris and S. Joseph (eds.), *The International Covenant on Civil and Political Rights* (Oxford, Clarendon Press 1995) pp. 597-627 at p. 620.

has been placed on race and ethnicity.[17] A series of laws has been adopted to curb various forms of discrimination based on race, colour and ethnicity. The Race Relations Act 1976 regards a 'racial group' as 'a group of persons defined by reference to colour, race, nationality or ethnic or national origins and references to a person's racial group refer to any racial group into which he falls'.[18] Further refinement of the race discrimination law has been conducted through the Race Relations (Amendment) Act 2000.[19] Race discrimination legislation within the United Kingdom does not cover discrimination on religious or political grounds *per se*.[20] The boundaries between race, ethnicity and religion are fluid. As a consequence of this fluidity, while adherents of some religions such as Jews and Sikhs have been accorded protection under this legislation, Muslims are not considered a racial or ethnic group and are therefore unable to rely upon the existing race discrimination legislation.[21] As a religious minority, demand for a comprehensive legislation outlawing all forms of religious discrimination has been a top priority for Muslims. Recent developments at European level have made some, though limited, advances towards providing a regime of religious equality. The Employment Equality (Religion or Belief) Directive prohibits direct and indirect discrimination, harassment and victimisation on the grounds of religion and belief with respect to employment and vocational training; the legislation applies to higher education institutions.[22] It nevertheless remains the case that, unlike Northern Ireland, English law does not provide a comprehensive cover for religious discrimination.[23]

Related to the issue of discrimination is a more specific concern emanating from the restrictive and arbitrary approaches adopted towards blasphemy laws in the United Kingdom. In its current form, the common law offence of blasphemy is confined to vilification, ridicule or use of defamatory language

---

17 See A. McColgan, *Discrimination Law: Text, Cases and Materials* (Oxford, Hart Publishing 2000).

18 Race Relations Act 1976, Section 3(1). McColgan, *supra* n. 17, at pp. 409-433.

19 Race Relations (Amendment) Act 2000, available at: <http://www.opsi.gov.uk/ACTS/acts2000/20000034.htm>.

20 S.H. Bailey, D.J. Harris and D.C. Omerod, *Civil Liberties: Cases and Materials*, 5th edn. (London, Butterworths 2001) p. 1111.

21 See *Mandla* v. *Dowell Lee* [1983] AC 548; *Seide* v. *Gillette Industries Ltd.* [1980] IRLR 427, 430 (EAT).

22 Employment Equality (Religion or Belief) Regulations 2003 (SI 2003/1660).

23 On the position of Northern Ireland, see Fair Employment and Treatment (Northern Ireland) Order 1998 (as amended).

in relation to the Christian faith. In order to commit the offence of blasphemy, there is no requirement of establishing intent to blaspheme. In this regard, extraordinarily for a criminal law offence, it is one of strict liability.[24] It is sufficient that the offending materials are blasphemous and that there was intent to publish.[25] Its non-applicability to Islam emerged as a substantial issue during the campaign to have the novel *The Satanic Verses* banned and its author, Salman Rushdie, tried for blasphemy.[26] The Salman Rushdie affair, as it came to be known, attracted global attention after the *fatwa* (legal opinion) of the late Ayatollah Khomeini sentencing Rushdie to the death penalty. Khomeini's *fatwa* provided substantial ammunition to the critics of Islam, who criticised Islam as a religion that abhorred free speech and propagated violence and murder. However, all efforts to have the publication banned or prevent the sale of the book were unsuccessful.[27] Nor was there any success in having Salman Rushdie prosecuted for blaspheming the Islamic faith.[28] Recourse to legal remedies proved ineffective in the United Kingdom. Attempts to bring a private prosecution were unsuccessful in the United Kingdom in *R* v. *Chief Metropolitan Stipendiary Magistrate, ex parte Choudhury*,[29] while the European Commission on Human Rights struck out an application as manifestly ill-founded since Article 9 of the European Convention on Human Rights did not provide for absolute protection of religious sensitivities.[30] Such discrepancy in the application of laws relating to religion has not only infuriated the Islamic community but has also been the object of criticism by human rights scholars. Bailey, Harris and Jones make the striking remark that:

> *Ex p Choudhury* raises a question that has become increasingly relevant as the United Kingdom has become a more multi-religious society. Is it defensible that in *R v Lemon* the publisher of a poem that offended Christians could be guilty of blasphemy when in *Ex p Choudhury* the publishers of a novel that contained passages that were at least equally offensive to Muslims could not? The Law

[24] See 'Criminal Law: Offences against Religion and Public Worship', Law Commission Report No. 145 (1985) para. 2.18 (ii).

[25] Ibid.

[26] See S. Rushdie, *The Satanic Verses* (New York, Viking Penguin Inc. 1988).

[27] See C.P. Munro, 'Prophets, Presbyters and Profanity', *Public Law* (1989) p. 369; P. Kearns, 'Obscene and Blasphemous Libel: Misunderstanding Art', *Criminal Law Review* (2000) p. 652; P. Kearns, 'The Uncultured God: Blasphemy Law's Reprieve and the Art Matrix', 5 *European Human Rights Law Review* (2000) p. 512.

[28] Bailey, Harris and Omerod, *supra* n. 20, at pp. 1045-1053.

[29] [1991] 1 All ER 306, [1990] 3 WLR 986, Queen's Bench Divisional Court.

[30] *Choudhury* v. *UK*, Applcation No. 17349/1990, 12 HRLJ 172 (1991).

> Commission addressed this question in their 1985 Report when recommending the abolition of the offences of blasphemy and blasphemous libel (the written form of blasphemy).[31]

Similarly, according to Ghandhi and James:

> The injustice of preserving the status quo is manifest. The publication in September 1988 of Salman Rushdie's book *The Satanic Verses,* as is very well known, caused outrage among both British and non-British Muslims. Copies of the book were burned publicly across the world. Riots on the Indian subcontinent resulted in deaths. The Ayatollah Khomeini issued his notorious fatwa, which is still in existence. Yet the Divisional Court concluded that, *inter alia,* the blasphemous libel of Allah (Almighty God), the prophet Ibrahim, Muhammad the Holy Prophet of Islam and the religion of Islam was not an offence known to English law. The damage done by this book to interdenominational harmony was enormous and its effects are still being felt by the author today. Yet, by contrast, an insignificant 18-minute video *Visions of Ecstasy,* which would probably have passed into a minute and unnoticed public circulation if the Board had decided not to ban it, was entitled to the protection of the full panoply of the English law of blasphemy. Such disproportionality brings the law into disrepute. The alternatives are extension to other religions (discussed above) or complete abolition.[32]

After 2001, under Tony Blair's premiership, the Labour government attempted to introduce legislation to outlaw religious hatred.[33] The Racial and Religious Hatred Bill as introduced in the British parliament suffered from significant difficulties. Its attempt to fuse threatening words and behaviour against unbelievers with abusive or insulting words raised considerable opposition. The path of the Racial and Religious Hatred Bill in parliament, especially in the House of Lords, has been rocky.[34] It was amended significantly, and the government's attempt to resurrect some of the provisions failed in February 2005 before legislation was finally adopted.[35] In its current

---

31 Bailey, Harris and Omerod, *supra* n. 20, at pp. 1050-1051.

32 S. Ghandhi and J. James, 'The English Law of Blasphemy and the European Convention on Human Rights', 4 *European Human Rights Law Review* (1998) pp. 430-451 at p. 450 (footnotes omitted).

33 See 'Religious Hatred Bill: The Price in not Right', *The Guardian* (31 January 2006) p. 28; 'Religious Hate Bill Lost after Blair Fails to Vote', *The Times* (1 February 2006) p. 1.

34 Racial and Religious Hatred Act 2006, available at: <http://www.opsi.gov.uk/acts/acts2006/60001--b.htm>.

35 Ibid.

form, the law is vague and ambiguous. The Act deals ambiguously with defining 'religious hatred', which means 'hatred against a group of persons defined by reference to religious belief or lack of religious belief'. No definition is provided as to the meaning of 'religious belief'. According to Section 29.B, a person commits an offence if he uses 'threatening words or behaviour or displays any written material which is threatening with the intention of stirring up religious hatred'. With an inherent lack of clarity, the legislation is a recipe for divisions and tensions.[36]

While this new legislation was ostensibly introduced to provide a more adequate cover to Muslim religious minorities, there is a real danger of increasing convictions being brought against Muslims. The legislation is divisive and presents a further risk to community relations. As the former Archbishop of Canterbury, Lord Carey, noted: '[the Act] has the potential to drive a wedge between the Muslim community and the rest of us'.[37] Muslim communities have also expressed concerns over the implications of criminal laws such as those incorporated in the Anti-Terrorism, Crime and Security Act 2001. This Act has created a new category of religiously aggravated offences, and there are fears that this provision may in fact be used to prosecute Muslims.[38]

A further complication arises as a consequence of differing modes of dress code, dietary requirements, prayers and religious festivities. A hugely divisive subject has been the wearing of headscarves in educational institutions and the workplace. While many institutions, particularly schools, tolerate the wearing of the *hijab*, there is nevertheless a considerable amount of controversy and resistance as to the extent to which Muslim girls can cover their bodies.[39] In a recent case, a female Muslim pupil named Shabana Begum challenged the decision of her school refusing to allow her to wear a *jilbab*.[40] Muslims also feel aggrieved at the insensitivity of wider British society to-

---

36 Ibid.

37 'Christian Group May Seek Ban on Qur'an', *The Guardian* (12 October 2005).

38 In advancing this point, Professor Walker notes 'one strongly suspects that the passage of such an offence in Britain would be more likely in the atmosphere prevailing after 11 September to provoke prosecutions of Muslims than those speaking against their faith'. C.P. Walker, *Blackstone's Guide to the Anti-Terrorism Legislation* (Oxford, Oxford University Press 2002) p. 183.

39 See Open Society Institute, 'Muslims in the UK: Policies for Engaged Citizens' (Budapest, Open Society Institute 2005) pp. 104-183.

40 See *R (on the application of Begum)* v. *Headteacher and Governors of Denbigh High School* [2005] EWCA Civ. 199, [2005] 1 FCR 530.

wards their religious obligations such prayers, fasting and religious holidays. A particular source of difficulty concerns attempts by Muslims to take off time to pray, especially on Friday afternoons. Legal challenges have proved unsuccessful in British courts,[41] as well as under the European Convention on Human Rights.[42] There is frustration that society rends to prejudge the identity and character of Muslims on the basis of stereotypical images rather than regarding them as individual citizens.

4. Policies and Practices of Engagement and Conflicting Positions Since 11 September 2001

An increasing amount of Islamophobia has been encountered since the tragic events of 9/11. Muslims, in particular the minority communities in Europe, the United States and Australia, became victims of 'Islamophobia'.[43] The concern for the Muslim diasporas in Europe and the United States has been so grave that, in its fifty-ninth session, the United Nations Human Rights Commission requested the Special Rapporteur on the contemporary forms of racism, racial discrimination, xenophobia and related intolerance to examine the situation confronting Muslim and Arab people all over the world regarding physical assaults and other forms of attacks against their place of worship, cultural places, businesses and properties since the events of 11 September 2001.[44] The tragic events of 9/11 placed a heavy burden on British Muslims. In the approaches adopted both in the media and, often, in political rhetoric, Muslims found their loyalties tested and were made to renounce violence and

---

41 See *Ahmad* v. *Inner London Education Authority* [1978] QB 36, [1977] 3 WLR 396, [1978] 1 All ER 574 (Court of Appeal). See also 'Religious Discrimination in England and Wales', Home Office Report (London 2001). Cf. *Yassin* v. *Northwest Home Care Ltd.* CRE Rep. 1993, p. 21 Ind. Trib. (which awarded compensation to a Muslim for having been dropped from a sales representative training programme because of the need to have a half-hour off for Friday prayers).

42 See *Ahmad* v. *UK* (1982) 4 EHRR 126.

43 Islamophobia has been defined as 'dread or hatred of Islam – and, therefore, fear or dislike of all or most Muslims'. The Runnymede Trust, *Islamophobia: A Challenge for Us All* (London 1997) p. 1.

44 See Commission on Human Rights, Sixtieth Session, Annotations of Provisional Agenda E/CN.4/2004/I/Add.1 para. 29. For further analysis, see J. Rehman 'Islamophobia after 9/11: International Terrorism, Sharia and Muslim Minorities of Europe – The Case of the United Kingdom', *European Yearbook of Minority Issues*, Vol. 3 (2003-2004) p. 3 at p. 217.

terrorism more than any other minorities.[45] There were also some irresponsible statements, such as the accusation made by former prime minister Margaret Thatcher against Muslim priests for not condemning enough the events of 9/11, or the observations made by the Italian prime minister about the superiority of the Western civilisation *vis-à-vis* the Islamic world.[46]

A. *Bombing campaign in Afghanistan and the Guantánamo Detention Centre*

The international community led by the United Nations was at the forefront of condemnation of the crimes carried out on 9/11. The UN General Assembly and the UN Security Council adopted a series of resolutions.[47] The United Kingdom – whose own citizens had also been murdered – very rightly supported the international community in condemning the atrocities. However, in its keenness to express solidarity with the United States, the British government also undertook certain extraordinary steps. This was evident in its unequivocal support for the military campaign against Afghanistan in October 2001,[48] as well as in the introduction of further stringent anti-terrorist domestic legislation.[49] While the United States, the United Kingdom and their allies claimed that the bombing campaign against the Taliban was justified under international law, in reality the legal situation was far more complex. In

45 Ansari, *supra* n. 3 at pp. 24-25.

46 'We must be aware of the superiority of our civilization, a system that has guaranteed well-being, respect for human rights – and in contrast with Islamic countries – respect for religious and political rights. Islamic civilization is stuck where it was fourteen hundred years ago.' Italian Prime Minister, Silvio Berlusconi, comments made in Berlin, 26 September 2001. These comments have been cited extensively: see A. Palmer, 'Is the West Really Best', *Sunday Telegraph* (30 September 2001) p. 14; A. Osburn, 'On the Brink of War: Reaction – Scorn Poured on Berlusconi Views – European and Muslim Leaders Express Disgust', *The Guardian* (28 September 2001) p. 4; 'EU deplores "Dangerous" Islam Jibe', BBC News, available at: <http://news.bbc.co.uk/1/hi/world/middle_east/1565664.stm>.

47 See General Assembly resolutions: Condemnation of Terrorist Attacks in the United States of America, UN Doc. A/RES/56/1 (12 September 2001); Measures to Eliminate International Terrorism, UN Doc. A/RES/56/88 (12 December 2001). See also Security Council resolution 1368 (2001) condemning the terrorist attacks of 11 September 2001 in New York, Washington D.C. and Pennsylvania, adopted by the Security Council at its 4370th meeting (12 September 2001); Security Council resolution 1373 (2001), adopted by the Security Council at its 4385th meeting (28 September 2001).

48 See <http://www.pm.gov.uk/files/pdf/culpability_document.pdf>.

49 See Anti-Terrorism, Crime and Security Act 2001 (discussed *infra*).

the absence of an express authorisation by the Security Council, question marks were raised regarding the legitimacy and usage of the right to self-defence.[50] The military campaign, accompanied by evidence of indiscriminate bombardment and civilian casualties, was an unfortunate development for the Muslim minorities of Britain.[51] As ordinary conscientious citizens of a civilised legal and political order, many Muslims expressed their concern about the resort to military action. An unrelenting military campaign with an open-ended agenda based on the amorphous though lethal 'war on terror' could devastate the families and surroundings of many of the British Muslims who had hailed from Northern Pakistan and Kashmir. As the 'war on terror' gained momentum, Muslim communities were targeted not only in Afghanistan, but also in other countries such as Pakistan, Saudi Arabia, the United Kingdom and the United States. While the scale of the US-led policies of kidnapping, detention, torture and rendition is yet to become fully apparent, the abuse of the principles of international humanitarian law was evident with the commencement of the bombardment of Afghanistan in October 2001.

A complicated aspect of the military intervention in Afghanistan has been the application of international humanitarian law to the persons captured by the coalition forces in the conflict. The matter was disturbing for the British government, since it transpired that a number of those captured were British citizens. On 11 January 2002, the first twenty captives from Afghanistan were transferred to Camp X-ray, a detention camp at the US naval base at Guantánamo Bay in Cuba.[52] Since that time, over 700 captives (including adults and children) have been sent to this base. A vast majority of the adults have been detained and held *incommunicado* without charges being brought against them. These men have been separated from one another and held in wire 'cages' measuring eight feet by six feet in conditions described by Amnesty International as 'falling below minimum standards for humane behaviour'.[53]

---

[50] See A.A. An-Na'im, 'Upholding International Legality Against Islamic and American Jihad', in K. Booth and T. Dunne (eds.), *Worlds in Collision: Terror and the Future of Global Order* (London 2002) pp. 162-172 at p. 168.

[51] See J.N.B. Frank and J. Rehman, 'Assessing the Legality of the Attacks by the International Coalition against Terrorism (ICAT) against Al-Qaeda and Taleban in Afghanistan: An Inquiry into the Self-Defence Argument under Article 51 of the United Nations Charter', 67 *Journal of Criminal Law* (2003) pp. 415-430.

[52] E. Katselli and S. Shah, 'September 11 and the UK Response' 52 *International and Comparative Law Quarterly* (2003) pp. 245-255 at p. 250.

[53] Cited in P. Thomas, 'September 11th and Good Governance' 53 *Northern Ireland Legal Quarterly* (2002) p. 366 at p. 379.

In these detentions at Guantánamo and elsewhere, the United States and the United Kingdom have shown disdain for accepted norms of international human rights law and international humanitarian law.[54] Particularly abhorrent have been the denial of rights under the third Geneva Convention relative to the Treatment of Prisoners of War[55] and attempts to try the so-called unlawful combatants in military commissions set up by the US president himself.[56]

In a report issued on 5 September 2002, Amnesty International stated that the continued detention of individuals in Guantánamo Bay was a violation of international law.[57] The organisation demanded that the detainees be entitled to fundamental rights as provided by international humanitarian and human rights law. Similar views were echoed by international law experts and the then UN High Commissioner for Human Rights, Mary Robinson.[58] In a report published in February 2006, the United Nations, led by the Special Rapporteur on Torture, Professor Manfred Nowak, heavily criticised the activities in the camp and called for its immediate closure.[59] The United Kingdom supported the US administration in its policies of detention of individuals at Guantánamo Bay. At the same time, it sought assurances that its citizens would be treated humanely and in accordance with the Geneva Conventions. In reality, the UK government's policies reflect disdain towards the fundamental human rights of its citizens who were detained at Guantánamo Bay. Since the detainees were predominantly Muslim by faith, their detention was

---

54 Katselli and Shah, *supra* n. 52 at p. 250.

55 See the Geneva Convention relative to the Treatment of Prisoners of War, adopted 12 August 1949 by the Diplomatic Conference for the Establishment of International Conventions for the Protection of Victims of War held in Geneva 21 April to 21 August 1949 (entry into force 21 October 1950), available at: <http://www.unhchr.ch/html/menu3/b/91.htm>.

56 D. Mundis, 'Agora: Military Commissions – The Use of Military Commissions to Prosecute Individuals Accused of Terrorist Acts', 96 *American Journal of International Law* (2002) pp. 320-328 at p. 325.

57 See Amnesty International's Memorandum to the US Government on the Rights of Individuals in US Custody in Afghanistan and Guantánamo Bay of 15 April 2002, available at: <http://web.amnesty.org/ai.nsf/recent/AMR510532002>.

58 See the statement made by High Commissioner for Human Rights on the detention of Taliban and al-Qaeda prisoners at the US base in Guantánamo Bay, Cuba, 16 January 2002.

59 See United Nations, Situation of Detainees at Guantánamo Bay E/CN.4/2006/120 (15 February 2006), available at: <http://news.bbc.co.uk/1/shared/bsp/hi/pdfs/16_02_06_un_guantanamo.pdf>.

also a major concern for British minority communities. The prolonged and arbitrary detention of Muslims heightened concerns of a foreign policy based on religious discrimination. Muslim human rights organisations regard the Guantánamo captivities as evidence that the United States and the United Kingdom were pursuing an Islamophobic agenda.[60] In so far as the British detainees at Guantánamo are concerned, all the men were eventually released, although no liability was accepted by either the British or the US government for the torture, humiliation and inhumane or degrading treatment suffered by these men and their families.[61]

B. The 'war on terror' and the invasion of Iraq

The fusion of the 'war on terror' with the threat to international peace and security allowed the United States to justify its invasion of Iraq in March 2003. It was argued that the threat from Iraq was so substantial and real that the international community had to take immediate military action. According to the Western leaders, led by US President George W. Bush, there was unequivocal evidence that Iraqi President Saddam Hussein had an arsenal of weapons of mass destruction that he intended to use against his neighbours and other states. The build-up to the invasion of Iraq also saw a human rights argument advanced by the United States and the United Kingdom. Saddam Hussein's dictatorial regime and Iraq's repression of its ethnic and religious communities were put forward as additional grounds for justifying invasion and removal of the regime. This argument was fallacious, since for years Saddam Hussein had conducted such action with the knowledge and support of the United States. Furthermore, the promotion and projection of human rights has only been a factor when its suits the political ambitions of powerful states; the worst violators of human rights in the neighbourhood of Iraq continue to be the closest allies and friends of the United States.[62] Indeed this

---

[60] See Islamic Human Rights Commission, 'Failure to Repatriate Britons Masks Islamophobic Policy' (11 August 2003).

[61] See T. Branigan, 'I am Just Amazed: He is Finally Coming Home', *The Guardian* (20 February 2004). On the futility of legal challenges, see *R (on the application of Abbasi)* v. *Secretary of State for Foreign and Commonwealth Affairs* [2002] EWCA Civ. 1316.

[62] Note the criticisms of human rights violations carried out by the United States' Middle Eastern allies, such as Saudi Arabia and Kuwait. See Amnesty International's 2004 report on Saudi Arabia, available at: <http://web.amnesty.org/report2004/sau-summary-eng>; and Amnesty International's 2004 report on Kuwait, available at: <http://web.amnesty.org/report2004/kwt-summary-eng>.

so-called 'war on terror' has provided an excuse for dictatorial and autocratic regimes all over the world to repress, torture and violate fundamental human rights – the international community is determined to remain tight-lipped so long as these regimes continue to purport allegiance to the ambitions of US foreign policy.[63] Such duplicity, double standards and selectivity have not only troubled Muslim communities but also others who retain an objective vision of law and politics. According to Ian Brownlie:

> The issue of selectivity can lead to claims of human rights violations being used as a powerful political weapon. Probably the most egregious example of this is provided by the case of Iraq. The Iraq-Iran War raged for eight years (1980-8). Iran was not the aggressor. During the conflict leading Western powers gave assistance to the Iraqi Government in the form of matrices for chemical weapons (which were used against Iran) and satellite intelligence. The Security Council took no action under Chapter VII of the Charter. In contrast, in the period from 1991 up to the United States' attack on Iraq in March 2003, the same State took a strong line on the bad rights record of the Iraqi regime, and the attack was justified in public statements in part by reference to human rights factor. Here is revealed a purely cynical version of human rights, contingent upon collateral political considerations.[64]

Amid the global public opposition to the invasion of Iraq, Muslim minorities remained strongly opposed. There were mass demonstrations, marches and protests on the streets of all major British cities. It would not be an exaggeration to state that, of all communities, the US and UK governments' decision to invade Iraq inflicted the greatest pain and humiliation on Muslim

[63] An Amnesty International report reinforces this point when it notes: '[t]he impact of the so-called "war on terror" (henceforth "war on terror") on human rights in the Gulf and the Arabian Peninsula has been profound and far reaching. Governments in the region and the US government have treated nationals and residents of the area with a disturbing disregard for the rule of law and fundamental human rights standards. The results have been mass arrests, prolonged detention without charge or trial, incommunicado detention, torture and ill treatment, strict secrecy surrounding the fate and whereabouts of some detainees, and apparent extra-judicial killings. These human rights violations have had profound effects not only on individual victims but also on their relatives and the general human rights situation in the region.' See Amnesty International, *The Gulf and the Arabian Peninsula: Human Rights Fall Victim to the 'War on Terror'* (22 June 2004), AI Index: MDE 04/002/2004, available at: <http://web.amnesty.org/library/Index/ENGMDE040022004?open&of=ENG-USA>.

[64] I. Brownlie, *Principles of Public International Law*, 6th edn. (Oxford, Oxford University Press 2003) p. 557.

minorities. British Muslims were not unanimous on the nature of the action that ought to be taken against Saddam Hussein's regime. While Muslim communities were not in favour of condoning the mass violation of individual and group rights in Iraq, there was a feeling that all necessary action must be taken under the auspices of the UN Security Council. Military action would only be permissible after all means of negotiation had been exhausted. Notwithstanding the difficulties involved in establishing a legal argument and in the absence of a Security Council resolution authorising the use of force, the UK government loyally pursued the US agenda of a predetermined invasion of Iraq. It is difficult to find any persuasive legal basis to justify the invasion and occupation of Iraq. Kofi Annan, the UN Secretary-General, declared the intervention unlawful, with many senior international lawyers condemning it as a substantial breach of law.[65] In the words of (the now retired Law Lord) Lord Steyn, in order to present justifications for the invasion of Iraq, the British government was 'scraping the legal barrel'.[66]

The failure to recover weapons of mass destruction and the continuing violation of human rights in Iraq have generated a huge backlash among British Muslims.[67] Muslim minorities have been extremely vocal in their opposition to the Iraq invasion; there have been calls for the withdrawal of troops and demands for an apology for taking Britain into war based on false pretences. In the build-up to the invasion of Iraq, the US and the UK governments not only exaggerated the threat from Saddam Hussein's regime but also avoided a proper debate on the future of Iraq post-Saddam Hussein. There was an immature, self-conceited belief about the righteousness of armed intervention and misplaced optimism about a meagre domestic response

65 The verdict of former UN Secretary-General Kofi Annan represents the position insofar as the United Nations and the Charter is concerned. He notes: 'I have indicated it [i.e. the invasion of Iraq] was not in conformity with the UN charter from our point of view, from the charter point of view, it was illegal.' 'Iraq War Illegal, Says Annan: The United Nations Secretary-General Kofi Annan has told the BBC the US-led invasion of Iraq was an illegal act that contravened the UN Charter', BBC News (UK edition) (16 September 2004), available at: <http://news.bbc.co.uk/1/hi/world/middle_east/3661134.stm>.

66 F. Gibb, 'Law lord damns "half-baked reforms and illegal Iraq war"', *The Times* (19 October 2005), available at: <http://www.timesonline.co.uk/article/0,,2-1832270,00.html>.

67 The Iraq invasion also proved embarrassing and in some cases disastrous. There were tragic consequences for over 100 families of servicemen and servicewomen who were killed on the battlefield. There were also tragic consequences for the families of David Kelly and Ken Bigly.

to the invasion. The US-led invasion has resulted in enormous suffering for the Iraqi people – many British Muslims have felt aggrieved at the violations conducted by the US and the UK officers in detention centres such as Abu Ghraib and in southern Iraq. As the occupation powers, the United States and the United Kingdom also remain ultimately responsible for the substantial human rights violations and sectarian violence.

C. *British government response to 9/11 attacks*

The British response to the events of 9/11 was to further consolidate its laws through the adoption of the Anti-Terrorism, Crime and Security Act 2001.[68] Much like the US Patriot Act,[69] it was passed with spectacular speed, with only the House of Lords providing some opposition.[70] The 2001 Act is a very substantial piece of legislation authorising draconian measures. Among its most contentious features was Part Four, which authorised the Home Secretary to issue a certificate against any non-UK national if there was a reasonable belief that the individual's presence in the United Kingdom constituted a threat to national security and that her or she was a suspected terrorist.[71] This certificate would authorise the continued detention of the individual concerned. The legislation raised substantial problems in the light of existing international and European human rights jurisprudence. The European Convention on Human Rights (ECHR), which was largely incorporated into British law through the Human Rights Act 1998, allows individual states to deport foreigners when their presence presents a risk to national security. However, under the Soering principle, foreign nationals must not be extradited to other states in cases where there is a real danger that they will be subjected to torture, inhuman and degrading treatment or punishment (contrary to Article 3 of the Convention).[72] In

68 Anti-Terrorism, Crimes and Security Act 2001, Chapter 24.

69 See the Uniting and Strengthening of America to Provide Appropriate Tools Required to Intercept and Obstruct Terrorism Act of 2001 (USA PATRIOT Act of 2001), Section 412.

70 'The moral panic that consumed the USA was reflected in its most constant ally, the UK.' Thomas, *supra* n. 53, at p. 380.

71 The provisions follow those of the US Patriot Act of 2001. Section 412 of the US Patriot Act authorises indefinite detentions of immigrants and non-citizens. Several thousand Muslims/Arabs have been detained under these provisions. See Thomas, *supra* n. 53, at pp. 377-378.

72 *Soering* v. *UK* (1989) 11 EHRR 439. See C. Van Den Wyngaert, 'Applying the European Convention on Human Rights to Extradition: Opening Pandora's Box', 39

the *Chahal* case, the European Court of Human Rights went further and decided that the right of individuals to protection against torture was absolute and therefore could not be trumped by considerations of national security.[73] For the British government, allowing individuals suspected of international terrorism to remain at large in the United Kingdom was no longer acceptable. The government therefore felt it necessary to derogate from Article 15 of the ECHR.[74] During the adoption of the relevant legislation, evidence was presented to the Parliamentary Joint Committee on Human Rights stating that such derogations would be unlawful.[75] It was also extraordinary that the United Kingdom was the only member state of the Council of Europe to have adopted such a derogation provision as a consequence of the events of 11 September 2001.[76]

Relying upon his newly found powers under the Anti-Terrorism, Crime and Security Act 2001, the then Home Secretary, David Blunkett, initiated the detention of certain individuals in December 2001-January 2002. The detainees – the so-called Belmarsh detainees – were detained without charges, arguably under inhuman and degrading conditions, prompting them to bring legal challenges under the Human Rights Act.[77] The case raised profound issues, including the limits of executive power, discrimination on the basis of nationality and the role of judiciary to pronounce upon fundamental rights such as the right to liberty and freedom.[78] On 16 December 2004, in an unprecedented sitting of nine judges, the Appellate Committee of the House of Lords declared Section 23 – the offending provision – of the Act as incompatible with the European Convention on Human Rights. The Committee consid-

---

International and Comparative Law Quarterly (1990) p. 757; R.B. Lillich, 'The Soering Case' 85 *American Journal of International Law* (1991) p. 128.

73 *Chahal* v. *United Kingdom*, judgment of 15 November 1996, 1996-V RJD 1831.

74 Human Rights Act 1998 (Designated Derogation) Order 2001 (Statutory Instrument No. 3644).

75 In its report, the Committee had expressed substantial concerns both about the invocation of a public emergency threatening the life of the nation and about the lack of adequate safeguards in relation to detention powers. See Joint Committee on Human Rights, Report on Anti-Terrorism, Crime and Security Bill 2001-02 HL, HC372 para. 30.

76 Thomas, *supra* n. 53, at p. 381.

77 *A* v. *Secretary of State for the Home Department* [2004] UKHL 56.

78 For commentaries on the case, see B. Dickson, 'Law Versus Terrorism: Can Law Win?', *European Human Rights Law Review* (2005) p. 11; C.P. Walker, 'Prisoners of "War all the Time"', *European Human Rights Law Review* (2005) p. 50; S. Shah, 'The UK's Anti-Terror Legislation and the House of Lords: The First Skirmish', 5(2) *Human Rights Law Review* (2005) p. 403.

ered three salient aspects of the case. The first one required a judicial response to the government's position that there was a public emergency threatening the life of the nation, thereby validating the derogation under Article 15 of the ECHR. While a majority of the Committee was prepared to defer the matter as one of political judgement on the part of government, there was a noticeable minority that felt that either the threat to the nation did not exist or was not so imminent as to sanction such a derogation.[79] Once it was accepted that there was a public emergency, the next issue was whether the detention provisions contained in the Act were necessary, proportionate and rational, or, as stated in the terms of Article 15, 'strictly required by the exigencies of the situation'.[80] The Committee resoundingly declared the detentions to be disproportionate and unnecessary and therefore incompatible with the grounds as provided in Article 15.[81] The Committee was also unwilling to accept that the detention of foreign suspected terrorists as contained in the 2001 Act did not constitute discrimination[82] – a view taken by the Special Immigration Appeal Tribunal[83] but overturned by the Court of Appeal.[84]

5. LAW AND POLICIES AFTER 7 JULY 2005

Amid the growing tensions and Islamophobia in the aftermath of the 7 July bombings and the failed attacks of 21 July, British society was suddenly reminded of the infamous 'shoot to kill' policy by the killing of an innocent Brazilian man at Stockwell underground station.[85] The government's response to the July bombings was aggressive. Presenting a whole raft of measures at a press conference on 5 August 2005, Prime Minister Tony Blair warned: 'Let no-

---

79 *A* v. *Secretary of State for the Home Department* [2004] UKHL 56, at 93, 96.

80 Article 15(1) provides as follows: 'In time of war or other public emergency threatening the life of the nation any High Contracting Party may take measures derogating from its obligations under this Convention to the extent strictly required by the exigencies of the situation, provided that such measures are not inconsistent with its other obligations under international law.'

81 *A* v. *Secretary of State for the Home Department* [2004] UKHL 56, 155.

82 Ibid., at p. 68.

83 See SIAC 2002 HRLR 1274.

84 For reported summaries of the decision, see the Incorporated Council of Law Reporting for England and Wales (ICLR), available at: <http://www.lawreports.co.uk/civoct1.2.htm>.

85 'Police shot Brazilian eight times', BBC News (25 July 2005), available at: <http://news.bbc.co.uk/1/hi/uk/4713753.stm>.

one be in any doubt, the rules of the game are changing'.[86] It is this rewriting of the rules and the responses of Muslim minority communities that poses a great challenge to integration and accommodation. Although ostensibly aimed at fighting terrorism, the government's measures have had a substantially negative impact in terms of community relations. Furthermore, the paranoia associated with the so-called 'war on terror' has led to profound limitations on fundamental rights. The curtailment of these rights is exemplified by the treatment of an 82-year-old Labour activist, Walter Wolfgang, at the 2005 Labour Party Conference.[87] Mr Wolfgang was stopped under Section 44 of the Terrorism Act 2000 for shouting 'nonsense' at Jack Straw's speech. He was bundled out and prevented from re-entering the conference. Similarly, John Catt was stopped and searched under Section 44 of the Terrorism Act 2000 for wearing a T-shirt with anti-Blair and anti-Bush slogans.[88] Another protester, Maya Evans, was convicted under Section 132 of the Serious Organised Crime and Police Act 2005 for reading aloud the names of (the then) 97 British soldiers who had been killed in Iraq.[89] These incidents reflect an unfortunate trend of intolerance and censorship of liberal values and unacceptable constraints on democracy.

The series of legislative and administrative measures planned after the 7/7 bombings included the introduction of new anti-terrorism legislation that aimed, *inter alia,* to extend the period of allowable detention without charge to up to ninety days, to introduce the offences of glorification of terrorism, dissemination of terrorist publications and training for terrorism and to expand the grounds for proscription of terrorist organisations. After significant debate in the UK parliament and the defeat of the government in the House of Commons, the ninety-day detention period was reduced to twenty-eight days.[90] However, it is contended that a four-week detention period without charge could nevertheless amount to inhuman and degrading treatment or punishment. Extended detentions are a fundamental assault on an individual's liberty and integrity and demand an appropriate justification.

---

[86] PM's Press Conference of 5 August 2005, available at: <http://www.number-10.gov.uk/output/Page8041.asp>.

[87] C. Hulme, 'Our Freedom is at Stake: Blair Threatens to Restrict the Rights of Terrorist Suspects', *The Guardian* (15 February 2006) p. 32.

[88] M. Berlins, 'When a Slogan Equals Terrorism', *The Guardian* (3 October 2005), available at: <http://www.guardian.co.uk/terrorism/story/0,,1583684,00.html>.

[89] 'Activist Convicted Under Demo Law', BBC News (7 December 2005), available at: <http://news.bbc.co.uk/1/hi/england/london/4507446.stm>.

[90] 'Blair Defeated Over Terror Laws', BBC News (9 November 2005), available at: <http://news.bbc.co.uk/1/hi/uk_politics/4422086.stm>.

Notwithstanding opposition from the House of Lords, the government was able to incorporate into the legislation the offence of glorification of terrorism.[91] Given the vagueness in defining the nature of terrorism, there remains a substantial risk of conflict with freedom of expression. Under the proposed legislation, anyone supporting armed resistance against a state or an occupation, however repressive and illegitimate it may be, will be committing an offence if it might reasonably be regarded by the public as a direct or indirect glorification of terrorism. Given that the definition of terrorism is widely contested, Muslim communities are fearful that any support for resistance movements in Kashmir, Afghanistan, Iraq or Palestine could well be regarded as glorification of terrorism. It is also worrying for many Muslims to note a further extension of the ban on political organisations under the new legislation, which runs the risk of repressing movements claiming the right to self-determination, such as those in Kashmir, Chechnya or Iraq. Furthermore, current proposals for screening clerics and closing down mosques is not only likely to violate the right of freedom of religion but also risks a violation of the right to freedom of expression as contained in Article 10 of the European Convention on Human Rights. It is akin to sending a message that 'Muslims cannot be trusted' and is bound to infuriate the Muslim religious communities.[92]

The government also concluded memoranda of understanding with several countries that would authorise deportation of refugees or stateless persons notwithstanding the presence of a well-founded fear of persecution. The government reinstated its intention to strip 'citizenship from those individuals with British or dual nationality who act in a way that is contrary to the interests of this country'.[93] These dangerously vague and arbitrary provisions now find a home in Clause 56 of the Immigration, Asylum and Nationality Bill, which sanctions stripping individuals of their citizenship if their conduct is 'not deemed for public good'.[94] The government also introduced a new test

---

91 M. Tempest, 'MPs Back Ban on Glorification of Terrorism', *The Guardian* (15 February 2006), available at: <http://www.guardian.co.uk/terrorism/story/0,,1710278,00.html>.

92 See Employment Equality (Religion or Belief) Regulation 2003 (SI 2003/1660).

93 PM's Press Conference of 5 August 2005, p. 2, available at: <http://www.number-10.gov.uk/output/Page8041.asp>.

94 Immigration, Asylum and Nationality Bill, Cl. 56. See the text of the Immigration, Asylum and Nationality Bill (as amended on report and ordered to be presented in the House of Lords on 7 February 2006), available at: <http://www.publications.parliament.uk/pa/ld200506/ldbills/074/2006074.htm>.

for acquiring British citizenship,[95] with government and opposition leaders calling for a redefinition of loyalties. Home Office minister Hazel Blears suggested the introducing of double-barrelled nationality, such as British-Asian, while the then Shadow Home Secretary David Davis suggested that multiculturalism was 'outdated'.[96] After the July bombings, former Conservative Party chairman Norman Tebbit made the claim that the July bombings could have been prevented had his infamous 'cricket test' been applied.[97]

In its pursuit of the 'war on terror', the labour government has expressed its willingness to compromise on the well-established principle of excluding all forms of evidence obtained through torture. In a case emerging from the Belmarsh detentions, the British government expressed a willingness to allow the use of evidence in courts against individuals that may have been obtained through torture in foreign jurisdictions. The Court of Appeal agreed with the government's position for the inclusion of such evidence.[98] However, on 8 December 2005 the House of Lords, again overruling the earlier Court of Appeal's decision, established the impermissibility of utilising evidence obtained through torture regardless of whether it was obtained in a foreign jurisdiction and by foreign agents.[99] The case of the Belmarsh detainees and the plight of the British men incarcerated in Guantánamo Bay (until January 2005) deeply affected the hearts and minds of their co-religionists. In the violations of human rights of these individuals, many in the British Muslim community perceived a religious conflict: a 'clash of religions' or possibly even 'a clash of civilisations' – it was as if Islam had been placed in the dock. As noted earlier, to further exacerbate the tensions, the government also introduced proposals for screening clerics and closing down mosques. There was also a concern that the new identity cards scheme would turn into a

---

[95] 'New UK Citizenship Testing Starts', BBC News (1 November 2005), available at: <http://news.bbc.co.uk/1/hi/uk_politics/4391710.stm>.

[96] 'Davis Attacks UK Multiculturalism', BBC News (3 August 2005), available at: <http://news.bbc.co.uk/1/hi/uk_politics/4740633.stm>.

[97] 'Tebbit claims "cricket test" may have stopped blasts', *Daily Mail* (19 August 2005), available at: <http://www.dailymail.co.uk/news/article-359738/Tebbit-claims-cricket-test-stopped-blasts.html>.

[98] *A* v. *Secretary of State for the Home Department* [2004] EWCA 1123 (Court of Appeal).

[99] *A (FC) and Others (FC) (Appellants)* v. *Secretary of State for the Home Department (Respondent)* (2004); *A (FC) and Others (FC) (Appellants)* v. *Secretary of State for the Home Department (Respondent)* (Conjoined Appeals) [2005] UKHL 71 (8 December 2005).

witch-hunt for targeting and harassing Muslim men.[100] Muslim communities have expressed their fear that, in the existing tense environment, these administrative and legislative measures, in particular the planned Terrorism Act with its detention powers, would result in injustices due to the 'rounding up of the usual suspects'.

6. Concluding Observations – Strategies for the Future

This paper has analysed the substantial issues faced by Muslim minorities in the United Kingdom. To overcome historical patterns of discrimination, a change of policy is required at both legislative and administrative level, as well as changes in society's approach towards minority groups. There is currently no comprehensive legislation to cover all forms of religious discrimination in Britain. Religious minorities such as Jews and Sikhs are covered (albeit indirectly) by existing race discrimination legislation, but Muslims have not been able to obtain protection under this law. Some piecemeal protection of employment and working conditions has been provided to religious minorities through European Union regulations.[101] This protection needs to be expanded to provide comprehensive cover in key areas such as social security, health care, education, housing benefits and student grants. Steps can be taken either through new legislation or the extension of current race relations laws. The United Kingdom also continues to show failings in equality provisions within national and international law. There is an urgent need to incorporate the International Covenant on Civil and Political Rights (ICCPR) of 1976[102] into UK law and to ratify the First Optional Protocol to the ICCPR.[103] Successive British governments have resisted requests to incorporate the ICCPR into the domestic legal system. It has also consistently refused to allow individuals to petition the UN Human Rights Committee. The British government's stance has been based on the view that incorporation of these

---

100 See the provisions of the Identity Cards Bill, as amended on report in the House of Lords on 30 January 2006, available at: <http://www.publications.parliament.uk/pa/ld200506/ldbills/071/2006071.htm>.

101 R. Rothwell, 'Terror Moves Stoke Muslim Fears' 102(33) *Law Society Gazette* (September 2005) p. 3.

102 Adopted at New York, 16 December 1966. Entered into force on 23 March 1976. GA Res. 2200A (XXI), UN Doc. A/6316 (1966), 999 *UNTS* 171; 6 *ILM* (1967) p. 368.

103 G.A. Res. 2200A (XXI), 21 UN GAOR Supp. (No. 16) at 59, UN Doc. A/6316 (1966), 999 *UNTS* 302, entered into force on 23 March 1976.

instruments is not required since sufficient guarantees of rights are provided through the European human rights system. This premise is incorrect – the ICCPR contains a number of rights that are highly valuable for minorities and are unavailable under the European Convention on Human Rights. The United Kingdom also stands out among Western European states for not having ratified the first Optional Protocol. Dame Rosalyn Higgins, former judge and president of the International Court of Justice, noted as follows some time ago:

> The reason used to be offered to the Committee [by the British Government] that there was no need for the Optional Protocol, as individual access was available to individuals under the European Convention, and that was heavily used. But of course this is not the same instrument, and some rights in our instrument [i.e. ICCPR] are more detailed. This is true, for example, of the fair trial provisions under Article 14, and we also have … some rights in our instrument that simply are not in the European Convention. I speak of family rights, Article 24; rights relating to participation in public life, Article 25; rights of aliens, Article 13; free-standing non-discrimination, Article 26; and the rights of minorities, Article 27. Those rights cannot be tested before the European Commission or Court. Their only guarantee is in the Covenant, and unless those rights are fully reflected in domestic law, there can be no judicial scrutiny of them.[104]

The United Kingdom has also failed to carry out many of the obligations contained in the European human rights system. This includes the non-ratification of Protocol No. 12 to the European Convention on Human Rights.[105] This protocol plays a key role in ensuring an independent right of equality and non-discrimination. There is also the need to fully incorporate the rights contained in Protocol No. 4[106] and Protocol No. 7[107] of the ECHR. Protocol No. 4 deals with right of freedom of movement,[108] while Protocol No. 7 ensures safeguards for the treatment of aliens.[109] These additional protocols

---

[104] R. Higgins, 'Foreword', in Harris and Joseph, *supra* n. 16, pp. xi-xviii at p. xvii.

[105] Protocol No. 12 to the European Convention for the Protection of Human Rights and Fundamental Freedom, ETS 177, opened for signature on 11 April 2000.

[106] Protocol No. 4 to the European Convention for the Protection of Human Rights and Fundamental Freedoms, ETS No. 46, entered into force on 2 May 1968.

[107] Protocol No. 7 to the European Convention for the Protection of Human Rights and Fundamental Freedoms, ETS 117, entered into force on 1 November 1988.

[108] Article 2 of Protocol No. 4.

[109] Article 1 of Protocol No. 7.

needs to be specifically incorporated into current European human rights legislation.

A highly significant strategy is to learn from the past experiences of the Northern Irish conflict, which demonstrate the need for religious discrimination legislation, as well as having an equality commission with strong regulatory, investigatory and enforcement mechanisms. Furthermore, and perhaps more significantly, it is imperative to develop a trusting relationship with Muslim communities. Instead of adopting vindictive, spiteful and aggressive measures, there is great merit in adopting policies that strike at the core of some of the fundamental problems of integration. On a broader level, the Northern Irish experience demands an understanding of the complexity behind the concept of terrorism and those who are engaged in political violence. This paper has demonstrated the difficulties created by a foreign policy that is duplicitous, with varying standards of human rights. The falsified intelligence presented prior to the Iraq invasion has unfortunately undermined public confidence and has led to a greater threat of terrorism. Many commentators would agree with Lord Steyn's position that '[a]fter the recent dreadful bombings in London we were asked to believe that the Iraq war did not make London and the world a more dangerous place. Surely, on top of everything else, we do not have to listen to a fairy tale.'[110] There is a need for greater transparency in foreign policy decision making.

---

[110] C. Dyer, 'He's Woven the Human Rights Act into Our Legal System: He Has a Terrier-Like Tenacity and the Courage of a Lion', *The Guardian* (21 October 2005).

Terrorism and Human Rights in the Field of Conflict

Patrick Sookhdeo*

The relationship between human rights and terrorism, particularly within conflict arenas, is a complex and changing one. In order to contextualise the discussion, reference should first be made to the relevant sections of the UN Universal Declaration of Human Rights and, in particular, to those articles that state that fundamental rights are violated when:

- a certain race, creed or group is denied recognition as a 'person' (Article 2);
- men and women are not treated as equal (Article 2);
- different racial or religious groups are not treated as equal (Article 2);
- life, liberty or security of person are threatened (Article 3);
- a person is sold as or used as a slave (Article 4);
- cruel or unusual punishment is used on a person (such as torture or execution) (Article 5);
- punishments are dealt arbitrarily or unilaterally, without a proper and fair trial (Article 11);
- there is arbitrary interference into personal or private lives by agents of the state (Article 12);
- citizens are forbidden to leave their country (Article 13);
- freedom of speech or religion are denied (Articles 18 and 19);
- the right to join a union is denied (Article 23); and
- education is denied (Article 26).

Secondly, common Article 3 of the Geneva Conventions states that those not taking an active part in war, including members of the armed forces who have laid down their weapons, are protected. It prohibits:

---

* Dr Patrick Sookhdeo, Senior Visiting Fellow at the UK Defence Academy.

- violence to life and person, in particular murder of all kinds, mutilation, cruel treatment and torture;
- taking of hostages;
- outrages upon personal dignity, in particular humiliating and degrading treatment; and
- the passing of sentences and the carrying out of executions without previous judgment pronounced by a regularly constituted court affording all the judicial guarantees which are recognised as indispensable by civilised peoples.

Article 147 of the Fourth Geneva Convention lays out the following 'grave breaches' of the rights of those not actively engaged in conflict:

> Grave breaches to which the preceding Article relates shall be those involving any of the following acts, if committed against persons or property protected by the present Convention: wilful killing, torture or inhuman treatment, including biological experiments, wilfully causing great suffering or serious injury to body or health, unlawful deportation or transfer or unlawful confinement of a protected person, compelling a protected person to serve in the forces of a hostile Power, or wilfully depriving a protected person of the rights of fair and regular trial prescribed in the present Convention, taking of hostages and extensive destruction and appropriation of property, not justified by military necessity and carried out unlawfully and wantonly.

These documents provide the parameters within which any discussion of human rights has cohesion and validity and provide a backdrop to the tension that exists between the rights of the minority terrorist groups and those of the majority.

It should be remembered, also, that the standards that organisations such as Amnesty International demand from governments for the protection of the human rights of their citizens have become more and more exacting. This is because the meaning of 'human rights' has expanded in scope. The concept of human rights today differs substantially from the eighteenth century notion of the right to life, liberty and security of person. This overarching idea has evolved into what is essentially a cluster of human rights. As one philosopher notes:

> Human rights now mean *specific* rights against enslavement, torture, arbitrary arrest and exile. There are a series of liberty rights involving the right to *movement*, to marry, to have a family, to divorce, to freedom of thought, and to religious practice. There are political rights to participate in 'genuine elections' and cultural rights to develop one's personality. Economic rights include the right

to work, to join trade unions, and to paid holidays. We also have welfare rights to social security, to health care, to special assistance for child care, and to free education. Although few, if any, countries today adequately abide by all of these rights, the Universal Declaration sees these as a 'common standard of achievement for all peoples and nations.'

A major shift in the way we define human rights has occurred. Our acceptance of the validity of this change will affect how we see human rights being applied, especially in areas of conflict. That such a change has occurred can be illustrated by comparing our reactions to historical events with contemporary attitudes.

In 1806 and 1857, the Sepoys mutinied in Bengal. They rose against their officers because of various orders that they found offensive: they were told to trim their beards, refrain from wearing caste marks and, in the later uprising, the additional offence of the greased cartridges added fuel to the fire. Following the suppression of the uprising, the British military had to decide on a way of dealing with the Sepoys that would be effective and a deterrent against further unrest. They engaged in a number of kinds of punishments, but the one that is most interesting – for reasons that will be explained below – was to tie the rebellious Sepoy, particularly if he was a Hindu, to a gun barrel which was then fired, blowing the unfortunate Sepoy to pieces. Maya Jasanoff graphically describes the scene:

> As for the mutineers themselves, they suffered British wrath almost immediately; thousands were degraded, flogged and summarily hanged. Grisliest of all were the fates of mutineers tied to cannon barrels and blasted into hash.[1]

Was that just pure cruelty for its own sake, sadism to satisfy the thirst for revenge amongst the soldiers? Actually, it was not. It was a deterrent. The motivation behind such a punishment was the understanding of the belief in reincarnation that is one of the basic tenets of Hinduism. After death, the body would be reincarnated – it would progress from one state to another. However, if the body were blown to bits, reincarnation would become a hazardous process, and so what seems to modern eyes to be an arbitrary punishment was, in fact, a very carefully constructed and devised *religious* punishment, the purpose of which was to ensure that Hindu soldiers did not rebel against the Crown. It is likely that those who were contemporary with

---

1 Maya Jasanoff, 'Secret Signals in Lotus Flowers', *London Review of Books*, Vol. 27, No. 14 (21 July 2005).

the events would not have seen the issues in human rights terms; the uprising would have been fuelled by religious or nationalistic sentiments, and the ensuing punishments would have corresponded to the brutalities and cruelties long endured under the Mogul Empire, to whom the British were successors. Did the British absorb such punishments within their armoury to ensure that they could keep their troops in order? Was that a breach of human rights, religious liberty and freedoms, or was it a necessary tactic to restrain a resentful minority for the sake of the majority?

The tension between human rights and dealing with terrorism can be further illustrated by a more recent example: the alleged massacre at Kunduz, Afghanistan, in November 2001. General Abdul Rashid Dostum of the Northern Alliance took control of Kunduz and accepted the surrender of about 8,000 Taliban fighters that included Chechens, Uzbeks, Pakistanis and about 500 suspected members of al-Qaeda.

It is alleged that the US forces allowed these fighters to surrender to Dostum and be arrested by him, which they did voluntarily. They were taken off and transported in containers to a particular fortress. About halfway there, a number of them (about 5,000 of the 8,000) disappeared, and those who arrived were in a desperate state. Given that the United States was working closely with Dostum, whose fighters were effectively surrogates of the Coalition forces, the question may be asked: ought they to have allowed these prisoners to be transported? If the United States took the view that such a decision was justified, then should they not have ensured their safe protection, in particular given the tensions between the Taliban and the Northern Alliance? And should they not in retrospect have accepted responsibility, given that about 5,000 or so were killed, as the evidence seems to suggest, and that a number of others, on arriving, had been treated brutally in various ways? Once again, when the issue of human rights is examined in a theatre of conflict, in a specific context, it becomes difficult to apply hard and fast solutions.

Guantánamo Bay is another case that throws up problems. If it was necessary to take prisoners, are they to be classed as prisoners of war? How are Taliban prisoners to be classified if they are captured on the field of conflict? Are they legally, according to the Geneva Convention, prisoners of war and to be treated as such, or are they insurgents? If they are defined as insurgents, then which category do they fall into? And if they have been transferred from Afghanistan to Guantánamo Bay and are allegedly subjected to certain abuses, how does such treatment of prisoners square with human rights law, in accordance with the relevant UN Declarations and the Geneva Conventions?

If Iraq is considered, the complicated question of the Baathists arises. It is well known that under Saddam Hussein's regime the Baathists practised a ruthlessly dictatorial policy. The restrictions on freedom of movement, speech and ideas were well known to all who visited or lived in Iraq when Saddam was in power. The possibility of disappearing was a real threat for many. After the 1991 war, it could be argued that the Coalition forces did not completely finish the job, with the result that the Shias bore the brunt of Saddam's revenge when they rebelled. After the second Gulf War, therefore, many Shias were naturally concerned about the advent of the Coalition forces, especially as the Baathists were still in positions of authority, in their booths or in their hotel rooms down the road, waiting hopefully for the return of Saddam. How could the Shias ever trust the Coalition forces, knowing that they had been betrayed in the past *by* the Coalition forces?

In order to remedy this, and to regain Shia trust, the Coalition forces tended to turn a blind eye to Shia violence against the Baathists. In recent times, this line of action has developed further. It was alleged that the former prime minister, Al-Jaafari, had a Baathist hit list, the object of which was to remove all Baathists who had held a position of power at any time.

The question where the concept of human rights comes into play is therefore legitimate. A people have been terrorised; they are living in fear. They see a future fraught with danger: the possibility that their enemies could turn on them once again to subjugate them violently or attempt to annihilate them remains a present threat. In order to pre-empt such dangers, it might be necessary to take out the agents who menace them – to imprison or kill them before they can return to threaten their existence. What, then, is to be the role of the Coalition forces? Should it be to ensure the protection of the Baathists, whose criminality is well known and who would very quickly return to their acts of oppression or should it be to stand by and let them die? In order to prevent terrorist acts, should the Coalition forces acquiesce in ignoring legal safeguards and in permitting pre-emptive use of force? These are pertinent questions that underscore the tension that exists in the arena of conflict between the need to maintain human rights and the need to combat terrorism.

The question becomes even more urgent in other war situations where Coalition forces are deployed, for example in the recent conflict in Afghanistan. What is to be done when insurgents are captured? Put simply, the response is this: they should be imprisoned. However, with no judiciary, no courts, no sentences, and no prisons in operation, all that can be done is to hold them there for a day or two and then let them out – only to find that a couple of days later they return fully armed to attack once again. There is a possible way out, namely to work with national forces, because the strength of their position is that they take no prisoners. The problem of interning prisoners without proper adherence to human rights and the legal safeguards regarding the capture and detention of insurgents simply disappears.

It appears, then, that conflicts such as those in Afghanistan and Iraq can exacerbate tensions between the demands of human rights and the protection from terrorism that the population ought to be able to expect. A choice has to be made by the Coalition forces. Should the national forces take responsibility and round up the insurgents, which would certainly result in them being killed, or do the Coalition forces detain them, watch over them for two days and then let them loose, only to find they return to the attack, causing further losses of manpower? There is, thus, a very real tension in terms of human rights in such a context.

Thus, it is argued that, particularly when civilian lives are themselves at stake due to the actions of terrorists, human rights as defined today are untenable. And this, it is maintained, is especially true when attempts are being made to gather intelligence. An example that illustrates how human rights seem to be at odds with the actual situation can be found in the recruiting of police in Iraq. Where should they be recruited from? It is pointless to talk about creating a new Iraqi police force that will be above reproach and will subscribe to human rights laws. The serious situation and the need to restore order demand rapid and effective action. It becomes necessary to compromise, to accept into the police force those who have been employed before in similar roles, such as sections of the military, particularly certain sections of Saddam's Special Forces, who are experienced but who are often brutal according to human rights standards. But then a problem arises: if these forces are used in a policing capacity, they will act as they have always done. They will be violent, they will kill, they will attempt to subjugate the population according to their own methods and they will have been given *legitimacy* by the present forces. But what can be done? Without a police force, it is impossible to maintain any semblance of law and order. But if, as in the case of Iraq, the police are recruited from an already existing group, the result is a force composed of what might be termed 'respectable thugs' who know no differently and who will ply their trade in the only manner they know. The question once again arises: how far should the Coalition forces go down that route?

Bruce Hoffman discusses the dilemma faced by those working in security in his essay 'A Nasty Business'. He quotes a British intelligence officer who claimed in 1985 that:

> If you have a close-knit society which doesn't give information then you've got to find ways of getting it. Now the softies of the world complain – but there is an awful lot of double talk about it. If there is to be discomfort and horror inflicted on a few, is this not preferred to the danger and horror being inflicted on perhaps a million people?[2]

Hoffman relates how he encountered this approach amongst Sri Lankan intelligence officers fighting the Tamil Tigers. They claimed that 'by going through the process of laws you cannot fight terrorism'. It can only be fought effectively by thoroughly 'terrorising' the terrorists.

One of the counter-intelligence officers interviewed explained how he had personally shot defenceless prisoners dead. He explained that he had arrested three prisoners; he knew that a bomb had been planted in Colombo, but none of the prisoners would talk about the location of the bomb. So he told them that if they did not tell him the location of the bomb he would kill them. They still would not talk:

> So he took his pistol from his gun belt, pointed it at the forehead of one of them, and shot him dead. The other two, he said, talked immediately; the bomb which had been placed in a crowded railway station and set to explode during the evening rush hour, was found and defused, and countless lives were saved.[3]

The words of General Adnan Tabit, special commander and special advisor to the interior minister, a senior commander under Saddam, will serve to further highlight the dilemma faced in conflict situations. General Tabit was sentenced to death for plotting against the former dictator and was tortured after his sentence was commuted. Now *he* was put into a position of power. When he in his turn engaged in torturing his forces, he said: 'This is a dirty war. We are the only ones with the nerves to fight it.' Perhaps it simply has to be accepted that the war against terrorism is a dirty war and that it has to be fought by the best means possible.

An interesting facet of the contemporary conflict with terrorism is the role of *religion* in fighting a dirty war. In one of my books on terrorism set within a cultural context, I looked at the way in which pig's blood was used in putting down dissidents. In Peshawar in 1882, during the period of the second Afghan War, a Pathan leader harassed British troops, continually shooting at

---

[2] Bruce Hoffman, 'A Nasty Business', in Russell D. Howard (ed.), *Terrorism and Counter Terrorism* (McGraw-Hill 2002) p. 343.

[3] Ibid., at pp. 342-343.

them. The commanding British officer decided to teach him a lesson by dipping bullets into pig's blood and shooting the Pathan, hoping that such a religiously abhorrent fate would put a stop to his activities. Unfortunately, it did not, because it so angered the Pathans that they wiped out the British force. The trampling of religious sensibilities in this case had the opposite effect to that intended. This example serves to emphasise the risky choices that face those engaging in the war on terror. A strict adherence to the constraints of human rights may produce better results in some cases, whereas in others the tensions between human rights and the good of the majority are more marked.

Another interesting case concerns an American general in the Philippines in 1911, known as Black Jack Pershing. In order to stop the insurgency that was taking place in that part of the Philippines, Pershing decided on a similar course of action to that taken in the example above: he threatened the prisoners he had taken that they would be sprinkled with pig's blood. That having failed, it was said he had them shot with bullets dipped in pig's blood, then dumped their bodies in pits that had been partially filled with the chopped-up remains of pigs. Muslims believe that when they die in battle they will go straight to Paradise, but any contact with pigs would defile them and jeopardise their hopes of entry to Paradise. Pershing's action so intimidated the insurgents that terrorism was effectively halted for fifty years. After September 11, a Jewish rabbi actually suggested a similar course of action. Later, in 2004, he proposed hanging bags of pigs' fat in Israeli buses as a deterrent to Palestinian suicide bombers, who frequently target buses. The issue of religion and warfare becomes crucial. Where does religion fit into human rights law? In Abu Ghraib, three men were allegedly made to masturbate. A bewildered American colonel asked why they should have been made to do this. There is a *fatwa* that says: 'If your semen falls to the ground, you are cut off from Paradise.' Was the aim to intimidate the prisoners into compliance? Can breaking human rights law by using religious methods be justified if the results lead to the end of terrorism?

There are two opposing arguments that the previous discussion throws into relief. There are those who criticise any contravention of human rights and those, like Bruce Hoffman, who argue that an increasing terrorist threat must lead to a more realistic approach and that full human rights are incompatible with counter-terrorism.

Those who advocate unconditional support of human rights are apt to make strongly argued statements, warning that governments can use the threat posed by terrorism as an excuse to reject human rights. Amnesty International cites Turkey, where suspected members of Hizbullah (not the organisation based in Lebanon) have been detained arbitrarily and tortured. The Turkish government appeared to become aware of the problem of human rights when it changed course in relation to the ongoing review of the 1982 Constitution, initiated as part of the effort aimed at meeting the criteria for EU membership. The review had previously suggested altering or removing articles that facilitated human rights violations. On 19 September 2001, the Turkish prime minister announced amendments that would 'eradicate terrorism'.[4]

Many organisations, such as Human Rights Watch, for example, argue for the retention of human rights as part of a counter-terrorism strategy. According to Kenneth Roth of Human Rights Watch, it is important to link anti-terrorism with human rights, because this will show most clearly the difference between terrorists and those who are fighting them:

> But what was overlooked, particularly in the initial reaction, is how important it is to see the campaign against terrorism also as a campaign for human rights. I believe that is a necessity if in the long term this campaign is going to be successful. Let me explain briefly what I mean by that and the ways in which the US in the global response to terrorism has in some important respects fallen short of making the fight against terrorism one that involves both security and the active promotion of human rights.
>
> What's wrong with attacking the World Trade Center? Why is that something that we call terrorism? At an instinctive level, we say, 'You're just killing innocent civilians.' But if you ask, 'What is the element of international law that makes that a crime?' it is the Geneva Conventions or the body of international human rights and humanitarian law that explain that regardless of your cause, regardless of whether you see yourself at war, there are certain lines you cannot cross, including one that says you can never deliberately attack civilians.
>
> So in that very straightforward sense, reaffirming a public sense of what is wrong with terrorism requires reaffirming the importance of human rights, building a culture of human rights, a culture where people do not believe that the ends justify the means, where they believe that there are certain limits that legitimately can be placed on political or military conduct. The bottom line should be that civilians are never deliberately killed which is a fundamental principle of human rights and humanitarian law.[5]

---

[4] Amnesty International, 'The backlash – human rights at risk throughout the world' (4 October 2001).

[5] Kenneth Roth, 'Human Rights and the Campaign Against Terrorism', transcript of speech made on 14 February 2002.

An important criticism of many anti-terror strategies that contravene human rights is that they are used to justify attacks against anyone the regime wants to suppress. In its annual survey of 2001, Human Rights Watch cited Russia, Uzbekistan and Egypt as the main offenders of waging indefensible wars against political opponents in the name of the war on terror. Human Rights Watch also alleges that Western countries are ignoring these abuses out of political expediency, commenting: 'These governments often embrace(d) human rights only in theory while subverting them in practice.'[6] Thus, it is the case that, particularly in countries with high levels of corruption, counter-terrorism measures are often used to clamp down on citizens who often have nothing to do with terrorism.

It is also argued that, in the long term, anti-terrorist policies that aim to win over the 'hearts and minds' of those who are potential supporters of terrorism are more effective than aggressive policies that may have only short-term success. In many cultures, a policy that aims only to subdue terrorism with overwhelming force and aggressive tactics will merely result in provoking further terrorist outbreaks. This, it is argued, is what the Russians, for example, have discovered to their cost in Chechnya.

This opinion is also advanced by those who maintain that human rights must form a part of a counter-terrorism strategy. The European Union Madrid Summit on democracy and terrorism in March 2005 argued for the latter position: 'Democratic principles and values are essential tools in the fight against terrorism. Any successful strategy for dealing with terrorism requires terrorists to be isolated. Consequently, the preference must be to treat terrorism as criminal acts to be handled through existing systems of legal enforcement and with full respect for human rights and the rule of law.'

A more pragmatic approach, on the other hand, takes a long hard look at terrorism, at effective means of dealing with it and at the human rights of the majority.

There are six main areas that need close examination: interrogation, deterrence, capture, detention of civilians, extended detention of suspects, prevention of terror acts, secrecy and lack of transparency. In all these areas, the tension between human rights and the need to fight terrorism is clearly discernible.

Anti-terrorist personnel can become frustrated with prisoners who are unwilling to give information, especially as intelligence is so vital in the battle against terrorism. It is clear that the interrogation of prisoners in counter-

[6] 'War on terror cloaks rights abuses', BBC News (17 January 2002).

terrorism operations has, in many parts of the world, resulted in prisoners being mistreated according to human rights standards. Amnesty International criticised a ruling in 2004 of the Court of Appeal of England and Wales which stated that evidence obtained through torture would only be deemed inadmissible in cases involving the expulsion of non-UK nationals 'if it were obtained directly by UK agents, or if UK agents had connived directly at its procurement'.[7] Evidence extracted under torture could be admitted if it were obtained by non-UK agents. This kind of compromise illustrates the tension between human rights and counter-terrorist necessity that has been demonstrated already.

It can also be argued that violent reprisals have to be taken against those believed to have committed terrorist acts as a deterrent to others who might follow suit. These reprisals can include imprisonment, the use of torture, and execution. Those who consider that human rights trump counter-terrorist measures hold that the death penalty is a breach of those human rights; this led to calls for its removal in the trial of Saddam Hussein, for example. The value of deterrence has, however, been illustrated by Bruce Hoffman above.

Those involved in counter-terrorism argue for the necessity of detaining civilians, often without the usual legal safeguards, because they are suspected of engaging in terrorism or of supporting terrorism and because terrorists frequently hide in civilian communities. It is felt that the level of proof demanded by normal procedures is too high to protect the innocent majority from the activities of the minority.

For the same reason, an argument can be made for the detention of suspects for an extended period of time without trial. Terrorist cases can be hard to prove, and the evidence difficult to gather. Those accused of such crimes are dangerous, and their detention for longer periods than usual is justified by the risk they pose for society. The most famous example of this is Guantánamo Bay, although calls for extended periods of detention have been made in many countries, including Britain.

It is clear, then, that human rights activists routinely criticise actions taken to prevent terrorist atrocities that involve ignoring legal safeguards, proceeding without the usual levels of proof and even permitting the use of pre-emptive force, detention or summary deportation, while a more realistic approach will lean towards the pragmatism displayed by those combating terrorism in the examples cited above.

---

[7] *Amnesty International Report 2005.*

Those who place a higher importance on the need to combat terrorism and protect the majority stress the necessity for secrecy in court procedures. It is of the utmost importance that the identity of those who provide evidence be protected, and the evidence provided should therefore not be examined in public in a court but in secret. In the United Kingdom, the Special Immigrations Appeals Commission (SIAC) certified that, if non-UK nationals were potential terrorists, evidence against them need not be publicly disclosed. This measure was criticised by Amnesty International, which disagreed that any evidence should be kept secret.

Paul Hoffman of Amnesty International also argues that 'the War on Terrorism which has been waged threatens to undermine the international human rights framework so painstakingly built since World War II… A "war on terrorism" waged without respect for the rule of law undermines the very values that it presumes to protect.'[8] These claims have been frequently and urgently made, but unfortunately those who make them have never been able to show persuasively that upholding human rights in their entirety effectively reduces terrorism (indeed, it appears to be on the increase), nor that granting potential and actual terrorists more rights and freedoms will make the majority population more secure from their attacks. Common sense suggests the opposite to be the case. Those who continually criticise counter-terrorist actions for contravening human rights must be realistic and must not demand the impossible. Rather than opposing every breach, however minor, of human rights, they should concentrate on those infringements that are most serious. This is especially true now that human rights have become so broad, as pointed out at the beginning of this paper. Human rights activists may need to accept that, in certain cases, the infringement of human rights in the name of security is sometimes justified.

The conflict in which we are engaged has brought a striking awareness of the significant tension between minority rights and majority rights – and it is a friction that will continue as long as terrorism lasts. In his article 'A View from the Eye of the Storm', Haim Harari writes:

> Do you raid a mosque, which serves as a terrorist ammunition storage? Do you return fire, if you are attacked from a hospital? … Do you raid terrorist headquarters, hidden in a mental hospital? … Do you shoot back at someone trying to kill you, standing deliberately behind a group of children? … All of these

---

[8] Paul Hoffman, 'Human Rights and Terrorism', 26(4) *Human Rights Quarterly* (November 2004).

happen daily in Iraq and in the Palestinian areas. What do you do? Well, you do not want to face the dilemma. But it cannot be avoided.[9]

Do those who blow up innocent civilians, who kidnap and murder their victims in barbarous ways, who view all those who live according to different principles as enemies deserving of subjugation or death deserve human rights? Could it be that the application of human rights to terrorists who are the minority harms the human rights of the majority? If that is the case, those who undertake terrorist acts forfeit their claim to full human rights as they are understood today. When the tension between human rights and anti-terrorist measures is examined, it seems that the conclusion to be reached is the realistic one that full human rights are incompatible with counter-terrorism. In other words, it may be necessary to deny the same level of human rights to terrorists as is enjoyed by the majority population. It must be argued, however, that there is an underlying weakness with this position in that suspected terrorists, who may later be found to be innocent, would also have to be treated for a period as terrorists in the process of seeking to eliminate terrorism. While some may have relatively few qualms about denying a measure of human rights to genuine terrorists, it is more difficult to sustain this argument for those who are merely suspected of terrorism. Yet, in the practicalities of real life, it is difficult to see an alternative if the majority population is to be protected. Perhaps, however, the idea that some suspected terrorists may later be discovered to be innocent should affect the balance point in the argument, that is, it should reduce the extent of human rights denial that might be considered justifiable.

Nevertheless, in general, it could be concluded that, for the protection of human rights in an increasingly complex and lawless society, majority rights should prevail over the rights of terrorists, and international law must 'adapt itself, as it has always done, to reality'.[10]

---

[9] Haim Harari, 'A View From the Eye of the Storm', FrontPageMagazine.com (15 March 2005).

[10] Ibid.

The Aftermath of 7 July 2005: New Trends in Terrorism

Michael Whine*

The multiple bombings in London on 7 July 2005 demonstrated the emergence of new trends in terrorism that had also started to manifest themselves elsewhere, most notably in Australia and the United States.

The first is that of the self-recruited group, composed of nationals of the target country, who draw inspiration from, but may not necessarily be under the direct operational control of, al-Qaeda. The group calling itself Jam'iyyat Ul-Islam Is-Saheeh, currently on trial in Los Angeles, is an example of this. This body of self-recruited Islamists allegedly led by an inmate at California State Prison, Sacramento, were apprehended before committing multiple bomb attacks on military recruitment centres and bases, the Israeli consulate and local synagogues.[1]

The Abu Bakr Group, named after its leader Abdul Nacir Benbrika, apprehended on 8 November 2005 in Sydney and Melbourne, appears to have been another.[2] The Samir Azzouz group, apprehended in Brussels, and the group

---

* Michael Whine, Community Security Trust.

1 For useful analyses of the self-recruitment process, see, for example, 'Between al-Andalus and a failing integration: Europe's pursuit of a long-term counterterrorism strategy in the post-al-Qaeda era', Egmont Paper No. 5, Royal Institute for International Relations (IRRI-KIIB) Brussels (May 2005); 'Radicalisation tendencies', Annual Report of the Dutch General Intelligence and Security Service (2004); Magnus Ranstorp, 'Al Qa'ida – An Expanded Global Network of Terror', *RUSI Journal* (June 2005); Fidel Sendagorta, 'Jihad in Europe: The Wider Context', 47(3) *Survival* (2005); 'The Jihad: Change and Continuation', 11(7) *IISS Strategic Comments* (2005).

2 Tracey Bowdon, 'Pre-dawn raids net terrorism suspects', The 7.30 Report, Australian Broadcasting Corporation, broadcast 8 November 2005, available at: <http://www.abc.net.am/7.30/content/2005/s1500243.htm>; 'Terrorism suspects to remain in high security prisons', *ABC Online* (12 November 2005), available at: <http://www.abc.

arrested in Holland in early October 2005 appear to be connected to the Maghreb and to Abu Musab al Zarkawi.[3]

From what we know about the first group of London bombers, they all seem to have been recruited in the United Kingdom, but two of them possibly trained in Pakistan. Mohammad Sidique Khan, the eldest of the bombers, was almost certainly the organiser and the controller of the others. He is known to have been a figurehead for local young Muslims from his regular visits to Islamic bookshops, local madrasas and, most crucially, the classes he organised in the basement gymnasium of a mosque in the Beeston area of Leeds. He is said to have met two of the others, Shehzad Tanweer and Hasib Hussain, up to five years previously and may have enlisted them at some point since then. The parents of Tanweer and Hussain told the press that their sons had come under the influence of a mysterious 'Mr K' – almost certainly Khan.[4]

In November 2004, Khan and Tanweer travelled to Pakistan and stayed there for three months, returning to Britain in February 2005.[5]

According to testimony given to the US authorities by Mohammed Junaid Babar, a Pakistani American computer expert who was arrested following a visit to Pakistan and who has since allegedly admitted his involvement as a planner for al-Qaeda, Khan attended a terror planning meeting in Waziristan on the Pakistan-Afghan border sometime in late 2004. It has also been claimed that Khan met Hambali and other leaders of the Jemaah Islamiah in Malaysia and the Philippines in 2001.[6]

Yet another report notes that an earlier planning meeting took place in March in the same region, at which the chief matter of business was plans to

---

net.au/news/newsitems/200511/s1505105.htm>; Roger Maynard, 'Australian police foil "catastrophic" attack and seize 17', *Times Online* (19 November 2005), available at: <http://www.timesonline.co.uk/article/0,,3-1864033,00html>.

[3] 'Counterterrorism Chief: suspected French terror cell had links to al-Zarkawi', Associated Press, 14 October 2005, quoted in *SITE Institute Bulletin*.

[4] Raymond Whitaker, Francis Elliot, Sophie Goodchild and Paul Lashmar, 'Circles of hate: Why the search for the London bombers is still far from over', *The Independent on Sunday* (31 July 2005).

[5] Francis Elliot, Raymond Whitaker, Paul Lashmar and Severin Casell, 'Revealed: British bomber had links with al-Qa'ida', *The Independent* (17 July 2005), available at: <http://news.independent.co.uk/uk/crime/article299680.ece>.

[6] '7 July bomber filmed last year', *BBC Online*, available at: <http://news.bbc.co.uk/1/hi/uk/ 4375598.stm>.

launch major attacks against Britain, and which was attended by Abu Faraj al Libbi, now said to be the senior al-Qaeda planner.[7]

According to speculative reports in the British media, it is likely that they planned the attacks then. Speculation also surrounds the video recording that Khan made which was released by Al-Jazeera after the bombings.

In the video, Khan claims responsibility for the attacks in the name of al-Qaeda but does not state that he had received orders from them. Although the video was released on 1 September 2005, it is possible that it was not made while Kahn was visiting Pakistan, seven or eight months earlier, but recorded in Britain closer to 7 July 2005 and taken by courier or posted to al-Qaeda contacts. In the video, Khan is shown holding a pen, whereas other suicide bombers have almost always been filmed with a weapon. The backdrop is also unlike others shown on al-Qaeda videos, lending further support to this theory. If so, some infrastructure in the United Kingdom remains in place, despite the many arrests in recent years.[8]

A connection between the three and the Pakistani Lashkar e Taiba (LET – 'Army of the Pure'), which is part of the wider al-Qaeda network, has also been suggested. Some LET contacts in Britain were detained in March 2005 when Palvinder Singh, Mohammed Khan and Frzana Khan were arrested and charged with terrorism-related offences. Their arrests were said to be part of a wider major operation to close down LET's British infrastructure.[9]

In a move to stem the flow of foreign-born Muslim students studying at radical madrasas in Pakistan, General Musharraf announced on 29 July 2005 that an estimated 1,400 foreign students would have to leave and that study visas would no longer be issued. However, this is unlikely to put a stop to their enrolment, given that many young people return to Pakistan on family visits, especially in the summer months, and many madrasas are located in areas of the country where the government does not exercise complete con-

7 Jay Solomon, Zahid Hussain, Keith Johnson and David Crawford, 'Pakistan Remains Terrorist Haven, Musharraf's Moves Fail to Rein in Militant Groups: Probing links to London', *The Asian Wall Street Journal* (22 July 2005).

8 The Al-Jazeera website carries more on the Al-Zawahiri statement. Aljazeera.net website, Doha, in Arabic, 2 September 2005, BBC Monitoring (which publicised the full text of both Khan's and Al-Zawahiri's online statements, noting the difference between the latter's video tape broadcast and the later text published online); Kim Sengupta, 'Defiant message from bomber was filmed on British soil, claim security services', *The Independent* (3 September 2005).

9 Solomon et al., *supra* n. 7.

trol, particularly in the tribal homelands in the North-West Frontier region abutting Afghanistan.[10]

The second trend, also seen elsewhere, concerns the composition of the group carrying out the attack. This was a mixture of 'born again' Muslims and criminals radicalised in prison and possibly recruited there who came together voluntarily or through the efforts of one individual or some outside agency to plan and carry out the attack.

Again there are strong similarities with the Los Angeles and Australian groups. None of the 7/7 bombers had been identified as having close links to known jihadi networks, and although they were clearly known to the relevant agencies they were not considered threats. The apparent loose arrangement of the groups includes the third and fourth members. Jermaine Lindsey, the Jamaican born convert to Islam who came from Huddersfield, 20 miles from Leeds, but was living in Aylesbury, appears at first sight to be the odd one out. However, we have since learned from press reports that his telephone number was stored on Hussain's mobile phone, and a bystander reported that the two had met in October 2004 in the Leeds Grand Mosque.[11]

The fourth member of the group, Habbib Hussain, may have been a late addition to the plot. He did not participate in the reconnaissance mission of 28 June 2005; he appears not to have been a member of the tight-knit group of Beeston-based Islamists who trained together and went white water rafting in June; he failed to detonate his bomb on the underground, detonating it on a bus near Euston Station after failing to make contact with the others from his mobile phone, and only after he had eaten a final meal at McDonald's at King's Cross Station. As a strict Muslim, which the others had become, he would not have eaten non-Halal meat, and indeed he was known more for his night clubbing and drugs usage than for his Islamist convictions. Again, the similarities with the Australian and American would-be bombers are there.[12]

Connections to al-Qaeda or other terrorist groups did not become apparent until well after 7 July 2005 and only emerged into the public domain later. The group may thus, in some senses, have been a self-directing one, probably able to choose the time and location of its attacks and with little element of

---

[10] Peter Foster, 'Pakistan to expel madrassa foreigners', *The Daily Telegraph* (30 July 2005).

[11] Jason Bennetto and Ian Herbert, 'London bombings: the truth emerges', *The Independent* (13 August 2005). Ben Taylor, 'London bombers filmed 18 months before attack', *Daily Mail* (26 October 2005).

[12] Jason Bennetto, 'Tube suicide bomber argued with cashier hours before blast', *The Independent* (31 October 2005).

outside control. No Internet or phone connections have so far been reported between them and any central command and control. As with the March 2004 Madrid railway bombers, this appears to have been a network based on personal contact, where a single person was a kind of catalyst.

Balthazar Garzon, the Spanish counter-terrorism magistrate, and Marc Sageman, the American researcher, have both described the spontaneously generated loose constellations of young Muslim men defined by a system of personal relationships that characterise this emerging trend of terrorism, rather than the hierarchically controlled discrete cells that characterised the 9/11 terrorists and their immediate predecessors and successors. For these activists, al-Qaeda is an ideological reference point and an inspiration rather than a superior level in the chain of command.[13]

The head of the French domestic security service recently noted that:

> We are seeing a terrorist threat that keeps changing… Often the groups are not homogenous, but a variety of blends. Hard-core Islamists are mixing with petty criminals … people of different backgrounds and nationalities are working together. Some are European-born or have dual nationalities that make it easier for them to travel. The networks are much less structured than we used to believe. Maybe it's the mosque that brings them together, maybe it's the prison, maybe it's the neighbourhood. And that makes it much more difficult to identify and uproot them.[14]

The US State Department's 2004 report on terrorism also refers to this new phase in the development of terrorism, one in which local groups inspired by al-Qaeda organise and carry out attacks with little or no support or direction from al-Qaeda itself.[15] The Australian Abu Bakr group had been under surveillance for over a year and included a mixture of known political activists and others who had no other profile, save for those surveying them. The stockpiling of dangerous chemicals purchased at local shops prompted their arrests before they could carry out their attacks. All were Australian nationals, although some are said to have been born in Lebanon. Benbrika himself was born in Algeria.[16]

---

13 Shann Waterman, 'Eurojihadis: A new generation of terror', UPI (2 June 2005). Marc Sageman, *Understanding Terror Networks* (Philadelphia, University of Pennsylvania Press 2004) pp. 137-173.

14 Elaine Sciolino, 'Europe Meets the New Face of Terrorism', *The New York Times* (1 August 2005).

15 Country reports on Terrorism 2004, US Department of State, Office of the Coordinator for Counterterrorism, Washington DC (April 2005).

16 Bowdon, *supra* n. 2; Maynard, *supra* n. 2.

The third emerging trend is that of minimal-cost terrorism. All in all, it is estimated that the 7/7 bomb components cost no more than a few hundred pounds.

Even if the cost of travel to Pakistan, which two of the bombers undertook, is factored in, the overall costs still total no more than a few thousand pounds. Such sums were easily affordable by the terrorists themselves without resorting to outside funding either from al-Qaeda or its offshoots, or the use of criminal enterprise, which has been a characteristic of other recent terrorist plots.

A UN report published in August 2004 quantified the cost of recent major terrorist attacks. It suggested that the Madrid train bombings in March 2004 cost only $10,000, that the Istanbul truck-bomb attacks in November 2003 cost $40,000, that the Marriot Hotel bombing in Jakarta in August 2003 cost $30,000 and that the USS *Cole* attack in October 2000 cost $10,000.[17]

Of course, these estimates do not take into account any training costs, the establishment of front companies or money-laundering enterprises, but they do reinforce the point that terrorism has become a cheap form of warfare and one we are likely to see more of now that al-Qaeda's funding role has been diminished, and as local groups enact the ideology. A report by Joshua Prober for the Washington Institute attempts to estimate infrastructure costs and lists the various associated costs of training, renting, accommodation, maintaining communication networks, purchasing electronic equipment and so forth. He makes the vital and obvious point that money will always be necessary to fund attacks, however cheap the component costs for the bombs may be.[18]

Prober quotes US Treasury Department Under Secretary for Terrorism and Financial Intelligence, Stuart Levy, who noted in August 2004 that:

> The cost of financing terrorist activity cannot be measured by the cost of a primitive destructive act. The maintenance of those terrorist networks, like Al Qaeda which threaten our national security, is expensive... Groups like Al Qaeda must spend money for many purposes – to recruit, train, travel, plan operations, and bribe corrupt officials for example.[19]

Levy observes that all terrorist acts leave a money trail that leads back to the originators. He argues that stemming the flow of funds can delay or prevent attacks even when the cost of the explosives remains relatively low. This is an

[17] Joshua Prober, 'Accounting for Terror, Debunking the Paradigm of Inexpensive Terrorism', Washington Institute, Policy Watch No. 1041 (1 November 2005).

[18] Ibid.

[19] Ibid.

important point, and one now aggressively pursued by the United Nations and many governments. However, as the two London attacks and the US and Australian plots have suggested, the self-recruiting nature of these newer, younger terrorists emphasises this emerging trend of few, if any, costs and a connection to al-Qaeda limited solely to ideology.

These terrorists, for the most part, may not have trained in Afghanistan, Pakistan, Iraq or Chechnya. Their connection to al-Qaeda is limited to inspiration. They can download bomb manuals from the Internet, and they can purchase the components at hardware stores and chemists. For this reason, and recognising and promoting the development, al-Qaeda and its offshoots have now launched an on-line 'virtual university' for would-be terrorists that provides them with all they need to carry out attacks.

In October 2005, a posting on the Al-Farouk jihadi forum (www.al-farouk.com) by Ahmad al-Wathiq bi-Llah, the 'Deputy General Amir' of the Global Islamic Media Front (GIMF), announced what it referred to as the 'Al-Qaeda University of Jihad Studies'. The accompanying statement explained that 'Al-Qaeda is an organisation, a state and a university, this is a fact which cannot be denied'.[20]

It goes on to note that: 'Since the events of the USS *Cole* and Manhattan, hundreds of Muslims from all corners of the world have joined this global jihadist university, studying all the sciences, rules and methods of jihad.'

According to press reports, Wassem Mughal, who was arrested and charged, along with two others, with terrorism-related offences at the Old Bailey during the first week of November 2005, had a DVD in his bedroom called 'Martyrdom Operations Vest', which contained information 'likely to be useful to a person committing or preparing an act of terrorism'. Another charge refers to a piece of paper allegedly found in his bedroom with information about a recipe for rocket propellant and guidance on causing an explosion.[21]

The police raid on the Manchester home of Anas al Liby in 2000 led to the discovery of the first known jihadi terrorist manual, although American anarchists and far right activists had posted bomb making manuals on the Internet years before.

[20] The Jamestown Foundation, 'An Online "University" for Jihad', 2(19) *Terrorism Focus* (17 October 2005).

[21] John Steele, 'Two in court accused of plot to build a car bomb', *The Daily Telegraph* (5 November 2005); Stewart Tendler, 'Two sent for Old Bailey trial accused of plotting explosions', *The Times* (5 November 2005).

Clearly, therefore, the Internet plays a vital role in educating would-be terrorists. As the post-9/11 investigations showed, it also plays a vital role in the command and control processes. However, it should be remembered that the Internet in itself does not lead to terrorism. This requires face-to-face interaction and the formation of social networks or cliques, which, as Sageman points out, are important in reinforcing individual commitment to jihad. No-one goes straight from reading terror manuals on the Internet to becoming a terrorist. Here, the role of the Salafi Islamist organisations has been sadly underestimated. Hizb ut Tahrir and Al Muhajiroun, or its successor, the Saviour Sect, and the Supporters of Shariah are vital in this process. They provide the conveyer belt that starts by radicalising young Muslims and ends with some of them becoming terrorists.

Sageman describes the highly connected hubs that have dominated the architecture of the Global Salafi Jihad: the Central Staff, the Core Arabs, the Maghreb Arabs and the South East Asian groups. These are all large clusters of activists built around hubs, which may in fact be dominant figures. As their importance diminishes, as a result of degrading or interdiction, the role of other groups will emerge and increase. Here the hub becomes ever more important: it is the centre that recruits, motivates and directs. In Britain, this role was filled, to a large extent, by Omar Mahmoud Othman (Abu Qatada), Mustafa Kamel (Abu Hamza al Masri) and, to a lesser extent, Omar Bakri Mohammed and others. This role may now revert to two other hubs. The first could be the returning Iraq veterans (although the police and the security services are alive to this possibility); the other will be what Sageman calls 'the larger disconnected and unorganised loose networks of small cliques and singletons' who are politicised and radicalised by world events and racism in society and whose frustrations are nurtured and channelled by the Salafi groups.[22]

The need for open-minded vigilance is therefore vital in the future. The security and law enforcement agencies are reported to have lost interest in Khan and other 7/7 bombers because they did not fit their preconceived notions of who is a terrorist.

Sageman's study and other studies prove that there is no typical terrorist profile. Salafi terrorists come from all socio-economic levels, nationalities, family backgrounds and levels of educational attainment. We adopt a narrow view at our peril.

---

[22] Sageman, *supra* n. 13, at p. 172.

Part II:
Foreign Policy and Human Rights

Geopolitics and Power: What Room for Human Rights?

Sir Jeremy Greenstock*

Since my expertise is not specifically in the corpus of human rights, in the law and in the implementation of the laws of human rights, I thought I should concentrate on the big picture: where human rights fits into world politics and what problems stem from that. I will set a context for what I am going to say. I will ask where the problems lie for human rights in the modern world. I will then look particularly at governments – why do they behave as they behave, and how do we get them to improve their approach to human rights? I will then look at the balance between the individual and the state in the light of the changes that are occurring at such a pace in our world, try and draw a few conclusions on foreign policy objectives in human rights against that background, look at the United Nations' approach to this and what the United Nations can do for it, and leave you, I hope, with a core message. That core message is that in the implementation of human rights law and human rights norms, governments are pivotal, but the good ones are not doing enough, the bad ones are not sufficiently constrained, and we must understand why both those things are true if we are to introduce some improvements and go in the right direction.

The United Nations is a vital centre of norms and actions for the pursuit of human rights, but the United Nations cannot do it on its own. Nor can governments, nor can civil society or the individual. The balance that we are looking for has to come from the interaction between all of those within a sensibly set, strategic context.

What about the context? Now, what kind of world are we living in? Globalisation, polarisation – which is dominant? We are living in a world which is

* Sir Jeremy Greenstock, GCMG, former UK Special Representative for Iraq and Ambassador to the United Nations.

globalised. The process has been going on for 100 years, but it has globalised in economics, in information, in communication, in movement, in technology, in global cultural exchange, all very beneficial things for some people in the world, but not all. It has polarised, at least has not globalised, in politics and in culture and the events we are going through in this decade are a clear example of the forces of polarisation against the background of globalisation. There is a tension between the two that is easily illustrated. When a major government reacted to an abuse, to a fault in the system or to a threat to its interest in a previous era, the action it might have taken, perhaps with some force and some brutality, would have been effective. However, in a *globalised* world, the capacity to use strength to mend a situation in the subjective perception of the operator is aggravated, is made worse, by the globalised effect of what it is doing. Iraq is a clear example of that – that an action that should have been done better, should have achieved its aims sooner, has been marred through its lack of support in a globalised world with immense opposition, a lack of legitimacy and in a failure to achieve the objectives.

It is clear to me that the corpus of human rights legislation in the world is, by and large, sufficient. We do not have a deficit of norms in human rights. There are always improvements that can be made. I think that in the Security Council we achieved some important steps forward on either side of the turn of the millennium – in passing Resolution 1325, for instance, on women's rights in the context of security, in what we have done on the protection of civilians, the abuse of children and other aspects of human rights. The Security Council, in the eyes of many members of the United Nations, was not supposed to be dealing with these, but the security situations that came up also brought in very strong human rights considerations. There was no dividing line that was clearly set in the procedures of the United Nations and, I think I will have to add, the General Assembly did not show itself equally effective in some of these areas.

I think that the statute of the International Criminal Court was an exceedingly important step forward for one of the things that I am going to talk about in some depth, which is the need to constrain the abusers and particularly the government abusers of human rights. The prescription of human rights, in the form of charters and declarations and covenants and resolutions, is largely there. It is the implementation that is insufficient and it is the implementation that we have to focus on.

Let us quickly ask for a moment: where do the abuses of human rights largely come from? Now this is of course a subjective question, but there is no doubt in my mind about the abuses of human rights that we have witnessed in our lifetimes, coming out of many places in Africa (Darfur, the Congo,

Somalia, and Zimbabwe spring to mind at this moment, but there are many other instances), out of China, Iraq, Iran, Chechnya, Haiti, Serbia, Abu Ghraib and Guantánamo Bay or even Northern Ireland. In mentioning those instances – and of course I am leaving out many others – I am illustrating the huge difference in the circumstances of the abuse of human rights that are going on in our lifetime.

Those instances were mainly concerned with poor government decisions, a lack of attention to human rights for the civilian, the man, the woman and the child. However, they have also come out of poverty, out of the breakdown of states, not particularly in any one instance anyone's fault, but, for example, more that the state could not hold together in Somalia, in Sierra Leone, in the Democratic Republic of the Congo. In addition, and let us not mince words about this – the abuse of human rights also comes from the excessive or indiscriminate use of violence, including by terrorism – sometimes by governments, sometimes by small groups, sometimes by criminals, often by terrorists. The excessive use of violence where the perpetrator sees the advantage of the instruments of violence, something which is very common now with powerful weapons in the hands of a few, causes the abuse of human rights.

So I thought I should cover two fields. Firstly, what governments are doing, and what we should be doing as governments. Secondly, the role of the individual and the balance between the individual and the state.

How do governments behave? And here I mean by governments those governments that are trying to do something about human rights and not always succeeding. I am not talking about those other governments that themselves abuse human rights. We will mention those at a later moment.

On the whole, in our countries, our agendas are often right, our rhetoric, our commitments are often right. Perhaps in some of our government agendas, human rights has got caught up too much with development policies and at other times too much with politics. I do not believe that human rights should be a subdivision of development policy, although development is extremely difficult unless we address human rights problems. Human rights has got to invade a larger part of the agenda than just the development area, but in practice, what happens with governments?

When the human rights problem is the crisis – as it was over Rwanda, in our dealing with the Balkans, is now in Darfur, was at particular times in Sierra Leone and the Congo – we are active, we are concerned, we pass resolutions, we do things, but just in the mention of those instances, what usually happens is that we do not meet the requirement to end that human rights abuse. The story of Rwanda was a clear example of governments failing to address the sudden acceleration of a problem from a local peacekeeping difficulty to one of the most awful abuses of human rights in the 1990s. That, to some extent, is now continuing in Darfur with the increasing killing of aid workers on top of the awful abuse of civilians, particularly women, in and around the camps in Darfur, with the Africans withdrawing their forces and the Sudanese government refusing to allow a new UN peacekeeping force to come in.

In Sierra Leone, there was an interesting instance which I was involved in, of a particular country, the United Kingdom, moving in without specific Security Council instruction and dealing with the security problem that was affecting the human rights of the Sierra Leone people. The United Kingdom carried out a military action and left, and it made the crucial difference. It was legal because it was at the invitation of the Sierra Leone government who asked for help because they were powerless to do it themselves, but it was not a UN action. It was a unilateral action to help a UN peacekeeping operation, and to my mind, that went well. It was a good decision by Tony Blair, very few people were killed, and it showed the bad boys on the ground – they were literally called 'the West-side boys', who were dealt with by the paras – it showed them that they could not go beyond a certain line in their abuse of the population. From then on, the peacekeeping operation in Sierra Leone began to bite, with a lot of help from other peacekeeping operations – the Indians, Bangladeshis, Pakistanis, Russians and Ukrainians all having a presence. It turned into a good UN operation to reverse the collapse of the state.

Normally, however, when human rights are *the* crisis, governments do not do enough. The United Nations is not capable, without governments, of filling that gap.

When it is not *the* crisis – I am thinking perhaps of Zimbabwe or Somalia or Burundi or, in quite a different context, the lack of individual and human rights implementation in China – when it is not *the* crisis, then the action taken is truly insufficient, because there are other priorities. I will come back to why governments act as they do, but neither when human rights is *the* crisis, nor when it is *not the* crisis, is the action sufficient.

My experience – I think it is our experience – is that the international community – whatever that means, but it normally means action through the United Nations – tends to do the minimum. There are reasons for that, but the actions of the Security Council, the actions of the security community in the world, the international community, are normally insufficient, because they are trying to get through that particular problem or crisis at minimum cost. That is actually a product of democracy – that the people have other priorities, they do not want their money to be spent on something that is not relevant to them. But at the United Nations we were constantly frustrated by the tendency of governments only to allow the minimum to be done to satisfy their constituencies that the problem was being dealt with.

That is, of course, because there are other national priorities. There are important reasons why the United States, Russia, China, the United Kingdom, France, African governments, the Cambodian government, the Congolese government, act as they do at particular times. They have other national priorities and even those countries that are particularly good at soft power operations, at passing resolutions, at allocating money, at persuading the world that something needs to be done – as in the European Union, as with Canada – are not themselves prepared to put harder resources on the ground to deal with the problem.

There are other causes of consistent abuses and here I think it is worth mentioning that one of the great downsides – of course there were so many other downsides – but one of the great downsides of 9/11, that strike by a small group of people who could not have cared less what damage they caused, was that the human rights agenda in the last five years has been downgraded. It was a huge disservice of al-Qaeda, particularly to the developing world, that this act changed the agenda in foreign policy, and it is an illustration of how national priorities can change.

In 1999-2000, I was under explicit instructions from my prime minister to try and get agreement in the Security Council on a set of norms for what was then called 'humanitarian intervention'. It was not possible to get agreement in the Security Council, because there was not sufficient trust in the international community that any agreement would only be used as the basis for the remedying of human rights abuses. There was always the worry that any basis laid down at a level equivalent to international treaty commitment might be used as the basis for unilateral action in other contexts. Russia and China had particular concerns about that at the time, and indeed the United States was not really willing to have a general agreement that might constrain its freedom to make its own foreign policy decisions on a specific occasion. That still affects the whole business of the responsibility to protect, which remains a moral responsibility which many other people are trying to turn into a political responsibility. The moral ground, as I have said earlier, has been well set out. How do we turn it into political action?

Why do governments behave like this? Well, here I am going to introduce a vexed word that we stumbled over many times in the Security Council and never got round, never really understood, never really acted on, and that is 'accountability'. There is a deep lack of understanding of where accountability lies in the international community, and that includes the whole responsibility to improve human rights. Why? Well, if you look at the real accountability of governments in the real world, in the decisions that they take in their closed rooms day by day – and there is something cynical in this, but there is truth in it as well – there is a descending order of priority. For most governments, the first accountability is to themselves, to their party, to their power base, to remaining in power. It is often very well covered by constitutions, by speeches, but when you look and analyse the actions, the first accountability for most governments is to retain the reins of power, usually legally, and that also needs quite a lot of thought and focus.

The second accountability is to their domestic constituency. There is a cost to taking any action on security or on human rights and that cost has got to be explained to the people who are providing the resources – the taxpayer in a democracy. That is a true accountability, an acceptable accountability, and could easily be the first accountability for very good governments.

The third accountability is to national interests in the international context. It should never be forgotten that the highest level of political decision making in our globalised world *remains* at the national level. There is no supranational government in this world at the moment. The European Union is an example of extremely close cooperation between national governments, perhaps the closest that there has been in history, in terms of so many governments and such a large volume of population sharing certain policies by treaty. Nevertheless, the decision to go with each policy and to commit resources each year is a national decision. Therefore in international affairs, national priorities are going to rule and the national interest in the international context is an accountability for any responsible government.

The fourth of the four accountabilities I am going to mention and the least compelling is to norms, is to the standards, the charters, the declarations, the treaties, the resolutions in international law and international life. They are important and they are particularly important in rhetoric, but they are not as compelling a force on government action as the other three accountabilities that I have mentioned. In terms of this list, the adherence to norms is minimalist in most governments in the modern world. Of course there are other pressures on governments. The pressure of events is perhaps the strongest. We are always saying to each other now that everything is so short-term, the media dominate, governments have to react in the short term. They do. That is their compelling need to survive, to react, to govern, to deal with the short-term issues and the headlines, which are, in this world, very strong forces acting on them. There is one other consideration as to why governments act or fail to act as they do, and that is that for any one government initiative, the scale of the problem that they are trying to deal with is so much greater that they feel that what they do is just a drop in the ocean. The buck is easily passed when you know that from your seat and with your resources, you cannot mend the problem unless there are enough allies, enough co-contributors, to meet the size of the problem.

How can we influence governments to do better? We have to look at their accountability. We have to try and make the implementation of human rights part of the interests, the self-interest, of a government, which in the long term it is, but in the short term rarely is. Out of that consideration came Robin Cook and the – often – misquoted ethical foreign policy, which was really a foreign policy with ethical dimensions. In early summer 1997, Robin Cook set out twelve points on ethical dimensions of foreign policy. His intention was as follows: 'Of course we cannot fulfil all of these. The point of setting it out is to show that there are objectives which we must follow and just because we cannot do all of it, or some of it in all places, does not mean that we should not try to do some of it some of the time somewhere.' He was very clear about that. That is a very important injunction, and has been mischievously rubbished in our media and elsewhere.

We have to make sure that domestic opinion is mobilised, the second accountability. Taxpayers must understand that it is in their long-term interests that there should be an ordered world without the abuse of human rights, wherever they can help to mend them. In a democracy, in countries that are not a democracy, their interests are going to be better ordered if there is a stable and a prosperous world, so it is a domestic interest that international human rights should be addressed and that needs to be brought out, pushed and discussed, including by the media, all the time.

In that area of thinking, I would put the reactions of the American people to their government's actions since 9/11. Trace the shift in American opinion about what their government has been doing since 9/11 and you will see a very considerable movement of domestic opinion in the United States of worry about the moral and political standing of their government in addressing the wrongs in the world. Of course it has happened even more forcefully elsewhere.

It is easy to say, but difficult to act upon – the United Nations is important. We must maximise the use of the United Nations in the international arena, and here I think it is worth adding as a parenthesis a comment on what the United Nations really can do to help the implementation of human rights beyond governments. A forum is needed to develop norms. The United Nations has been excellent on that. There is a need for a forum for collective action to bestow legitimacy on action in dealing with abuses. The United

Nations is the only place for that. The United Nations has good agencies and some bad committees. The good agencies that do the specific work on health and refugees and food and human rights itself are, to my mind, excellent agencies, led better or worse at particular times, but they are good agencies. The intergovernmental action on human rights – now the Human Rights Council – is a much more doubtful area of really effective action.

The United Nations is also a very important resource for non-governmental activity. There is this equivocal relationship between NGOs and the United Nations, between civil society and the United Nations, which Kofi Annan tried to do a tremendous amount about in his time as Secretary-General, but governments are jealous about their monopoly of intergovernmental action at the United Nations. There is a tension between governments and non-governmental bodies at the United Nations. I think that the trend still needs to go further in the direction of non-governmental action.

I took great care at the United Nations to regularly meet the collective committee of NGOs and make it clear that the United Kingdom took NGO concerns into account in addressing what was in front of the Security Council. But the United Nations cannot do these things on its own. It cannot have the buck passed to it because governments will not act. It is not that sort of body. In intergovernmental action, the United Nations is its member states, and if the member states cannot agree, they cannot shift the problem off to a United Nations that is powerless unless it is given power and resources by the member states.

Indeed, as I said earlier, governments cannot do it on their own. They actually need the United Nations. Civil society cannot do it on its own. It needs governments; it needs the United Nations. These three areas need each other.

It is extremely important that the non-governmental sector keeps going. The trend is in that direction. It must include not just NGOs but also the corporate sector, parliaments, churches, all the institutions of civil society as well as the NGOs that directly address human rights, as well as the individual. We have to enlarge the area of individual responsibility, because unless we all feel to some extent personally accountable, none of these other things will happen. The individual is the building block of every institution, and therefore there has to be a heightened awareness and a sense of responsibility in the individual in society if all of the institutions are to work better on the question of human rights. In this area, the function of education in international responsibility is exceptionally important and is not given enough attention, including in the United Kingdom's school curricula.

To a great extent the individual has gained with globalisation, if the law around him is working. The effect of the spread of the freedom of choice, of democracy, of openness, pushes things the way of the individual. This is not completely a zero-sum game, but the corollary is that the state becomes weaker in controlling the individual. The state used to have a monopoly of power, of arms, of use of force, of information, and of status. That has faded with globalisation, so the individual has gained in terms of his or her own protection from power, and human rights have gained in that bad governments have found it more difficult to abuse human rights without the victims having recourse, without finding that there is punishment for abuses. However, there is another consideration: that the individual needs the state to be effective. The individual cannot exist without a social and political structure. It is the first duty of government, after all, to provide security. To what extent must the provision of security rank above freedom or the protection of human rights?

There have to be limits to absolute freedom and there have to be limits – it is a strange phrase, perhaps – but there have to be limits to absolute human rights. The Universal Declaration on Human Rights is the fundamental document beyond which really nothing else needs to be said, but in that Declaration there is a right not just to a safe existence, a subsistence life, there is a right to a civilised life, which is extremely difficult to deliver in many territories, whether or not governments are trying to do that.

How can we try to get the balance between the individual and the state, between freedom and security from the pressures that we see in the modern world? Individuals as well as governments have to understand the compromises that have to be made.

In all of that, what should our foreign policies be aiming at? Well, first of all, in what I call the 'case action', when we have to take action because something is happening in a particular case – we must keep going. We have to do it. We have to do it to the best of our ability. If constraints block the perfect answer, fine, but we must try. We have to keep going on case action.

But what about the general international atmosphere? First of all, we need agreement on definitions and on what 'human rights' means. There is no universal agreement on what human rights are, and 'human rights', the phrase, is often seen by part of the world as a cover, as a pretext for the fulfilling of the agenda of another part of the world. That problem is still there. We have to go on talking about it. To my mind, it is an endless conversation, but it must be a conversation and not a war.

Secondly, there must be constraints, constraints within international law on governments that abuse human rights. They must not feel that they can get away with it. Gradually, millimetre by millimetre, we are making advances in that area. It is becoming more difficult, but it is not just the action of the

United Nations or other governments that is necessary. It must be the action of forces everywhere to punish or constrain those who are abusing their people.

We must involve the people, beyond their governments, and that has to be a factor in foreign policy and not just in civil society. We must bring in civil society and NGOs, parliaments, business, churches and individuals who are the voters and who apply the real pressure in the end – or lack of pressure if we as individuals do not act. In all of that, foreign policy must continuously aim at a collective understanding of the strategic framework for human rights implementation, including many of the things that I have discussed, and the United Nations has to be part of that.

So, to return to the core message, governments are pivotal and the pressures on them to deliver a strategically coherent policy on human rights and international security must be a very high priority. The good governments are not doing enough, the bad ones are not sufficiently constrained. We must change that. The United Nations is a vital centre of norms and implementation action, but it cannot do it on its own, nor can governments, nor can the individual. The balance has to come in the interaction between all of them within a high priority conversation on the right strategy.

That leaves many questions to be asked and answered, but it has to be the framework within which all governments should act on human rights.

Comments on *Geopolitics and Power*

Rosemary Hollis*

This paper offers some thoughts in response to Sir Jeremy Greenstock. They are the thoughts of a political scientist who has been fascinated by the study of international relations and who has understood politics to be all about the pursuit of power.

Sir Jeremy Greenstock's observations provide some evidence for the kind of statements that I might wish to make about the behaviour of actors on the international stage. His list of government priorities was especially useful for understanding the behaviour of state actors internationally. He stated that the first priority for most governments is accountability to themselves – in other words, to perpetuate themselves in power, no doubt within the system. So this would be to win the next election, if that is the system. Subsequently, their responsibilities are to their domestic constituencies, and after that, to promote national interests in the international context. Finally, they have an accountability to the existing norms, standards, treaties and charters that are out there, and that will tell us a lot about what behaviour to expect, as opposed to what we might like to see happen.

In describing what it is that may restrain governments from acting always in accordance with international human rights law, with upholding international human rights law and holding accountable those who fail to do so, Sir Jeremy Greenstock assumed that these were things of which there should be more. In his core message he assumed that the good governments were not doing enough and the bad ones were not sufficiently constrained.

I want to step one stage back from that, to ask: why would we make the assumption that more upholding of human rights is a good thing? That it should be something that we expect of governments? Why? If the way the world works is about actors pursuing power, maintaining power, wishing to

* Dr Rosemary Hollis, Director of Research, Chatham House.

justify their actions, why not have a *realpolitik* position which says might is right, the strongest will win, and we are in a Hobbesian state of nature where you really have to pursue your own self-interest. It is nice, if you can, to be pleasant to other people in the process, but you really cannot expect people to act out of anything other than self-interest. Therefore human rights are doomed unless they happen to coincide with self-interest.

My response to that is that I do not think you can make a national interest argument go very far in defence of human rights and in defence of the human rights of others. Obviously, if we are talking about the rights of soldiers taken prisoner in war, there is a self-interest in that 'do unto others as you would have them do unto you'. However, I do not think that is sufficient to explain why we might assume that human rights and the defence of human rights is 'a good thing', and that therefore it is a necessary premise for a discussion of what the problems are.

I start from the assumption that man does not live by bread alone. We are learning more and more about how we do live in the context of the war on terrorism, because some of the champions of the war on terrorism are claiming that what is being defended here is values. The British prime minister and the US president say: 'They hate our values. They resent our freedom. We are at war with them because they want to undermine our values. They want to take away our democracy. They do not want us to bring democracy to the peoples of the Middle East.' What on earth is that all about?

My position here is that human rights lawyers do us an enormous service in getting us better in touch with what we actually mean when we make a statement like: 'We are defending our values, we are defending our freedoms', and we claim some kind of moral justification for our position. I think I would attribute to theologians, philosophers and lawyers key roles in enabling us to understand better what we mean when we say that we act in the name of certain principles and values. I would further say that none of us is correct if we claim that we are operating without any values. None of us is totally self-interested. All of us have to derive some meaning in life for ourselves, and the value system that we espouse is the bedrock of our understanding of our meaning in life.

I believe that all actors in the human drama have an implicit or explicit value system. When we claim to be acting in accordance with that value system, we all benefit from the work of lawyers who have tracked the evolution of law and who can give us reference to the corpus of law; we all benefit from theologians who can tell us what, in their theological tradition, constitutes a just war and an unjust war; we need both in order to act more clearly and consistently in accordance with the values that we claim – mere opinion or majority opinion or public preference will not do. That is why we should worry about the ability of governments, NGOs and the United Nations to uphold international law, to apply standards across the board.

The second broad point I want to make, is that if we take all the belief systems that are being espoused – especially those that are overt, like Islam, Judaism, Christianity, Hinduism, Buddhism – if we take them all, I suspect that through some level of dialogue, we would be able to establish that, in all cases, there is no support for torture; in all cases, there is no support for arbitrary arrest, detention without trial; and in all cases, there is a concept of justice. Therefore I think there is sufficient basis to establish some universal principles of human rights that will be the practical basis for action.

The third area that I want to touch upon comprises a couple of practical conundrums where I see these issues coming to the fore. How do we read them?

The first is the application of the European Neighbourhood Policy, which is a policy devised principally by the European Commission and accepted as the umbrella policy of the European Union towards its Mediterranean neighbours. The application of that policy is inclusive of the promotion of human rights legislation in relation to Europe's Mediterranean neighbours. I want to take the case of Egypt specifically, because the European Union officials and policymakers face a specific problem in trying to persuade the Egyptian government that Europe should have anything to do with their human rights record inside Egypt, or that the promotion of human rights should be a plank in the European Union's policy towards its neighbours.

The second is the question of what was the correct position for European Union member governments, and the British government in particular, to take in the context of the crisis and war in Lebanon that erupted in 2006?[1]

In the case of Egypt and human rights, along with an Arab colleague, I have interviewed many Egyptians and established that, whilst there is a small body of opinion inside Egypt that is very supportive of the international community holding their government to account on the basis of human rights, it is largely irrelevant to the mass of the population, because they are largely unaware of any of this. Survival, scraping together a living and trying to attain basic security in terms of simple human needs, is the principal preoccupation of the majority of the Egyptian population. The position of the

[1] Lebanon became the scene of renewed and deadly fighting in July 2006, when Israel launched a major military campaign against the Lebanon-based Shia Muslim armed group Hezbollah, sparked by the movement's capture of two Israeli soldiers.

government is: 'This is none of your business, you outsiders, and we know exactly what we are doing and, by the way, if we did not handle legal issues and counter-terrorism issues in the way that we do, you, the Western players, would be deeply upset, because your problem with al-Qaeda would be worse.'

What should the European governments do in that case? My colleague and I differed on the issue of how great the ambitions of foreign governments should be in terms of interventions, but I think we could agree that, at the moment, the European Neighbourhood Policy aspires to achieve too much, and aspires to change too much. European governments are probably on shaky ground in terms of knowing really what they are doing and what democratisation and its full consequences would mean in Egypt. They are even on shaky ground when it comes to helping with education, thinking they should have a role in the curriculum that is taught in the schools that they would like to help the Egyptians build. Again, in terms of culture, heritage, and notions of rights, they are on shaky ground.

I would suggest that a minimalist notion of where to focus would point you towards trying to combat torture in jails, and one of the practical things that it turns out European police forces could do for their Egyptian counterparts would be to instruct them in interrogation techniques which do not use torture.

I leave open whether another point of action would be to demonstrate that we do not need Guantánamo in order to interrogate suspect terrorists outside Egypt.

I refer to the last message of Sir Jeremy's analysis, which was essentially:

> The good governments are not doing enough, the bad ones are not sufficiently constrained. We must change that. The United Nations is a vital centre of norms and implementation action, but the United Nations cannot do it on its own, nor can governments, nor can the individual. The balance has to come in the interaction between all of those within a high priority conversation on the right strategy.

Turning to my second area – the correct position for European governments to have adopted on the conflict in Lebanon. I was fortunate enough to chair a meeting addressed by international lawyers on this very issue. I shared in some of the frustrations of other non-lawyers at that event over the fact that the lawyers unfortunately could not give us the answers.

I have tended towards the view that an international lawyer is like a scientist or a medical doctor who will have a definite answer on what the human rights position is or what the international human rights legal position is.

Therefore we should be able to establish whether Israel's response to the detention of two of its soldiers and the killing of others was disproportionate or not. We can establish whether enough was done and whether, in the conduct of hostilities, the parties engaged were guilty of war crimes.

I have now discovered that it is nowhere near as simple as that, but I would suggest that human rights law, as explained by lawyers, is vital to the international debate in crises such as that one, so that we are at least clearer in assigning blame and in establishing what can and should be done in international terms in those circumstances.

Comments on *Geopolitics and Power*

Sir Franklin Berman*

It is really quite hard to comment on so thoughtful and well-balanced a paper as Sir Jeremy Greenstock's. On the other hand, it would not be much help if I simply were to say: 'Yes, I agree.' [In fact, if after years of sitting together and serving together in the Diplomatic Service I were to turn to him and say: 'Jeremy, that was excellent, I agree', he would probably fall of his chair in astonishment!]

Perhaps there is one point on which I am not sure that I do totally agree, and I was intrigued to see that Dr Hollis also picked up the aphorism that the good governments do not do enough and the bad governments are not sufficiently constrained – I think it is probably the other way round. It is the good governments who are not sufficiently restrained and it is the bad governments who do not do enough, but the art is to decide what exactly it is that the bad governments should be doing in the areas in which they are failing.

In any case, what I am going to do is to step aside a little from the main theme of the paper and give some broader background from my own professional point of view, that of a lawyer/diplomat. If Rosemary Hollis said that she felt somewhat overawed by the eminent human rights lawyers, I am the one who ought to feel overawed because of the depth of their expertise, because human rights, even amongst lawyers, is a subject which raises huge passions and because it may seem that something of what I am going to say will sound a bit sceptical. This is unintentional – it is informed far more by what I have always regarded throughout my career as being important, namely that there are limits to what you can ask the law to do for you and that you must be conscious of those limits. If you demand too much, then you damage an institution on which, in the end, you depend in an important way.

* Sir Franklin Berman, KCMG, QC, Visiting Professor of International Law, University of Oxford; former Legal Adviser to the Foreign and Commonwealth Office.

I would like to structure my remarks around three broad points and then say something about law and policy. Firstly, what is a human right? Secondly, what are the sources of human rights, looked at from the legal point of view – where do human rights come from? Thirdly, what is the consequence of the fact that something is, properly, a human right?

I start with the first: what is a human right? This may address directly one of the sources of frustrated puzzlement that Dr Hollis referred to. We talk very easily about human rights, but the question 'what is a human right?' is a rather important one. It is important not least because there has been, I think, latterly an enormous amount of inflation in the use of the description 'human right', and inflation, as we know in economic and other fields, leads ultimately to devaluation.

There is apparently an issue now – if you simply confine yourself to the newspapers – which journalists tend to find as being 'an abuse of human rights', things which previously just were international crises, were wrongs, were problems, are now almost all described as 'an abuse of human rights'. It raises the question as to why this is done. No doubt the answer is because some special magical quality is thought to inhere in a human right, which I will touch on a little later when I talk about consequences, and the consequences raise all sorts of issues about the power of particular kinds of legal rules.

Is there a touchstone for what sort of right is a human right? It seems that such a touchstone does not exist. What is a human right? A human right is something we call a human right, something which occurs in a legal instrument, which calls itself an instrument on human rights. Something is a human right because it is in that instrument, but beyond that, it is all rather grey and indeterminate.

One way to talk about it would be to say that inasmuch as we recognise nowadays that international law is not just about rights and obligations between states, it also deals with relations between states and the individual, then anything touching the individual is a human right. However, I think this goes too far, because there are all sorts of provisions of international law – dealing with ordinary travel, dealing with trade, dealing with economic activity and finance, which directly benefit individuals – which one would not really think in any sensible way of describing as human rights.

So I do not pursue the point beyond that, but I do insist upon the fact that there is not a self-evident answer to: 'What is a human right?' Is this particular claim or entitlement properly called a human right or not? There is no touchstone from which to decide.

My second question is to ask, looked at as a particular institution of the international system, where do human rights come from?

Well, those of us who are familiar with the way the international legal system works know that there are two primary sources of rights and obligations in international law. One is treaties and the other is customary law. Treaties are instruments which are written and which are agreed to specifically by states party to them. Custom is an expression of the broadly established practices of the world at large, practices which are undertaken in the consciousness that these represent legal rights and obligations, and that should apply to human rights as well. Most of what we talk about as human rights is in fact a reference to the leading treaties on human rights, and there is a very substantial and impressive body of treaty law on the subject, most of it post-dating the Universal Declaration on Human Rights. I agree with Jeremy Greenstock when he said that there is no deficit of norms. There is a substantial quantity of norms, but it would be a good thing if we could have some better implementation and, where necessary, enforcement of norms. Incidentally, I think there is a difference between implementation and enforcement, which I shall mention later on.

So is that the source, then, of human rights? Let us have an answer which I think would be broadly accepted by most human rights lawyers. They would say that nowadays there is also a customary international law of human rights. What the content of the customary international law of human rights is, is not so clear. This is because here there is no written instrument, there is no international agreement whose articles you can look through one by one and see what the rights are that are documented in it. No doubt candidates for a customary law of human rights would include the clear-cut examples that Rosemary Hollis has referred to, but beyond that, they would be questionable.

However, how does something that was enumerated as a treaty come out of the customary law of human rights? Well, it ought to depend – as with all customary law on widespread, quasi universal practice undertaken because of a sense of international obligation. Unfortunately, if you use that as the touchstone for a customary law of human rights, you would not come off very well at all, because of the very phenomena that Jeremy Greenstock referred to – the widespread abuses throughout the world. This has led many lawyers to ask the question: 'Well, is there not some deeper origin to a customary law of human rights? Can we not go back to what one of our leading general instruments in the field talks about: general principles of law as recognised by civilised nations?' Note that by saying 'recognised by civilised nations', yet another slightly scratchy, irritating phrase is introduced into the discussion.

These are profound questions, and having raised them, I have to leave them there, simply adding the point that the relationship between treaty law and customary law is much, much more complicated than appears at first sight. Treaties are instruments which derive their legal force from the fact that they are agreed to, so one of the characteristics of a treaty is not only that it is clear and definite, but also that you know exactly who is bound by the treaty. The states who have concluded the treaty are bound by it, but not those who have not concluded the treaty. However, the relationship between treaties and custom, the way in which the negotiation of treaties feeds into the creation of a wider international custom that affects everybody and is legally binding on every state in the world, is a very complex process indeed and one which defies easy description.

Now I have to say I find there is something rather perverse in the attitude of a lot of lawyers and diplomats and governments who think that the customary route is an easy route to follow because it avoids those tiresome details, like getting governments actually to commit themselves formally to international instruments.

Why are these points important? They are important because I, like Jeremy Greenstock, have spent a whole lifetime not simply in defining national interests, but in trying to get other governments to agree to forms of behaviour which we think either represent our national interests, or which we think conform to international norms. Imagine the real world problems of holding states, usually reluctant states (such reluctance may be an underestimate of the highest order), to norms of behaviour which they themselves have not endorsed, to which you cannot show a specific endorsement of some form. Therefore, if you are relying on something which is custom or which is a general principle, you have to find some direct association with that.

This leads us onto what I think is the biggest and most troubling question of all, which Rosemary Hollis has already mentioned, and that is values. Here there is a big distinction between defence and enforcement. It seems to me that a state is always entitled to say, whether or not you use the words of Tony Blair: 'We defend our values.' A state is always entitled to defend its values, as long as there is not something in those values which is in itself deeply offensive. However, when it comes to imposing behaviour on others, then I do not think it is any longer a question of our values. It has to be universal values. Universal values track very closely the issue of customary international law, which has to be a universal concept, a universal quantity.

And therein lies the rub. What exactly are the universal values, and where did they derive from? One way to look at them is of course to find that they have an association with religious beliefs, something I always find slightly uncomfortable. This has connotations of superiority, and additionally one has to admit that over the years of human history, religion has not had a glorious record in maintaining the brotherhood and sisterhood of the human race.

So where else do they come from, these values, if not from religion? Well, they have to come from somewhere, they have to have a moral base somewhere, but it has to be a moral base that is evident to all and can be shared by all. There are enormous arguments in the diplomatic human rights field about relativity – about the relativisation of rights.

There have been waves of anguished discussion, through various international conferences in which the opposing arguments are vigorously pitted against one another. Universality is thrown against particularity and it is very difficult indeed sometimes to discern what are the universal values. I always recall in this context the rather interesting and significant fact that if you look at the two leading United Nations instruments on human rights – the two international covenants on civil and political rights and on economic, social and cultural rights – in each case, the first article, the first substantive right documented is the right of self-determination, and the right of self-determination is defined as being the right of each country to define its own social, economic and political systems without outside interference. In other words, there is an inbuilt tension and there are no automatic and self-evident answers. So if Dr Hollis found the international lawyers disappointing in not producing self-evident answers, then I apologise, but that is just the way the world is.

Finally, the question of the consequences of something being denominated a human right raises the question: are some rights different from others? The orthodox answer – which I think is the proper answer in the international legal system – is 'No'. Rights are rights, obligations are obligations. And when you look at what the rights and duties of a state may be in particular circumstances, you weigh up all the issues that come into play, all the rights and obligations which are asserted, and you assess them in the same way as you would others.

However, to many that might seem a slightly abhorrent point of view, because they would say: 'Human rights are surely different? There is something different about them.' But it is not enough just to say that. The question is: 'Why?' Where can you find an adequate basis for saying that human rights are different?

Over the last twenty to thirty years, we have had huge discussions in the international legal field about what is referred to as 'relative normativity' – are some obligations superior to others, and if some obligations are superior to others, why is that so? This is a very difficult question to answer, but if they are superior to others, what are the consequences that that has in the international system? These are very difficult and puzzling questions, because the system does not provide an answer, and if there is no answer, you begin to ask yourself: 'Is the whole construction, the notion that there may be some obligations that trump others because of their very nature, something slightly disturbing?' Perhaps there are a few absolutely fundamental, core, elemental concepts that are necessary for international society to function, which include not just those tentatively put forward by Dr Hollis, but other fundamental concepts, such as the fact that a state may not invade another state, may not annex its territory and take over its people. But can we go beyond these?

I have to come from there to another characteristic of human rights, and that is indeterminacy. The fact that one can describe something as a human right does not usually answer the question: 'What conduct does that right require to be followed in particular circumstances?' If you get beyond just the slogan 'human rights' and begin to look at the instruments that define human rights – like those UN covenants I have referred to – you will see that at least half, if not the majority, of the rights are not stated in absolute and categorical terms. They need to be weighed up against the other interests of society in relation to particular questions.

So human rights are not absolute in that sense. They have a degree of indeterminacy about them, which requires that judgements need to be made all the time, and that is precisely why these international treaties are so important – they do not simply set up codes of conduct, but create machinery under which the conduct of those subject to the codes can be assessed and monitored and, most importantly, in most cases, set up machinery in which individual judgements can be made on individual complaints. Here there is a long history of what has been happening in our courts and between the courts and the government since the European Convention on Human Rights was given statutory force shortly after Labour came to power.

The point is simply that you need to make judgements which are very fact-specific and not absolutely clear-cut in advance. What is more – we come back to values again – when you make the judgement, values enter into the kind of judgements you are making. In fact, very often, the way the legal text is written seems to say: 'and you have to make the values enter into the judgements you are making.' That is fine, within the contours of the national system, but when you try to apply it on the international front, you should never underestimate the sheer difficulty of the task of carrying it out in a way that carries ultimate conviction at the global level.

Well, that is an issue of compliance, though there are other issues of compliance too, because not all human rights are the same. We talk in the technical jargon about different generations of human rights and I am never quite sure I get them straight, but one can move from what we used to regard as civil and political rights – things which are clearly defined, where the individual has rights and where you can see a clear-cut remedy for the individual against the state – to other kinds of rights which tend to be in the economic, social and cultural fields, which are rights of a more programmatic kind. You cannot achieve them automatically, today, tomorrow, but you are under an obligation to work towards a more divine state of being. Then there are further generations of rights which are collective in that they are not seen to inhere in every individual, but in society or in groups of individuals taken as a whole. I raise all of that not just because you would see the levels of indeterminacy increase as you went through the generations, but because it raises another question – that you can have conflicts within a system of human rights.

A first-generation right of the individual – such as the right to liberty or the right to freedom of speech – can come into conflict with a third-generation right of the society within which that individual lives, and there you have two human rights pitted against one another. You cannot say that because they are human rights, one must override the other. You have very difficult issues of accommodation to reach, and, as I have said before, if those are difficult within the context of one society, they are ferociously difficult within the context of the international community as a whole.

So enforcement has to be not of our own values, but of the values that we all share, and one of the values we all share is peace and cooperation. Peace and cooperation and self-determination are quite hard to reconcile with enforcement, in the sense of the compulsory imposition of particular forms of conduct. That is why I think that what Sir Jeremy Greenstock said about the crucial function served by international validation through the United Nations of action to vindicate behaviour in the human rights field is so vital and, for my money, trumps any amount of unilateral intervention, however well-meaning and however well-argued.

I finish with a brief reflection on law and policy and policy and law. Just because something cannot be said to be clear-cut international law does not mean it is not good policy. There are many areas in which governments should be encouraged to pursue good policy and to use all of the means at their disposal – and incidentally, I think there are a lot of means other than either military intervention or naming and shaming. There are other forms of influence which governments can use, like withholding or granting benefits as a way of encouraging good behaviour. I do hope that whatever we do in the name of good behaviour returns to the question of values, so that we can clearly be seen to be speaking in the name of international values as a whole, and not simply those of one society or group of societies.

Such a comment was not intended to be cynical, but intended to be realistic. Such a realistic concluding note is an upbeat one, because the very fact that human rights have been so mainstream means that you can no longer conduct diplomatic debates and ignore these considerations – and I think that is an extremely good thing.

Response

by Sir Jeremy Greenstock
to the comments made by
Rosemary Hollis and Sir Franklin Berman

I should like to reply to Rosemary Hollis's contention that you cannot take the national interest argument too far in the pursuit and implementation of human rights. I know exactly what she means and I agree with her, but I do not think I was saying what Rosemary was indicating. Quite clearly, an over-active unilateralist approach to the implementation of human rights because you are dressing up your national action in that clothing is unhealthy. What I think we have to establish is that there are norms which are in the national interest to uphold, and there must be compromises on some national priorities if you are not to damage your longer-term universal priorities. For instance, I think that what the United States and the United Kingdom have been doing over the past three years in Iraq has taken us into that territory where an attempt to address one wrong (calling the action various good things) has not been accepted as being good in the long-term interest of those nations. Something has gone wrong in that approach. From that, I come back to what Rosemary Hollis, Frank Berman and I all agree upon, which is that respect for the collective corpus of norms has to be established. The United Nations represents this collective approach to acceptable behaviour. There is nowhere else where you find it so clearly, so usefully, and where action can be taken, if it is rightly handled by governments, with such legitimacy and with such effectiveness.

The heart of our problems on human rights is twofold. One is bad action by those who have power or the use of force in their hands, and the second is the failure to establish a strong enough supranational or universal set of values and norms and standards and treaties and laws that take priority in political decision making. In the short term, the politician will have a narrower view of a range of priorities than is consistent with that collective set of norms. That is not a prescription for doing the whole thing better. It is a statement of the problem – that if we have globalisation, we have not yet got the instruments that deal with the consequences of globalisation. It has gone more wrong over the past five years than it should have done, because those with the most power have not always used that power with the respect for the longer-term strategy of an ordered world.

Turning those good words into action needs something that I meant to mention and did not, which has not been mentioned by Rosemary or Frank, and which I think should be brought out. This is the need for leadership. You have got to have respected leaders fulfilling what I am trying to say. There is a requirement on people to respect the generally agreed norms and not take advantage of freedoms through criminal and violent action. I suppose Nelson Mandela comes closest in many of our minds to somebody with the international status and record to set that kind of leadership. He will forever be associated with the priority of reconciliation over revenge, both in South Africa and internationally, and his moral status can promote that kind of leadership which we would follow if it was applied to other issues and was implementable.

I would say that in my lifetime, and particularly in recent years, we have not had the quality of leadership in these areas that an ordered world requires. I am not just talking about Washington and London, although they have to answer some questions. I am also talking about the leaders of religions and cultures and faiths and governments that have not stood against abuses when it is their obligation to do so, particularly in the condemnation of terrorism. It would be a quite different scene addressing this awful scourge that has taken over our priorities if those closest to the cultural areas where terrorism seems to be coming from, and the ideologies – I will not call them the religions, because they are not – where terrorism is coming from, if men and women of stature stood up against them, even when it is politically inconvenient. That is the kind of leadership that we require in this modern world.

The Politics of the UN Commission on Human Rights/Human Rights Council

Sir Nigel Rodley*

The UN Commission on Human Rights – which has now been transformed into the Human Rights Council, which is what I am going to be dealing with in this paper, is an intergovernmental body. It is a body composed of governments. It, in turn, has created a system of special procedures composed of individual so-called experts. A special rapporteur on torture is one of the special procedures of the Commission on Human Rights, now the Council, so you have the rather odd business of this governmental body looking to individual, independent expertise in order to do certain kinds of work. An example of another form will be brought forward when Françoise Hampson talks about the Council's formalised expert programme in the form of the Sub-Commission on the Promotion and Protection of Human Rights.

That is on the intergovernmental side, sometimes known as the charter-based side, but there are also the human rights treaties that set up their own machinery for monitoring their implementation (and I avoid the term 'enforcement'). So there is a Committee against Torture, for example, under the Convention against Torture, and that is a quite separate body from the Special Rapporteur on Torture, who reports to the Commission, though they do in fact cooperate a lot. As Special Rapporteur on Torture, I cooperated substantially with the Committee against Torture set up under the Convention.

These days I am the UK nominated and elected member of the Human Rights Committee established under the International Covenant on Civil and Political Rights. Look what it means in terms of acronyms – CHR for Com-

* Sir Nigel Rodley, KBE, Professor of Law, Human Rights Centre, University of Essex; member of the UN Human Rights Committee; former UN Special Rapporteur on Torture; Founding Head of the Legal Office of the International Secretariat of Amnesty International.

mission on Human Rights, HRC for Human Rights Council, HRC for Human Rights Committee. Life is going to get worse rather than better! What the Human Rights Committee is trying to suggest is that the new Council be UNHRC, as it was the UNCHR, the UN Commission on Human Rights, and that the Human Rights Committee should just remain as HRC, unaffected by all this political change in nomenclature and structure, which I will mention presently.

Let me just say one thing about the whole business of international human rights law and the machinery set up in the United Nations to deal with it. That is, that it has got nothing whatsoever directly to do with resort to coercion, and in particular armed force, in order to achieve certain objectives which might or might not include the protection of people from massive and gross violations of human rights. In other words, you do not have to be in favour of humanitarian intervention, especially not unilateral humanitarian intervention (humanitarian intervention outside the framework of a Security Council mandated exercise) in order to be an international human rights lawyer. I suspect that most international human rights lawyers are extremely cautious, as I certainly am, about the whole humanitarian intervention discourse.

The main body dealing with human rights was the UN Commission on Human Rights. It was the only subsidiary body of the Economic and Social Council, a principal organ of the United Nations, consisting of a little under a third of the membership of the United Nations envisaged in the Charter of the United Nations. The Charter envisaged that the Economic and Social Council would set up functional commissions, but only one particular mandate was mentioned, this being the human rights mandate, so already the Charter envisaged special attention for human rights issues. This was in some ways a trade-off for the failure of the framers at San Francisco to agree on a Bill of Rights that would go into the Charter. So this commission was to establish what would become the International Bill of Human Rights, the two covenants that Sir Franklin Berman mentioned, plus the optional protocol to the Covenant on Civil and Political Rights, and of course, preceding both of them, the landmark Universal Declaration of Human Rights, which was a resolution of the General Assembly and therefore not per se binding. People often forget that the UN Charter has certain clauses about human rights requiring states to cooperate with the United Nations to promote and ensure respect of human rights and fundamental freedoms, and many would argue that the Declaration is simply a catalogue of those human rights whose respect is already mandated by the Charter.

Certainly the view taken in the first twenty years of the United Nations was that the Commission on Human Rights, and the United Nations in general, could only be involved in standard setting. It could hear no evil, speak no evil and see no evil as far as actual human rights performance was concerned.

Slowly – and I am compressing the history into a nutshell – slowly from the late 1960s onwards, the United Nations started to take an interest in certain country issues, starting with South Africa. Within a matter of months they also looked at the Occupied Territories of the Middle East in the context of the Six Day War, which was going to be the hallmark of much that was to come. The United Nations had basically become a political organ. It consists of governments and finds it much easier to deal with those who do not have very many friends than to deal with those who do have many friends. I will return to this point.

Nevertheless, the United Nations did start looking at country situations, and when it ran into political difficulties and could not deal with certain countries doing really nasty things, such as, for example, disappearances in Argentina in the late 1970s, it set up its first thematic mechanism – the Working Group on Enforced or Involuntary Disappearances – in 1980. When the resolution that would set it up was being negotiated in the corridors, no mention was made of any countries, but everybody was calling it the Argentina Resolution. They were working to try to deal in a politically neutral way, but nevertheless a real way, with violations of human rights, without having to go through a process of trying to find the votes when there might not be the political will to secure those votes. This would be easy with respect to Israel or South Africa, but not so easy with respect to a large country like Argentina, which has many grain contracts and so forth.

We now have a whole series of so-called thematic mechanisms. They started with the Working Group. There is a Special Rapporteur on Summary and Arbitrary Executions, and by 1985 a Special Rapporteur on Torture had been appointed. There are now some twenty-three mechanisms, covering the whole field of civil and political rights, as well as economic, social and cultural rights.

There were still debates in the Commission about individual country situations, and there was still the problem about it being very easy to investigate, report on and adopt resolutions in respect of other countries.

It was, if you will, the famous double standard, and the first article I ever wrote about human rights dealt with it in the context of the United Nations and human rights in the Middle East in the early 1970s. The manifestation to which I was drawing attention was precisely the way the United Nations had taken on the Middle East and the way that it was not taking on other situations, and that the United Nations was doing it in a way that prejudged investigations. That continued, but it was not just a one-way street. I challenge anybody to find a country of any colour, however devoted to human rights, that has even in the corridors been prepared to seek discussion on a draft resolution that might look at the situation in Saudi Arabia. Let us not assume that the double standards are all from one direction. I shall be returning to this point briefly – the problem with governments is that they behave like governments.

So what were the criticisms levelled at the Commission on Human Rights? Well, one of them was the double standard, and the United States made this point vigorously throughout, and increasingly so, especially when the representative of Libya became the Chair of the Commission. The fact that she was a perfectly good Chair of the Commission, discharging her responsibilities conscientiously and impartially, was beside the point. Libya having its representative as the Chair was somehow seen as an assault, especially in the context of the United States having not been elected to the Commission for the first time ever, which was another element that led the United States to make a rather sustained assault on the legitimacy of the Commission.

There were also more institutional arguments, namely that human rights were too important to be left to a functional body of the Economic and Social Council, which, even though technically a principal organ under the Charter of the United Nations, still reported to the General Assembly. Thus it was thought that the Commission on Human Rights was pretty low down on the institutional pecking order.

So with all of that, there were demands for renewal and reconsideration. The first proposal, a proposal which I still regret was not more widely discussed, was made by the so-called High Level Panel set up by the Secretary-General in 2003 and reporting in 2004.[1] It suggested either an amendment to the Charter that would make a human rights organ a principal organ of the United Nations or, failing that, at least an organ of the General Assembly that would be universal in membership. In other words, all the members of the General Assembly would be entitled to be members of it.

There was another difficulty with the Commission on Human Rights, and that was the tilted nature of the membership. A certain number of seats are allocated to each of the five UN geographic regions. What would happen was that, very often, those regions would agree a slate. They had four seats, they

1 See: <http://www.un.org/secureworld>.

had four candidates, and that was that: they automatically became members. It did not matter if they were Uganda, Libya – everyone can choose their own bogey person! If the region put them forward, they would be members, and then what would happen? Of course, the ones that were the most neuralgic about their human rights records were the ones that would lobby hardest to be nominated and elected, and indeed the regions had fixed slates all too often. It was primarily in the West that the slates were not fixed and there would be run-offs in which Spain could beat the United States occasionally, but other regions were rather more disciplined than the Western Europeans and others in that respect. The idea was essentially that the Commission on Human Rights was not just a cross-section of the membership of the United Nations, but that it was a tilted cross-section, tilted towards the human rights violators who had the greatest interest in being on the Commission in order to defend their interests.

Universality would solve that at a stroke. Now the argument against was obviously that a universal body – all 192 members – would be unwieldy. However, the fact remains that the General Assembly meets for three months a year and gets things done, and indeed it has not been unknown for really key issues to prosper at the level of the General Assembly and then come back to the Commission where they could not prosper because the habits of blocking were already too well entrenched. Indeed, it required a General Assembly resolution on disappearances to make it possible for the Commission on Human Rights to deal with the issue of disappearances in the way I mentioned.

The Americans argued for a smaller body, basically a body of those who respect human rights. The Secretary-General, in a report entitled *In Larger Freedom*,[2] decided to side with the United States and called for a body smaller than the fifty-three members of the Commission on Human Rights (without suggesting a figure). It was this approach which prevailed, and on 15 March 2006 the General Assembly resolution creating the Human Rights Council was adopted. This was one of those historic moments at the United Nations where people actually clap at the end. The clapping was not as loud as for the International Criminal Court, but it was there! I hasten to point out that I had nothing at all to do with the negotiations, but I did have the pleasure of being at the General Assembly.

It was interesting to see the politics in action there. The United States was represented by the ineffable John Bolton, making a statement about how the

2 See: <http://www.un.org/largerfreedom>.

United States was not going after the vote this time round. The United States was going to watch the new Council constructively, and it hoped it would do well. John Bolton mentioned that one of the tests would be how it would deal with such countries as Belarus, Burma, Cuba, Iran, Sudan and Zimbabwe. Just one or two days later, the overdue national security strategic statement came out, the first one since 2002 when they talked about pre-emptive action, and they listed as countries of strategic concern Belarus, Burma, Cuba, North Korea, Iran, Syria and Zimbabwe – there was a more than 50% overlap of countries. Earlier that day they had already agreed the budget for the new Council, so the United States decided – obviously under incredible pressure from their colleagues in the western group – to back down. They did vote against the Council, but they decided not to make it a big issue.

Cuba, on the other hand – because politics come from all sides – denounced the whole new Council and all its works, because it was built on looking at countries' human rights performance. The whole Council, as far as Cuba was concerned, was built on looking at countries' practices rather than trying to achieve cooperation amongst countries, as should be the case for the United Nations, and so Cuba viewed it as an American plot. It was a nice microcosm of a moment, showing how politics are at play, fermenting all the time. There is no escaping it when governments are involved.

What are the differences between the Council and the Commission? First of all, the General Assembly elects the Council, not the Economic and Social Council, so the 192-member body elects, rather than the 56-member body. Second, there are no permanent seats. A state can run for two three-year terms and that is it. They have to stand down for at least one year. Third, there is an absolute majority needed. In other words, a half of the membership can prevent a state being elected to the Council, even if there is an uncontested slate put forward by a regional block. The fact that they put forward some sort of international pariah does not ensure that that pariah will necessarily get elected. If you can muster half the states to vote against, they will not get elected.

It is also possible to remove by a two-thirds majority countries that are seen as not playing the human rights game correctly, though I doubt very much that this is going to happen. It is worth noting, however, that when there were fifty-three member states, twenty-seven came from the Afro-Asian region, and twenty-six – one fewer – came from the other regions combined. Under the new system for the Council, the forty-seven members (reduced by six from the Commission on Human Rights) are comprised of twenty-six Afro-Asian members and twenty-one others, so there are five more in the

Afro-Asian group than all the rest combined. This may not herald some of the more hoped-for changes in policy. Again, I am not casting any aspersions on any particular group or groups from one or other region, but I am willing to make the point that those two regions cooperate very strongly to protect their own regional members from unwanted scrutiny, not least through the G77.

Another element that was designed to mark a difference was the creation of a peer review system. The basic idea is that the new Council will scrutinise every single member of the United Nations in terms of its human rights performance, starting with its own members during the term that they are elected, so priority has to go to scrutinising those members. It is all to play for as to what such scrutiny will be, and some fear it might be rather superficial. It is hard to imagine, frankly, how it can be very serious, but a working group was set up to report on what the review might include. Some are afraid that it might affect the reviews that are done by the treaty bodies under the treaties that I mentioned – so the Human Rights Committee reviews periodic reports of states parties, the Committee against Torture the same, and the same with the other committees. I have a hunch that in practice the nature of the review that an intergovernmental body can give is going to be rather limited. The only fear might be that as they all give each other clean bills of health, it is then used against the committees when the committees do not give similar clean bills of health when applying the treaties under which the committees are set up.

The Council can now meet not just once for six weeks a year, but for ten weeks a year. Previously, the Commission could only have a separate meeting, an extraordinary meeting, if over half the members required. Now it takes only a third.

It is not surprising – and should not be surprising – that since the first regular meeting of the Council in June 2006, there have already been two extraordinary sessions, both on the Middle East. Developments in Gaza and Lebanon occurred early on in the Council's life, but it is very clear that there was already a coherent, planned attempt to move away from any suggestion that there had been non-consideration of one region. When the Council first met, the understanding was that there would be no country resolutions, not in June at any rate, until the Council got its procedures sorted out. Then very suddenly a group of countries decided to come up with a resolution that dealt with the Occupied Territories. It was a very brief resolution, but it was jumped on by the Council and adopted.

How should one assess the prospects? In terms of political bias, it is so far hard to be terribly optimistic, with the manifestation of the so-called double standard. That nevertheless does not mean that the whole system is not worth the candle. Certainly it is going to be no worse than the old Commission. It could possibly be a bit better, with some of the built-in inhibitors. A number of countries that might otherwise have been expected to stand and that had stood in the past actually did not stand, such as Zimbabwe, Sudan, Burma and Belarus. Cuba did stand and got elected by an overwhelming majority. Iran stood and did not get elected. So it is now no longer so easy for the bad guys to get elected, and that has to be a good thing.

Second, some substantive work has been done. Most of the work had already been done, but there was a fear that it would get lost. The Council forwarded two landmark human rights instruments – the Convention against Disappearances and a Declaration on Indigenous Peoples – to the General Assembly, and these went to the General Assembly in the autumn of 2006. The work of the Special Procedures will carry on. So far, in formal terms, all that has happened is that the General Assembly has continued the mandates of all the procedures pending a review of all the procedures, but it is expected that the procedures will essentially survive intact.

It is probably worth remembering that, despite Rosemary Hollis's *realpolitik*, the whole human rights project has been totally counter-intuitive from a *realpolitik* point of view – at least if you accept what I dare to suggest as a view of *realpolitik* as utilitarianism at the transnational level. This is rather more simplistic than the view of Hans Morgenthau, the founder of the theory (who actually was a believer in international law), who was a rule utilitarian, not an act utilitarian.

The fact remains that we have an incredible body of international human rights law, all of which should not have been there if countries behaved in a linear, simplistic way. All the machinery that I have just referred to that is doing reports on all sorts of countries, on all sorts of neuralgic human rights issues, they should not be there. They were not there and yet they happened, and they happened despite the fact that it was not in the interests of, or at least the narrowly focused interests of, the countries in question that they should happen. So by and large, something substantial has occurred in the last fifty years, and I have no reason to expect that this will not continue. Maybe the new Council will be not a lot better than the old Commission, despite all the brouhaha, but it is unlikely to be any worse and it may indeed even be somewhat better.

Running to Stand Still: The Reform of the UN Human Rights Machinery (not including the Council)

Françoise Hampson*

I am delighted to be able to take part in this conference, because the CNRC conference on counter-terrorism in which I also participated provided an opportunity to listen to speakers from a range of disciplinary perspectives. It is actually quite rare to get the chance to mix international relations, diplomacy and law, and I find these CNRC meetings a very enriching environment.

I have just returned from six weeks in Geneva with the Sub-Commission on the Promotion and Protection of Human Rights and two of its working groups, and we were meeting against a backdrop of informal private sessions, informal public sessions, formal regional public sessions, and every permutation of meeting there could be of members of the Council, because, by the ambitious target date of January 2007, they want to review the entirety of the non-treaty mechanisms. This review by the Human Rights Council is taking place by virtue of the General Assembly resolution that actually set up the Council.

All we know is that, at the end of the day, there has to be some system of universal periodic review, some system that deals with complaints, some system of special procedures and some system of expert advice, but all the details remain to be worked out.

Before getting into the issue of the transition and what is likely to happen to the pre-existing human rights machinery, I want to flag an issue to which I shall return in the end, and that is: does it matter? In other words, does it matter what happens to the UN human rights machinery? Not to the Council

* Professor Françoise Hampson, Human Rights Centre, University of Essex; member of the UN Sub-Commission for the Promotion and Protection of Human Rights.

– that clearly matters – but to the infrastructure that the old Commission created. Is this simply an esoteric question only of interest to human rights lawyers, or is it actually important in a wider sense? Clearly, it is important to victims of human rights violations, but is it also important to states trying to reduce the risks of instability, and is it important to states trying to avoid accountability?

The political level of decision making – whether it be the Security Council, the General Assembly, the former Commission and now the Council – very clearly matters. I have very little patience with those who profess outrage at the idea of any human rights decision ever being taken by a political body. I do not see how you can ever get something taken seriously unless at some point it does become the province of a political body. The only question is: at what stage does it become political? There was no thus objection to the previous Commission and now the Council being political bodies, provided they did not pretend that they were other than political bodies.

But what about the allegedly non-political human rights machinery that we are dealing with here, none of which is supposed to be political in the sense in which the Commission was political. Does that machinery matter, either in its own right or as something that feeds into the political process? I hope to show first, that it matters, and secondly, why it matters. However, before that, I need to explain a little about what that machinery is at present, and how it may be changed.

I suspect that those who are not immersed in this area will be amazed at the sheer quantity and range of UN human rights machinery. There are more than fifty-five mechanisms that the Human Rights Council is having to review. Now this is partly because of how the machinery was created – different types of machinery were introduced at different times to meet specific needs, and once you had created, for example, a country special rapporteur, well, there was a precedent. Once you had created a Working Group on Disappearances, there was a precedent, and so you got a very haphazard evolution of the actual machinery.

In order to understand the evolution, it might be useful to take a historical approach, but even that would be very likely to lead to confusion! So instead I have decided to look at the machinery by type.

The main distinction is between the treaty bodies, which owe their authority in relation to a particular state to ratification of the treaty, and other bodies, which ultimately derive their authority from the UN Charter. I would add that to Sir Franklin Berman's list of sources, as it seems to me that in the human rights sphere there is something which is not treaty law and which may not be custom, but seems to be derived ultimately from Charter law.

As far as the treaty bodies are concerned, there are seven main treaties. These are the covenants on civil and political rights and economic, social and cultural rights. There are two treaties on discrimination: one on racial discrimination, the other on discrimination against women; a Convention on the Rights of the Child; a Convention against Torture; and the newest one: the Migrant Workers Convention, which unfortunately has only been ratified by states from which the migrant workers come and not by the destination states.

There is a potential addition, as the General Assembly will be invited to open for signature and ratification a convention on forced disappearances. But in addition to these seven treaties, there is quite a large range of treaties which are about human rights issues, but which do not have monitoring bodies. For example, there are a couple of treaties in the anti-slavery field, where there are norms but no machinery is envisaged for actually giving effect to them. I will be concentrating here on the seven main treaties, the ones that do have monitoring bodies.

These main treaties have in common certain elements. First, whether they have jurisdiction in relation to a state depends on ratification, and that is the free choice of sovereign states.

Second, they all engage in monitoring – in effect, monitoring implementation – and the people who are doing that are, in theory, independent experts. I do not question their expertise; but in some cases I question their independence. They monitor implementation on the basis of a report coming from the state.

Many of these treaty bodies have the theoretical possibility of inter-state complaints – one state making a complaint against another state – but that requires separate acceptance and has never been used at the international level, only at the regional level in Europe.

Many of these treaties also have the possibility of dealing with individual complaints, but again, that needs to be separately accepted by states.

What are the problems with the operation of the treaty bodies? There follows a brief and perhaps simplified summary, but one which should help our discussions. First, anything that depends on ratification means you have all the problems of those states that choose not to ratify. With some treaties this is a really big problem, but there are some remarkably surprising ratifiers, who must have thought that nobody would pay any attention if they ratified! For example, before 1990, Iraq, with its impeccable human rights record [*sic*] had ratified the treaties, and Uruguay also ratified fairly early. There are also some surprising non-ratifiers. I was sad to see, for example, that Turkey has not ratified the Convention on the Elimination of Racial Discrimination.

One of the biggest problems with the operation of the treaty system is the business of submitting reports. It is an absolutely huge burden for states, and obviously the more treaties they ratify, the heavier the burden. It is a burden for small, developing states, either because of lack of resources, or a lack of know-how (how do you compile a report?). However, it is also a problem for developed, well-heeled states, because of the volume of issues on which they have to report and the sophistication of their bureaucracies, hence the need for interdepartmental cooperation to compile a report.

It is not surprising that many of these reports are submitted late, but that is just as well, because the treaty bodies only meet two or three times a year and they simply would not be able to cope if all states submitted their reports on time!

It seems to me this is a serious structural flaw if the system can only work as long as states do not meet their treaty obligation to submit periodic reports. This is, in large part, because of the inadequate time given to the treaty bodies, both in general, but also specifically for the discussion of the reports with the states concerned. As all states have to be treated equally, there is in effect a maximum of nine hours to discuss either with Tuvulu or with the United States or Russia the entirety of their obligations under the Convention on Civil and Political Rights. That is simply not serious.

At one time, I was opposed to the role of the Committee of Ministers in the Council of Europe in the field of human rights, as I questioned how they, as diplomats, could ever be allowed to deal with purely legal issues. Something that played a decisive role in changing my view was that, in ensuring that the judgments of the European Court of Human Rights were respected, the Committee of Ministers made it clear that the judgments were non-negotiable. The Inter-American Court of Human Rights envies the Committee of Ministers element of the European system. I am not suggesting there should not be any political input into the formulation of recommendations, but once they have been formulated, they need the support of some form of political body to give them clout.

What about the proposed reforms of the treaty bodies? This is being discussed, as far as one can tell, purely within the framework of the treaty bodies, not taking account of other reforms. It is important that one should not confuse reform of the Charter mechanisms and reform of the treaty bodies. However, we now have got the first opportunity in a generation to look at reform of the human rights machinery, and if that reform is to be coherent, then it is important that someone somewhere looks at both parts, even if the two parts are not allowed to leak into one another. It is the only way to ensure coherence.

Ideally, one needs to find some way of reforming the treaty bodies that does not reopen the treaties, because if changes need to be made to the treaties, then this is a hostage to fortune. The proposal that there should be one treaty body for all the treaties is, to put it politely, insane! To take the crudest possible measure: since the current treaty bodies meet for more than fifty-two weeks of the year, I do not see how, if you only had one treaty body, you could have improved scrutiny, unless that body were to make massive overtime. There would be the obvious problem that different states have ratified different treaties, the expertise of some of the treaty bodies and their particular focus would be lost, and it would be very difficult for one treaty body to adopt the very different style and approach of, for example, the Human Rights Committee, the Committee on Economic, Social and Cultural Rights and the Committee on the Rights of the Child. They work in very different ways.

There has been a significant increase in the proportion of the UN budget being used for human rights, but that is, in effect, because such a low amount was being spent on it initially. The amount of that increase does not appear to have been used to support the work of the treaty bodies and, anyway, it is still too low. In my view, the Covenant on Civil and Political Rights and the Covenant on Economic, Social and Cultural Rights ought to have their own full-time bodies, and there should be more time made available for the other treaty bodies too.

There are various possible solutions to these very genuine reporting problems, and while there is no time to go into them here, the goal needs to be the more frequent examination of more limited issues in greater depth. There is a need to improve follow-up, which could be done in two ways. If there were to be a focus on implementation, which seems to be much favoured everywhere, then the treaty bodies are the best bodies for dealing with implementation. I will argue in a moment that the rest of the human rights machinery is, in my view, not particularly suited for looking at implementation. However, implementation is not simply top-down. There is a bottom-up element. It is not simply what laws a state has put in place and what policies they have adopted. It is what happens in practice, and that means what happens when someone says they have been ill treated or have had an interference in the right of freedom of expression. This is part of the right to a remedy. So when looking at the issue of implementation, there has got to be the closest relationship between a right and a remedy, and it needs to be part of the test used by the treaty bodies.

Why has the domestic system not itself corrected the problem before it reached the international level? One might have thought that states would be very keen on this, because in the long term it would reduce international scrutiny, or at least the need for it. But if treaty bodies are to engage in this much more systematically, they are going to need assistance from NGOs, both domestic and international, and national human rights institutions in order to get the necessary information, as states will only adopt the top-down approach.

There may also be a role for the UN Human Rights Council in creating political authority in order to give effective strength to the recommendations of the treaty bodies, on the assumption that the recommendations themselves would be non-negotiable. They ought to see how they can help give more effect to the need for follow-up.

What about the non-treaty machinery? Basically, there are three types. There is the Sub-Commission on the Promotion and Protection of Human Rights, the special procedures, and a country-specific procedure, the 1503 Procedure.

First of all, the Sub-Commission. The oldest subordinate machinery, it is a 'think-tank plus', which consists of allegedly independent experts. Currently, my colleagues in the Sub-Commission include a serving ambassador and three former ambassadors. Interestingly, they are not always individuals who would be regarded as non-independent – academics from certain countries that feel they have to conform to what the state expects of them – so you cannot make a simple equivalence between an ambassador and someone who is not independent. It is more complicated than that, but I would reject the argument you sometimes hear from some developing countries that the only people with expertise are in fact their own civil servants – that is an unhelpful argument, as I am sure their human rights NGOs would endorse.

Originally the Sub-Commission was intended to guide the political body with regard to normative development on the basis of studies. In my view, there is still a need for normative development, but principally not in the form of treaties, but in the form of soft law, such as principles or guidelines for the implementation of particular treaty norms. The Sub-Commission can also pass thematic resolutions, which some NGOs seem to find useful since they have been quoted in the past few years in the US Supreme Court and the European Court of Human Rights. Until 2000, the Sub-Commission could pass country resolutions, but that was allegedly responsible for the politicisation of the Sub-Commission and so we lost that power. However, it does not seem to have corrected any of the things it was supposed to correct.

In the totality of the UN human rights machinery, one of the most important features of the Sub-Commission is that it is the part that is most open to NGOs. They can participate very actively, in particular in the working groups of the Sub-Commission. It has three main substantive intersessional working groups – one on slavery, one on minorities and one on indigenous peoples – and NGOs are sometimes co-authors of reports in those working groups, so it is a very active role.

What is the problem with the Sub-Commission? First, a lack of rotation. There are at present two members of the Sub-Commission who have been there for more than thirty years, there are many members who are unwilling or unable to produce reports, and there is a lack of support for the production of studies on the part of the Office of the High Commissioner for Human Rights. I was staggered to learn this year that, in the early years, when a member of the Sub-Commission was producing a report, there were three or four members of staff who were devoted full-time to writing that report. In effect, the alleged author simply gave a political imprimatur – 'political' with a small 'p' – to the product, whereas now, if you do not do it yourself, it will not get done. I have certainly never had even a paragraph's worth of support from the Office of the High Commissioner, as it does not have the resources. There were always difficulties in the relationship between the Sub-Commission and the Commission. This is hardly surprising, as subsidiaries always seem to have difficult relations with the parent body at some stage.

What about reform? Here, I think you begin to get a symptom of the problems that are arising with reform of the machinery other than the Council. Some – notably the Western group – are in favour of scrapping the Sub-Commission. Others – unfortunately including human rights 'bad guys' – are in favour of the status quo. This makes it very difficult to improve the Sub-Commission, because those in favour of keeping it do not want to improve it. They want it to remain weak, and those who do not want it as it stands want to abolish it rather than improve it. The Sub-Commission has shown that it cannot improve itself, so that any improvements need to be effected by the Human Rights Council, and I suspect that this will not happen.

The second type of machinery consists of the special procedures. In my view, they are one of the most successful elements of the UN human rights machinery. Special procedures can be taken to include: country special rapporteurs, thematic special rapporteurs or working groups and special representatives of the Secretary-General. It is valuable that some people who reflect on ideas rather than monitoring are involved in these activities.

The country-specific rapporteurs are very dependent on the degree of co-operation they receive from the state in question and, not surprisingly, that is often a problem. It is clearly very difficult politically to actually get the decision to appoint a country special rapporteur, but once they are appointed, they are normally allowed to get on with the job. The exception was the termination of the mandate of the Special Rapporteur on Iraq, who was an Egyptian American who dared to criticise American policies in Iraq, so the mandate was not renewed. He sees some sort of causal connection here!

There are also thematic investigative special rapporteurs, and in a sense a parallel here is perhaps with investigative journalists, on topics such as torture, arbitrary detention and other similar examples. An example of a thematic reflective procedure is a Special Rapporteur on the Impact of Foreign Debt on the Enjoyment of Human Rights. There is a real issue there, but why you need a special rapporteur is not clear to me.

The system of appointment varies. Some rapporteurs are appointed by the Secretary-General, some by the president of the Council, working through or in consultation with the Office of the High Commissioner for Human Rights and regional groups. But what has made the system work is that there seems to be, in effect, a roster – some sort of quality-control mechanism. There is an attempt to make sure that the special rapporteurs come from different areas of the globe and also to try and ensure that there is a vague attempt at equitable gender distribution. What has made the difference is that many of them have been quite extraordinarily independent and creative individuals. They report to the Commission, the Council and the General Assembly. What matters about the special procedures and what is most different from the treaty bodies, is that all members of the United Nations are potentially subject to their scrutiny. You do not opt in to anything. You do not ratify anything. By virtue of being a UN member, the Special Rapporteur on Torture, for example, can raise issues about your state's conduct in the area of torture.

What are the problems? It is not surprising that with over fifty-five special procedures in place, there is not merely a risk of overlap and duplication but that it occurs in practice. For example, if in a particular country human rights defenders are arbitrarily detained, during which time they are tortured and possibly killed, that falls under the remit of the Special Representative of the Secretary-General on Human Rights Defenders, the Special Rapporteur on Torture, the Working Group on Arbitrary Detention and the Special Rapporteur on Summary, Arbitrary and Extrajudicial Execution. However, the problem of overlap and the potential problem of duplication is much reduced by the fact that, in recent years, the special procedures have increasingly been engaging in joint visits and joint statements. They are doing what they can to reduce this issue.

Again, there is a huge problem of inadequate resources. In effect, special procedures need to engage in their own fundraising to get adequate levels of support, and this is a special difficulty for those who come from the developing world, where they may have less access to funding. They may know the system less well, and so will have less access to non-UN funds. There is clearly a need for rationalisation.

Partly because of the lack of resources, another problem is a lack of follow-up. Special procedures can raise individual cases with governments as well as raising general issues, but in practice, because they have so many thousands of cases each year, they cannot actually follow them up to see what happened next.

What about reform? It is likely there will be a reduction in the number of special procedures, which is not necessarily objectionable, but my concern would be what criteria are used for choosing which ones should go, as I suspect that the ones that will be eliminated, or where there will be an attempt to eliminate them, are the ones where the mandate holders have shown most independence and have been most awkward. For example, there is a real risk that the Special Representative of the Secretary-General on Human Rights Defenders will come under huge pressure, because she has taken it upon herself to consider, amongst other categories of human rights defenders, those dealing with lesbian and gay issues.

In addition there is a real risk that the Human Rights Council, or the states members of it, will try to clip the wings of the special procedures by limiting their scope for interpretation of their mandate, limiting the activities in which they can engage. I hope this has not occurred, but if the use of non-UN resources by special procedures is prohibited, that would also have serious consequences.

It is not at all clear that, even with a ten week per year meeting time for the Human Rights Council, that it will spend enough time interacting with the special procedures. This was one of the main weaknesses of the old Commission system. There were these wonderful reports and nothing happened with them. They were public, but apart from that, as far as the old Commission was concerned, they seemed principally to gather dust or to be used as ammunition in some sort of political fight with the state in question. There is a real need for the Council to sort out how it is going to work more effectively with the special procedures.

The last current mechanism is the confidential country procedure, also known as the 1503 Procedure. There is a practical problem. Petitions arrive at the United Nations, saying: 'Dear Mr Secretary-General, here is my problem. I want the United Nations to address it.' In that situation, the United Nations had to create a committee to do something with the petitions, and it created an elaborate system that started out with the Working Group on Communications of the Sub-Commission. It was decided from the start that this procedure was going to be confidential. A very high admissibility threshold was set, one that is so high that in practice I think it is not used. A consistent pattern of gross and reliably attested violations of human rights has to be established. That means, technically, a one-off massacre of 5,000 people is not a pattern, which is why some flexibility has been used in the admissibility criteria.

The application is sent to a government for comment. The government's comment is obviously part of the confidential procedure. Then the Working Group on Communications has three choices. It can send it up to a working group of the Commission, now the Council, it can keep the case pending, or it can drop it. In 2000, a reform to the procedure at the level of the Commission meant that the working group there that dealt with these confidential communications, instead of simply preparing them for discussion within the Commission, in fact acted as a filter instead. There is thus an awful lot of material going in at one end of the system, and very little coming out the other end. Basically, three states a year might be perceived to have caused some element of concern.

There are problems with the Working Group on Communications – because it acts as a filter – but there are also problems with the operation of the Working Group of the Sub-Commission. Three apparently innocuous rules or principles, when taken together, end up yielding results which might give the appearance of bias.

This system predated the special procedures, and not enough has been done to ensure coherence between the 1503 Procedure, which is confidential, and the special procedures, which are anything but confidential. The problem at the moment is that there are big delays in the 1503 Procedure. There is also a lack of transparency – which to some extent is inevitable, because it is a confidential procedure – but it is striking that the applicants or the petitioners do not get to know the results. A state is in breach of its human rights law if it conducts investigations and does not tell complainants the results, but that is precisely what the UN system is doing.

As far as reform is concerned, it is not clear how that is going to be handled and in which direction it is going. It is clear from the General Assembly resolution that some form of complaints procedure must be set up. I have no confidence that the system will be improved, as I do not think there is enough political will to improve it.

When one looks at the issue of reform and how the Council is going to handle reform of the human rights machinery, there are two kinds of risk. The first risk is that things will not be improved. For example, I do not think it is likely that the 1503 Procedure and the treaty bodies will actually be harmed, with the possible exception of the Universal Periodic Review (UPR), but the opportunity to improve the system will not be seized in many areas. In the case of UPR, everything that I have seen so far suggests that, to mix metaphors, it will be a toothless fig leaf! States will produce a report which will be the basis of a discussion for three hours every three years and that will be that.

Does this matter? It matters hugely, because what comes out of the political body – the Commission and now the Council – is, to a very large extent, the product of the work that has been done by the independent experts and the machinery other than the Council. In other words, what comes out of the Council to a large extent depends on what goes into it. States can avoid the treaty bodies by simply not ratifying treaties, but at the moment, they cannot avoid the special procedures. This is why it is so important to protect not just the existence of the special procedures, but their effective independence and their manner of functioning.

The reform of the UN human rights machinery has been the victim of the attempt to reform the United Nations more generally. Where not much, if anything at all, was achieved in other areas, with the exception of the responsibility to protect, the United Nations had to deliver the Human Rights Council to save face, to show that it could actually reform itself, but in so doing, Pandora's Box has been opened. It is tragic that the best that we can hope for is that as little harm as possible is caused to the pre-existing machinery, when what was needed was increased resources and improved coherence in the system as a whole, with more focus on implementation at the domestic level.

There is a joke doing the rounds in diplomatic circles in Geneva that it took sixty years for the Commission on Human Rights to discredit itself, but only two weeks for the Human Rights Council to do so. I hope that this will be proved wrong.

Human Rights and Foreign Policy in Developing Countries: Reflections on the International Bar Association's Work in Swaziland and Afghanistan

Phillip Tahmindjis*

I work for an international NGO – the International Bar Association. We have 30,000 members around the world and represent over 200 bar associations and law societies, so if you take into account their membership, we represent over a million lawyers around the world!

The topic covered by this paper raises a number of issues. Amongst these are the actors now working in the area of foreign policy and human rights. Apart from states and their agencies there are now NGOs like us, and many others. As we rely substantially on grants to be able to carry out our activities, the influence of the funding priorities of our funders on what we do, or are able to do, is significant. Another aspect of this, of course, is the tremendous impact of multinational corporations. That is itself a topic justifying deep study, but suffice it to say here that there is a changing emphasis on the issues. It seems to me, that certain issues and actors that may have traditionally been seen as being at the periphery of both human rights and foreign policy are now becoming more central.

A second issue that arises when we talk about human rights and foreign policy is the impact a government or an agency like the IBA has when it goes into a country with a human rights brief, and the extent to which foreign policy impacting on human rights is seen as being something foreign in that country. In other words, as a form of neo-colonialism. This has an impact on the notion of universality and relativism in human rights.

* Dr Phillip Tahmindjis, Programme Lawyer of the International Bar Association.

A third issue that arises is that for human rights in foreign policy to be effective, and this particularly strikes me with the work that the IBA has done so far, one must consider the overriding importance and significance of domestic legal systems – both sets of domestic systems – that in the country, for want of a better term, 'exporting' the foreign policy, and also that in the recipient country. There is a symbiotic relationship between foreign policy and the domestic legal system in each country, and this illuminates the issue of how effective change may be and whether human rights have helped to tip the balance in this regard.

I must make a caveat at this stage and say that this paper by no means presents a detailed analysis. I have picked only two countries, and I have picked them for two reasons, the first being very practical: the IBA has worked in Afghanistan for the last two years and in Swaziland for the last four, and I am the person managed both of our projects there.

But there is also another reason – because I could have picked other countries – for picking those two countries, there are interesting and valuable similarities and differences between the two. Both are poor, developing countries. Both are heavily reliant on foreign assistance. Swaziland is a Christian country, Afghanistan is Muslim. Swaziland is relatively stable and safe. As we know only too well, Afghanistan is not. The legal system in Swaziland is a Roman Dutch system, but essentially a common law system overlaid with customary law. The legal system in Afghanistan is a civil law system, basically a mishmash as a result of its chequered history, together with Sharia law and customary law.

Both countries now have a constitution. Swaziland's was passed and implemented only in 2006. The Swaziland constitution incorporates a Bill of Rights. The Afghanistan constitution has human rights provisions included in it. Swaziland is Africa's last absolute monarchy, but has constitutional overtones, because it now has a constitution. Afghanistan is a nascent democracy, at least in Kabul – in the rest of the country, that is questionable. Both countries have universal suffrage for people over the age of eighteen and both countries are parties to the major conventions on human rights – the Covenant on Economic, Social and Cultural Rights, the Covenant on Civil and Political Rights, the Racial Discrimination Convention, the Women's Convention, the Torture Convention and the Convention on the Rights of the Child. They are parties to all of those. They are not parties to any of the optional protocols, however, with the exception of Afghanistan, which is a party to both optional protocols under the Children's Convention. In addition, Swaziland, being in Africa, is a party to the African Charter on Human and People's Rights.

The issue these facts raise is: do any of these differences impact on any of the outcomes that we may see with respect to human rights work in each country? An interesting difference from the IBA point of view is that the driving force in our work in Afghanistan is government-funded. Our work in Swaziland is funded by an independent foundation. Does this have an impact?

In essence, the aim of these projects is to promote stability and justice through promoting the rule of law. Human rights is now seen as an inextricable and essential element of the rule of law. All of this, though particularly in Afghanistan, is now overlaid, post-9/11, with the war on terror.

Very briefly, our aim in Afghanistan is to establish a bar association, as they do not have one. This is part of the justice pillar under the Bonn Accord of 2001. Our work there is funded by the Swedish foreign ministry, so this is the government-funded project that we are doing. I would also add that Sweden very generously funds the IBA to undertake human rights training for lawyers in Palestine and that it also funded an analysis of the amendments to the Criminal Code of the former Yugoslavia when they introduced genocide and humanitarian law provisions into their domestic code, having one eye to the fact that the International Criminal Tribunal for the former Yugoslavia will cease operation in the not-too-distant future.

Swaziland turned out to be a three-pronged project. Initially, it was to comment on the draft constitution and to analyse it. However, there was a rule of law crisis when the entire bench of the Court of Appeal resigned after the prime minister said that the government would not follow two decisions of the Court of Appeal which had struck down a royal proclamation. The prime minister said: 'Royal proclamations are not debatable … it is unSwazi what the Court of Appeal has done. We are not following these decisions.' The entire bench resigned and went back to South Africa – they were all South Africans, white South African males. There were no Swazis on the Court of Appeal. So the IBA went in and undertook a human rights fact-finding mission and wrote a report with recommendations.

Thirdly, our work involved capacity building with the Law Society. The Law Society initially consisted of the president of the society's briefcase! There was no office, no staff, they did not even have a list of their own members and because of that, they could not collect dues, not knowing who to collect them from. They 'sort of' knew who all the lawyers were, because there are only about 200 of them in all of Swaziland, but nobody had actually made a list. They were doing no continuing legal education, they were providing no civil society leadership, and one of the main things we were funded to do was go in and build capacity with them. I am happy to say that they are well on the way now to doing the sorts of things that we would consider a Law Society should do.

This work has all been funded by the Open Society Initiative for Southern Africa, a branch of George Soros's charitable foundation, the Open Society Institute. This obviously raises an issue alluded to previously, and that is: what is the impact of this on the accountability of NGOs?

I would, with respect, challenge the premise on which this question is based – I think NGOs do have a lot of accountability, firstly to their own membership – if you look at a big organisation like Amnesty, it has a huge annual council meeting that reports to all of its members, and also to the media. We all put out press releases and, to that extent, we are publicly accountable because of that. But there is also accountability to our funders. We are restricted by the amount of funding that we can get and by the funding priorities that the funders set. We may be proactive in certain areas, and if that proaction coincides with a funding priority from a funder, that is excellent, but quite often it does not, and so to that extent, the driving force, when you are talking about NGO work in human rights, is not just what the NGO might want, but what it can get funding to do. So the question of who really is driving this – the IBA, or George Soros, or NGO X, or the Ford Foundation, or the MacArthur Foundation, or Bill Gates, with his billion-dollar foundation – is a very important one.

These questions also raise issues of the general categories or approaches to this area of human rights and foreign policy that have arisen in the past. Some refer to the realist school, the approach by writers like Hans J. Morgenthau, who allege that the national interest is power, not human rights. There is also the Statist/Legalist school, which claims that international law is based on state sovereignty which, together with the rule on non-intervention, limits the pursuit of power, and the relativist or pluralist approach that focuses instead on self-determination and diversity. This is not the place to analyse these approaches, but I will say that these issues, together with the expanding actors' base which I mentioned above, may require a rethink of the traditional categories, which do not really fit with what is happening in practice on the ground.

First, Afghanistan, which is clearly a country in crisis. Its legal profession is very small: in Kabul there are about 100 lawyers, perhaps a few more. Some of them are women, although men are definitely the majority. Because of the nature of legal practice in Afghanistan up to now, most of these lawyers work as civil servants. They are employees of the Supreme Court, attorney general's department, ministry of justice and so forth. The number of lawyers who practice in the way in which we would consider private practice – in setting up your own office – is only a handful.

Now that has had a tremendous impact on two things. Firstly, on the nature of what it means to be a lawyer and what a lawyer does, because when lawyers are basically civil servants, you think of them in that sense, rather than in a wider sense. Secondly, when you are setting up an association for these lawyers, it impacts on the notion of what that association is or should be doing. In Afghanistan, there is in fact a lawyers' union, but it acts like a trade union. It looks after employees' rights and has never done things that we would consider a bar association ought to do, such as contribute to law reform, require continuing legal education, contribute to the admission procedures to the profession, set ethical standards for the profession, discipline its own members and so forth. None of that has happened.

Legal education also is a problem in Afghanistan, so the question of just what law is going to be practiced is itself an issue. At the moment, every judge on the Supreme Court of Afghanistan is a Sharia lawyer. There are no civil lawyers on the bench yet, but more appointments are due. The lack of civil lawyers on the court is going to create a major problem, because the first bank has just opened up in Kabul and commercial issues will start to be litigated. Until now, all transactions have had to be in cash, usually in US dollars. So the very issue of what law can apply in a changing economy and whether the courts can cope with the change is a significant issue. In addition, there are virtually no law books, or copies of statutes in Afghanistan, because the Taliban burnt them. The best repositories of Afghan law are in fact located in university libraries outside Afghanistan.

The issue of admission to the profession and recognition of legal qualifications is a big problem, because particularly during the Taliban regime many people fled to places like Pakistan. Many of those who fled are returning now, some holding up pieces of paper that say: 'I have a law degree from the University of X' – sometimes a real university, sometimes a fictitious university, almost always a forged piece of paper. How can you determine whether these people ought to be able to practise or not?

I mention all of these facts because there are fundamental conceptual issues that have to be grappled with, and which in our jurisdictions we regard as axiomatic. We would not even have to think twice about them. There are different governments and different NGOs working in the country on many of these problems – most of them with different priorities – and this is only in the justice sector, leaving aside other essential matters such as reconstruction of infrastructure, healthcare, the heroin problem and so forth.

There can therefore be a clash of priorities and fragmentation in the work. There can also be overlap in what some of the agencies are doing. There are at least two agencies dealing now with legal aid. When the IBA came in and said: 'The bar association ought to be associated with legal aid', both of these agencies were concerned, and perhaps being territorial, they thought: 'My God, here is another one coming in, trying to do this!' What we did was to assure them that we were not there to work in opposition to them, we were not there to reinvent the wheel. The bar association ought to be plugged into the work that they were already doing, and we are now working in cooperation. Strategising can be crucial.

The problem, too, was that many organisations were going to the minister of justice with similar projects, similar claims and similar demands. The minister became tired of this and set up a coordinating committee, saying: 'I am listening to one lot of arguments, one lot of recommendations. All you people get together and come up with a coordinated approach.' The IBA was one of the organisations on that committee, but it was because of the action of the minister himself that this occurred. There remain huge conceptual and strategic issues that have to be grappled with.

There are also major translation issues. When you translate the word 'lawyer' from English into Dari and then translate it back again, because of the context in which lawyers have worked, the translation sometimes comes back as 'civil servant' or 'criminal lawyer'. The translation of 'bar association' sometimes comes back as 'association of criminal lawyers', because that is what the private lawyers were doing, substantially criminal law. We had to sit down with some other NGOs to try to create a glossary of translation terms.

I raise these issues – translation, conceptual issues, essential strategising and so forth – because what has happened in the context of Afghanistan, which I have not seen anywhere else, is that issues arise that could be called 'pre-human rights issues'. These are more fundamental things than we would normally have to consider, as an essential first step just to get on that bottom rung of the human rights ladder, before you even start considering, for example, the 1990 UN principles on the role of lawyers.

What we have in a situation and in a context like Afghanistan is not just what is usually called 'transitional justice'. 'Reparative justice' is what is needed, and in my view it is absolutely essential is that the approach to it is contextual. It cannot be, or be seen to be, a foreign organisation running a state's foreign policy on human rights through a bar association in Afghanistan. It has got to be contextualised, to make the end product sustainable. so that it will not fail as soon as we leave the country. Local issues such as the importance of religion, the existence of ethnic allegiances, and poverty, must be recognised if whole-country coverage of a bar association is to be achieved.

What did we do? It is important to say in this context that the Swedish government was not proscriptive regarding implementation. They gave us a general mandate: 'Set up a bar association. Here is $200,000. Now go and do it!' They were very generous and also very general in their mandate. It meant that we managed the project ourselves. We networked, we ran seminars on the role of lawyers and the work of a bar association, we ran a major conference in Kabul, and we organised two round tables with the government and stakeholders. I will summarise by saying that, as a result of this, the draft legislation to implement the bar association was approved. It went to the parliament and hopefully will be an effective and efficient law.

I will add, however, that the way in which we were able to work and which helped to make our efforts effective, was that, for example, in the conference we ran, there were over 100 people including as many Afghani lawyers and government people as we could find. The conference was a combination of presented papers and small-group discussions on bar association issues, with reporting back to the plenary so that a consensus could be determined. The participants were astonished that we did this, because this may have been the first time that a foreign organisation actually asked the Afghanis what they wanted, rather than telling them what it felt they needed. This was very important, and it was because of this that we convinced the minister of justice of the importance of the project; the minister then made the bar association a top priority.

We then asked the participants: 'What do you think about the independence of the association, the ethics of the association, continuing legal education and so forth?' We got very strong, positive reactions. They were in complete agreement with things that accorded with human rights and the 1990 UN principles. However, things that we thought might contribute to a good affirmative action strategy were not wanted. For example, Afghanistan is a very patriarchal country, and we had heard stories of problems faced by women lawyers. Lawyers in Afghanistan are often associated in the public perception with their clients and their cases, so it is regarded as unseemly for a woman lawyer to be involved with a rape trial, for example. We have also heard stories of women lawyers who have said: 'Oh, I was going to do an important case, but I could not go to the court on the day. My husband insisted that I cook his lunch that day and I could not go.'

We thought about creating a bar association with two divisions – one for men and one for women – so that the women would not be overborne by the men. However, the consensus of the women lawyers at the conference was overwhelmingly: 'Don't. We do not want to be marginalised, we want to be mainstream.' We dropped that idea. Listening to what they wanted was a very important strategy and helped us gain the support of the government.

Our suggestions had always been based on human rights, and in this instance we were able to use them as architectural norms to create a space for the return of the rule of law in Afghanistan. Our success so far can, I think, be put down to a combination of hard work and being able to garner the support of the local lawyers, other NGOs and the minister. It took us eighteen months to get that level of support, but once we did, it took only six months to bring a draft of the enabling legislation to fruition. That hard work was principally undertaken by some very able people we were able to engage as a result of the grant. Nevertheless, the impact of working under a grant, and not being able to sustain competitive salaries for a long period, can be a crucial factor in the competent delivery of human rights.

However, in Afghanistan there are other factors that can be even more debilitating for human rights delivery: poverty, the lack of education, the presence of warlords in the cabinet, and the fact that 60% of the country's economy is produced through the heroin trade.

With respect to Swaziland, I will briefly draw the background. Sharing many similarities with Afghanistan, including being land-locked, Swaziland also exhibits substantial differences. It is the smallest country in the southern hemisphere, of 17,000 square kilometres bordered by South Africa and Mozambique. Its primary industry is timber, and it was formerly a substantially subsistence farming country, from which people were encouraged to switch in order to earn foreign currency from sugar production, a strategy which proved to be disastrous when the world price of sugar fell. Severe droughts have devastated the countryside, it has a 40% unemployment rate and it has the highest rate of HIV infection in the world. It was a British Protectorate until 1968, when it gained independence and adopted a Westminster-style constitution. It is a member of the United Nations, the OAU and the Commonwealth.

The country's constitution was abandoned in 1973 in what has been described by some commentators as a coup driven by the palace. The previous king, King Sobhuza, was concerned that the trend in elections indicated that support for the palace-supported political party was slipping. After a public meeting, a royal proclamation – which was produced at the same meeting – abolished the constitution and banned political parties. Until 2006, Swaziland was without a constitution. It was governed by a combination of royal proclamations, a parliament of which two-thirds of the members were appointed by the king, an executive consisting of a prime minister and a cabinet – all appointed by the king – and a system of common law and customary courts.

The legal system I have already described. I will simply add that the systemic issues which impact upon human rights, in addition to those mentioned, are the traditional subjugation of women in a strongly patriarchal society, a near-feudal system of land tenure, and chronic underfunding of the courts and the law school. (When I visited the law school, the Dean had a PC on his desk, but he had not been able to use it for over twelve months as it had broken down and they did not have sufficient funds for repairs.) While King Mswati III is, in effect, Africa's last absolute monarch and spends $50 million on a private jet while 70% of his subjects live below the poverty line, he is nevertheless revered by the overwhelming majority in this very traditional land.

It was into this context that the IBA, through a series of grants from OSISA, a private funder, undertook the three projects I mentioned earlier: capacity building for the Law Society, reporting on the rule of law crisis, and analysing the new draft constitution.

For brevity, I will concentrate on our work with the constitution, an interesting document which attempts, through the introduction of a Bill of Rights, the fusion of human rights into the context of an absolute monarchy.

I should state at the outset that the effectiveness of the IBA's work in Swaziland has been greatly enhanced by the fact that we have enjoyed the support of a single funder, with a single set of priorities, over a sustained period of almost three years. The OSISA priorities have also been substantially congruent with those of the other main human rights drivers in the region: the Commonwealth, the United States, women's groups and, now, the Law Society, which is starting to take its place as a leader of civil society. International foreign policy is largely congruent with internal movements towards reform of the system. There are not the conflicting priorities as in Afghanistan.

The outcome of the new constitution has been both positive and negative. These were pointed out in detail in the IBA analysis and report, which contained fifty-eight recommendations for amendment. We know the report was considered in detail by the Swaziland Constitutional Review Commission, headed by the minister of justice, Prince David, who is the king's brother. Little in it was changed, however. It does not substantially alter the king's powers: there is no longer rule through proclamations and a system of informal and unelected committees, but the king still dominates parliament, directly appointing thirty of the 100 members and he still picks the prime minister and the cabinet. The constitution is silent on political parties (and members are 'independent') and recently the media were warned by the government not to be critical of the king. As with the situation precipitating the rule of law crises a few years before, the notion of the 'cultural uniqueness' of Swaziland was the justification.

The constitution does contain a rather extensive Bill of Rights, which covers fundamental human rights. This includes the right to association, so the issue of the legality of political parties will certainly be raised at some point. Indeed, the IBA received funding from the (former) British High Commission in Swaziland for human rights training for the country's judges and magistrates. This took place in 2005 and specific examples used in small-group discussion sessions addressed this very issue. The congruence of policy between a public and a private funder has therefore helped to establish at least the possibility of reform.

Where there has been a distinctly positive outcome, however, has been in the area of women's rights. Swaziland has strong cultural traditions which include and are supported by patriarchy. Traditionally women cannot own property in their own name, a situation particularly exacerbated when the husband dies and the relatives proceed to take the property used in the marriage as the widow has no automatic entitlement to it. Article 29 of the Constitution now states: 'Women have the right to equal treatment with men and that right shall include equal opportunities in political, economic and social activities. ... A woman shall not be compelled to undergo or uphold any custom to which she is in conscience opposed.' While this provision also will need to be interpreted by the courts, it is a clear indication that despite 'cultural uniqueness', strong traditions may be overturned. A principal reason for this must be the internal context: the position of the king remains too powerful to be altered; but traditions with respect to women's rights have been directly challenged because the influence of women's groups in Swaziland has been consistent and effective.

Overall however, there is still relatively little reliance on human rights. The banned political party PUDEMO has been the target of government action, including having treason charges brought against thirteen of its members. They have made a complaint to the African Commission, but of the five heads of argument in that complaint, only one relates directly to human rights. It is apparent that human rights is still regarded as 'new' in Swaziland, despite the African Charter having been in existence since 1981. Work done through the Law Society of Swaziland may now help to dispel this sense of the 'foreign'.

One of the lessons we have learned from Afghanistan and Swaziland is that for human rights in foreign policy to be effective, there needs to be a functioning domestic legal system receptive to those rights. We have also found that the iconic power of the nature of human rights – quite apart from the detail, and indeed contrary to the expectations of the drafters of the Universal Declaration, considering the expansion today of human rights to multinational corporations – is very, very strong. Jack Donnelly has referred to this as 'the language of legitimacy.' Nevertheless, human rights are vague and contested, but that is the case all over the world, not just in developing countries, not just in Muslim countries, Christian countries and so forth. Consider the right to marry – unquestionably a human right, but it is controversial now, with respect to same sex marriages, for example. The fact that it is vague, the fact that it is contested does not matter, and whether they are developing or developed countries, Christian, Muslim, conflict-ridden or not, does not really matter fundamentally, at least in these two examples. Similarly, with respect to foreign policy, we must now ask ourselves: foreign policy by and through whom? NGOs and non-state funders now play a significant role, and the focus is increasingly on civil society and its issues rather than on state interests. These 'foreign policy' issues now integrate more with domestic issues.

I will conclude by saying that human rights and foreign policy are often classified as part of the spread of democracy, or now of the rule of law as well, but it is really more than that. It is human rights as part of an iconic, fundamental notion that allows the law to be seen by foreign policymakers as no longer just a technicality that they have got to put up with, but as being part and parcel of the foreign policy process.

Protecting Citizens from Torture Abroad: Are Governments Doing Enough?

Carla Ferstman*

The organisation of which I am director, REDRESS, works with victims of torture to assert their rights to justice and to reparation; the relationship between foreign policy and human rights is central to our work, both at the national and the international level.

Torture is one of those crimes that all, or just about all, governments would publicly agree is a horrible practice, that can never be condoned and that must be eradicated. Where there is disagreement is on the nature of the responsibilities of governments to take proactive steps on behalf of victims. This is all the more obvious when one looks at what governments are doing to protect their nationals and, indeed, long-term residents who are tortured abroad.

To make diplomatic representations or to take a stand against torture when it involves another country undoubtedly has very serious foreign policy implications. It is this relationship between a government's prerogative in the domain of foreign policy, on the one hand, and a government's responsibilities to prevent its nationals and others with close links to the state from being tortured, on the other, where this is most at issue. My focus will be on this relationship, considering both the general situation and the particularities that are associated with what has come to be known euphemistically as the 'war on terror'.

Today, in a world where travel is commonplace, it is very easy to imagine the prospect of someone being detained whilst travelling abroad. The notion that some detainees are at risk of torture, or indeed that they have been tortured, is not altogether surprising. Governments, through their consular departments, have a mixed record in such situations, both in making repre-

* Carla Ferstman, Director of REDRESS.

sentations to ensure that torture does not occur in the first place, or to remove the national from the risk of further torture, or after the fact, to ensure that the victim receives some form of redress.

Looking at the general situation, the main issues are, firstly, the nature and adequacy of this response. In other words, whether government officials, usually consular departments, fought hard enough or fought at all, whether they shouted loud enough, whether their policy of quiet diplomacy was accountable to victims and family members, or indeed needed to be, and whether they obtained the desired result.

The second issue is whether the nature and adequacy of this response had enough to do with the precarious situation of the victims or whether it was, or whether it was perceived to be, subsumed by the desire on the part of the government concerned to maintain good foreign relations.

The war on terror exemplifies the issues just listed, considering governments' responses to the detention of their nationals in Guantánamo Bay, detention centres in Afghanistan or indeed other locations. The context in which counter-terrorism measures take place also adds several additional dimensions. Firstly, whether governments were complicit in torture or ill-treatment: by sharing inconclusive intelligence information about their nationals that led to their arrests abroad; by accepting or facilitating the hand-over of their nationals to other governments or operatives where there was a real risk that their nationals might end up in a location where they would face torture or other forms of cruel, inhuman or degrading treatment or punishment; or by participating in the interrogation of their nationals detained abroad, by putting questions through the interrogators or by being physically present at those interrogations. Also at issue, legally speaking, is the extent to which governments are able or indeed obliged to take up the cases of their nationals when torture is at issue, and the obligations they have towards dual nationals and long-term residents.

The law on what governments should appropriately do to safeguard the interests of their nationals, dual nationals or even residents who face torture abroad is not altogether clear in these very complex situations and can be approached from a number of disparate angles.

The first angle is to look at the law through the lens of foreign policy. Under international law, any step a government takes in respect of its nationals abroad is in its own right. It is acting to safeguard state interests, not the interests of those nationals. If the government decides to take any measure, the decision is its own prerogative, and following from this first proposition, it is not the job of courts, the judicial branch, to decide on the appropriateness of actions taken by the executive in the conduct of foreign relations.

But we can also look at this issue from another angle, through the lens of human rights. We know that the development of human rights law increasingly recognises the duty of states to ensure protection of fundamental human rights. The Torture Convention refers specifically to the obligation to take effective legislative, administrative and judicial or other measures to prevent acts of torture and it also makes specific reference to the possibility for one state to bring a claim against another to protect these rights. As far as I am aware, the right, in the Torture Convention, to bring a claim against another state has never been used. If it has been used, then it has been used very sparingly.

While recognising that the law was in a state of development, the Special Rapporteur of the International Law Commission, in his report on the International Law Commission's draft articles on diplomatic protection, had this to say about the relationship between human rights and diplomatic protection: 'Today, there is general agreement that norms of *ius cogens* including torture reflect the most fundamental values of the international community and are therefore most deserving of international protection. It is not unreasonable therefore to require a state, as opposed to allow a state to react by way of diplomatic protection to measures taken by a state against its nationals which constitute a grave breach of a norm of *ius cogens*. If a state party to a human rights convention is required to ensure to everyone within its jurisdiction effective protection against the violation of the rights contained in that convention, and to provide adequate means of redress, there is no reason why a state of nationality should not be obliged to protect its own national when his or her most basic human rights are seriously violated abroad.'

This was the statement of the Special Rapporteur of the International Law Commission. But in coming to this proposition, he cited a number of national jurisdictions which recognise an obligation in some circumstances to afford diplomatic protection and noted that, while his suggested approach conflicted with the traditional view that it is the state's prerogative, his view could not be dismissed out of hand, as it accorded with the principal goal of contemporary international law. And what is the principal goal of contemporary international law? The advancement of the human rights of the individual, rather than the sovereign powers of the state.

Considering these vast principles, and the traditional dichotomy between the sovereign authority of the state and the protection of human rights of the individual, it is through this contrasting set of views that we could look at the law in the United Kingdom with respect to these complex questions, in particular with reference to the detainees who have been, or continue to be, languishing in Guantánamo Bay.

In the case of Feroz Ali Abassi, which arose from a judicial review of the failure of the government to make representations, UK courts upheld the traditional view that diplomatic protection was the sole prerogative of the state, but recognised that nonetheless, in some cases, there could be a legitimate expectation that the executive would consider taking some action, and their failure to do so could be subject to judicial review. This is quite an important inroad in that, if the government has acted in a way which gave rise to a legitimate expectation of action, then the individuals concerned could, in principle, seek to make good that expectation.

Another issue which relates to this complex issue of diplomatic protection is the issue of nationality.

On the issue of nationality, the traditional view is that a state is only allowed to make diplomatic representations in respect of its own nationals, its citizens, but the law relating to dual nationals, people who have more than one citizenship, is somewhat unclear, a little bit murky. There is generally a right to make representations in respect of dual nationals, but some commentators understand that there is an exception with respect to the ability for one state of nationality to make representations against the other state of nationality. But other commentators have seen it in a very different light, and have enabled the state of nationality to make representations so long as it is the primary, the dominant nationality, so there are some differences of view here.

However, traditionally when it comes to residents – these may be people who have lived in a country for more than twenty years, long-term residents – a state does not have the right to make diplomatic representations. Yet if we look to the International Law Commission's recommendations, they extend to enabling a state to exercise diplomatic protection in respect of stateless persons, so persons who would have no other state to represent their interests, or recognised refugees habitually resident in the state seeking to exercise diplomatic protection. These are some of the legal issue which impact on the considerations at hand with respect to what governments should be doing to protect their nationals abroad and whether they are doing enough.

I would like to discuss one case, which is actually going through the courts currently in this country, which raises some of these complex issues, and here it is the case of British long-term residents and persons recognised as refugees in this country who remain in Guantánamo Bay.

To put it in context: there were a number of British nationals in Guantánamo Bay, but they were all released or returned to the United Kingdom following representations made by the British government. However, the remaining detainees with ties to the United Kingdom are long-term residents and some of them have refugee status. One of them is an Iraqi national who had been living in the United Kingdom since 1983. Another is from Jordan, and had been in the United Kingdom since 1994 with refugee status, and a third is from Libya, and had been in the United Kingdom since 1986, also with refugee status. Two of these individuals were arrested in Gambia in 2002, where they had gone to set up a peanut processing plant. They are Bisher Al Rawi, an Iraqi national, and Jamil Al-Banna from Jordan.

Six days before they went to Gambia, Gatwick Airport authorities had detained and questioned them for two days about a suspicious package that was found in their luggage. It was considered at the time that this suspicious package could be some type of improvised explosive device. Later it turned out that the package was a battery charger, but apparently information about this suspicious package was passed onto authorities, believed to be US intelligence, through the UK security services. Somehow they failed to mention that actually they had confirmed that this was in fact a battery charger, so the initial information that it was a potential explosive device was the information that was passed on.

Needless to say, when the two individuals eventually arrived in Gambia, they were arrested and questioned by US investigators. They were then transferred to a US base in Afghanistan and then sent to Guantánamo Bay.

One of the other long-term residents was initially arrested in Pakistan in 2002 and was then transferred to Bagram Air Base and then to Guantánamo Bay. As for the two who were in Gambia, when they requested to see British Consular officials, the surprised Gambian investigator said: 'But it is your government, Britain, the MI5, who called the CIA and told them that you and Bisher were in Gambia and to come and get you. Britain sold you out to the CIA.'

The UK government ostensibly refused to make representations on these persons' behalf to seek their release, so the residents petitioned the High Court to review the decision not to intervene and not to provide them with assistance. The case turned on the following specific points.

The first issue was obviously nationality. The High Court indicated that, despite the long-term residence and refugee status of the individuals concerned, with respect to the judicial review the foreign secretary was entitled, as a matter of law, to draw a distinction between nationals and persons with other ties and connections to this country.

What the High Court said with respect to policy considerations is interesting. The claimants had argued that, despite the government's submissions to the contrary, a formal diplomatic intervention might have actually made a huge difference in their case. The government had made submissions to the Court that in fact they did not think that that was the best approach. The

Court did not wish to evaluate the value judgements put forward by the government as to what would be the best approach in this type of case, because clearly the Court saw this as a domain of foreign policy into which the Court should not enter; that separation was clearly maintained in the High Court's decision.

Developing the lines of the Feroz Ali Abassi case, the Court was willing to consider whether the foreign secretary appropriately exercised his discretion. In other words, it was clear that there was a discretion and it was the discretion of the government to decide what to do in the case, but if there was a failure to exercise this discretion in an appropriate way, the Court could, in a relevant circumstance, request the government to reconsider the matter.

To take the implications of this case a little bit further, it has been suggested that one of the reasons for the failure of the UK government to make diplomatic representations on behalf of the British residents was not because the representations would have been counterproductive or ineffective but, on the contrary, for the very reason that they might indeed have been effective! That perhaps is a bold claim, but according to the statements, the foreign secretary specifically alluded to this and pointed to the security threats that the claimants continued to pose and that they would pose should they be allowed to be returned to the United Kingdom. He considered that this material was relevant to his assessment, and that a fair balance between the interests of the claimant and the general public interest did not require him to make a formal request to the US government, which the claimants had demanded.

Actually, when we look closer, we have, on the surface, an issue which relates to nationality and whether or not a diplomatic representation should be made, but below the surface there is a suggestion that what is at stake here is whether these individuals should indeed return to the United Kingdom. It is also important to note that none of the detained claimants had meaningful ties to any other country and that some of them had been recognised as refugees who risked persecution or torture were they to be returned to their countries of nationality, makes it clear that these individuals could not rely on their countries of nationality to make diplomatic representations on their behalf.

In a related way, this may put claimants on a collision course with another foreign policy, the policy of deporting foreign nationals who are said to pose a security risk. This is particularly relevant in this case, and worrying with respect to the claimants from Jordan and from Libya, with whom the United Kingdom has signed controversial memoranda of understanding. That is that they might receive transfers on the understanding that the receiving governments would refrain from using torture, and, as the UN Special Rapporteur on Torture indicated not long ago: 'Diplomatic assurances with regard to torture are nothing but attempts to circumvent the absolute prohibition of torture. The Council of Europe should call on its member states to refrain from seeking and adopting such assurances from states with a proven record of torture.'

The decision of the Court of Appeal will be interesting for a whole range of reasons, and if positive it can possibly chart important new ground, not only for British residents languishing in Guantánamo Bay, but for many other cases as well. What is very important about the High Court's decision is that it recognised that the executive has an obligation to justify its position with detailed evidence and arguments – even though it is within the executive's discretion to make diplomatic representations, the discretion must be reasonably and fairly exercised.

The case does not go so far as to recognise a duty of states under international law to make representations on behalf of their nationals or anyone else when torture is at stake, but as the Special Rapporteur of the International Law Commission on Diplomatic Protection has noted, this area of international law is still very much evolving, so an international law obligation is not yet clear.

Of course it is certainly open to the British government to create this obligation in its national law, as a number of other countries have been seen to do. The UK government has regularly taken a very firm stance on the prohibition against torture and this may be an opportunity for it to demonstrate its firm commitment to the principle.

We have to look at the law as a tool and not as a barrier. If it is a barrier, then certainly the accountability at issue is to ensure that the law ceases to be a barrier and reflects what it needs to reflect.

Part III:
International Development and Human Rights

Democracy, Development and Violence

Paul Collier*

This paper focuses on the interconnections between democracy, development and violence. In many ways, its scope goes beyond *The Bottom Billion*,[1] which was written largely in 2005 and tells the story from the 1960s to the millennium. This paper starts with a very brief account of one of the key themes of this story and then moves on to developments during the present decade, which have created new opportunities and challenges.

In a nutshell, the story of *The Bottom Billion* is that there was a class of countries – about sixty countries around the world – that had missed out on the economic development process. Those sixty countries had between them a population of about a billion people, so the typical country was very small. They were unusual in being very small, and they were unusual in having been stagnant during a period of four decades in which most developing countries were transforming themselves through accelerated development. They had missed out on global development, and so were gradually diverging from the rest of mankind. Societies that are poor, stagnant and small generally have a much higher incidence of large-scale violence than other societies. Thus, the background is that during the 1960-2000 period there was a rise in large-scale violence in the countries of the bottom billion and, generally, a fall in large-scale violence elsewhere in the world. International war did not disappear but became very rare, and violent conflict on any large scale thus became overwhelmingly a matter of internal conflict and civil war in these countries.

How has this story developed since? In the first decade of this millennium, there have been three important developments that need to be considered in

---

* Professor Paul Collier, Professor of Economics, University of Oxford; Director, Centre for the Study of African Economies

1 Paul Collier, *The Bottom Billion: Why the Poorest Countries Are Failing and What Can Be Done About It* (New York, Oxford University Press 2007).

order to update and potentially transform the story of the bottom billion. Moreover, each of them is a double-edged sword: they offer hope and opportunities but also dangers.

The first development, which occurred around the time of the millennium, is that a lot of these civil wars, which had been running for years, were settled. The average civil war lasts more than ten times as long as the average international war and is very hard to stop through internal processes. Around the time of the millennium, however, the international community woke up to this problem and intervened in an attempt to restore peace. There was thus a wave of peace settlements, which was obviously good news. However, the legacy for the present decade is that there are now a lot of post-conflict situations.

The second big change was the spread of democracy, which occurred during the 1990s as a result of the fall of the Soviet Union. The end of the Soviet Union produced a wave of democratisation in Eastern Europe, which was then copied around the developing world, especially in Africa. Thus, in the present decade, many more of the bottom billion countries have at least some of the trappings of democracy.

The third development, which occurred in this decade, is the global boom in commodity prices. While commodity prices were very depressed during the 1990s, the price of almost all non-agricultural commodities is above levels previously experienced. This is most obvious in the case of oil, but it is also true for most metals. This, in turn, has produced revenue booms across the bottom billion. Not all the countries of the bottom billion have benefited. It depends on whether or not they are exporters of these non-agricultural natural resources, but quite a few of them are.

Thus there are three new features that were not present in the 1980s and 1990s: lots of post-conflict situations, lots of new democracies and substantial revenues from commodity exports. I will now discuss the impact of these three developments, especially in terms of the level of violence.

Post-conflict situations are hopeful because peace is now the norm and internal large-scale violence seems to have gone out of fashion. However, our best guide is the past and, based on experience, post-conflict situations are very fragile. On average, 40% of post-conflict situations revert to conflict within a decade. They are thus high-risk situations, which makes them a double-edged sword.

Regarding the spread of democracy, one would hope that the implications of democratisation for violence would be pretty unambiguous. This has indeed been the core belief in the promotion of democracy in bottom billion societies. The reason why democracy should reduce the incidence of large-scale internal violence in these societies is that it reduces feelings of alienation and grievance, because a democratically elected government is more accountable to its citizens, which in turn means that there is less cause to resort to violence. At least, this is how it is supposed to work. Statistically – and this forms the whole basis of my own work – one finds that the effect of democracy on a whole variety of forms of violence – from rebellion and civil war to guerrilla activity and riots – is actually ambiguous and that it largely depends on the level of income. Above a certain income threshold, around $2,500 per capita per year, democracy does significantly reduce the risk of all these forms of violence. Below this income threshold, however, the opposite is true: democracy significantly increases the risk of all these forms of large-scale violence. This implies that there is evidently some other effect that counterbalances the accountability effect.

One of democracy's side effects is that it ties a government's hands as to what it can do in order to maintain internal security. Thus, the government is less subject to grievances, but it is also less able to repress. Repression is also a double-edged sword. If a government is less able to repress, society is less prone to violence, but repression may also be an effective form of keeping the peace. Two of the most violent political regimes in the world, those of Stalin and Saddam Hussein, provide a stark example of this dilemma. Both were replaced with more democratic forms of government, but this same process took the lid off internal violence. Thus, under Stalin and Saddam Hussein, the violence came from the top, and this actually replaced the violence from below. These are extreme cases, but the general tendency is that, as a country moves towards democracy and so reduces its capacity for repression, a lot of possibilities for organised violence are created. The question is then whether the increased scoped for organised violence is offset by the reduced sense of grievance. My research shows that, at low levels of income, the reduced sense of grievance effect – the accountability effect – is not very strong and that it only becomes more powerful at higher levels of income.

In order to understand why the accountability effect is weak at low levels of income, one needs to understand how democracy is conducted in some of these very low-income countries. The depressing answer is that it is easy to steal an election. That is to say, it is easy to win the democratic game by other means than being a good government. However, the accountability effect only works if the way to win an election is to be as good a government as possible.

Take, for example, a newly democratic country. The old government did not come to power through an election, but it has agreed to hold elections because the aid donors have so decided. However, the old government still wants to win, and it has several options in this regard. The first is that it tries to be a good government. This is very difficult, because the civil service was corrupted by the old government itself and is unable to deliver services.

Another option is to use the government's resources to bribe voters because the government is not subject to a whole lot of scrutiny. Thus, one finds that vote buying is a major strategy in the countries of the bottom billion. Vote buying is at the 'nice' end of how to win an election without being a good government. There are also some strategies at the nastier end. Vote buying is a matter of trying to get people to vote for the old government. However, if the leadership knows that some people will not vote for the old government under any circumstances, then the best it can do is to make sure these people do not vote for anybody else through intimidation. Thus, the money is used to hire a load of thugs who go along and 'encourage' these people not to vote.

Then, there is a third strategy that the old government can use as a back-up: it can turn out not to be very good at counting the votes. The old government can load the electoral commission with its cronies, thus assuring a certain victory. This combination of bribery, intimidation and miscounting is a much more reliable way of winning than being a good government. Looking at the Western world, where all elections are conducted based on an incentive system in which governments try to win by being good at what they do, the probability of winning is about 55% or 60%. Thus, even in the best of circumstances, trying to win by being a good government does not have that high a success rate, whereas in the new democracies of the bottom billion, incumbent governments have a much higher success rate than that. Either they are superb at being good governments, or they are resorting to techniques that imply that they do not need to be good governments.

In these societies, elections alone are by no means enough to produce the accountability effect. What is left, therefore, is the lifting of repression effect, which in these low-income societies increases the incidence of violence. My research has looked particularly at the interaction between democracy and post-conflict situations, and the findings show that post-conflict elections have been the international community's main strategy for establishing post-conflict peace. Take, for example, the Democratic Republic of the Congo (DRC). The international community's strategy was that there would be a transitional government and peacekeepers for a short time. Then, there would be post-conflict elections. These took place on 29 October 2006, so the date for the withdrawal of peacekeepers was 30 October 2006. The elections were thus the exit strategy for the international peacekeeping effort. The underlying theory was that the election would confer a sense of legitimacy upon whoever won. Under these circumstances, however, only the international community could regard the outcome of the election as conferring legitimacy, as it is accustomed to elections conferring legitimacy. Another group that might regard the election as legitimate is the group that wins. Unlike in developed countries, however, it says that it will act only in the interest of the people who supported it. On the other hand, those who lost the election will claim that the winners cheated and will rightly think that they are in danger unless they are protected by international peacekeepers. However, the international peacekeepers are leaving the country. That was the DRC strategy. Of course, in the end, the international community had to fly troops into the DRC, not out of it. And this is not just one specific case: this is the norm. Post-conflict elections postpone the risk of reversion to conflict. The year before the election, the risk of reversion to violence goes down a lot, because all the parties are trying to win the election. The year after the election, the risk of reversion to violence goes up even higher than it was before. So the net effect of the post-conflict election is to make the situation more dangerous, which means that it is absurd that the international community uses it as the benchmark, or the milestone, for the withdrawal of peacekeeping troops. If one thinks about it, given these results, the international community should be using post-conflict elections as the milestone for sending in international peacekeepers, not withdrawing them.

This brings us to the resource boom. This is the single biggest story in the countries of bottom billion at the moment, since about half of them have enjoyed a big surge in revenue. My research shows that the effect of the resource boom on violence is again a double-edged sword, with two opposite effects. One effect is that all this money has the potential to produce rapid growth and sustained higher levels of income, which systematically reduce risks. However, there is another effect of these resource revenues, namely a sort of 'honey pot' effect. The resource revenues accrue to the government, and capturing those resources becomes the main objective. Resource revenues thus finance conflicts and also become an object of conflict. An example of how the prospect of resource revenues can make it much harder to maintain peace is Sudan. Looking at the relationship between big commodity revenues, high prices and the growth of the commodity exporters over the past forty years, one finds that there is a difference between the short term and the long term. In the short term, everything is fine: the resource revenues produce a bonanza of growth, which is what we can observe now. If history repeats itself, however, this will last until about 2010. In the long term, say by 2025, growth will have peaked and the situation will have started to deteriorate.

If one tracks income relative to what it would otherwise have been for the average African resource exporter, it will be up by 10% by 2010 but down by

25% by 2025. The long-term prospects are dreadful if history repeats itself. These prospects depend on initial levels of governance. There is a threshold level of governance that determines the long-term effect of the resource boom, just like there is a threshold level of income that determines the effect of democratisation. Above this threshold, a country gets richer not only in the short term but also in the long term. This was the case in Norway. Norway did not crash as a result of its oil money: it is now the richest country in Europe. The threshold of governance is located around the level where governance was in Portugal in the mid-1980s. This was probably the weakest governance environment in Europe at that time, but it was still a much better governance environment than currently exists in many of the bottom billion. The long-term prognosis is therefore that, if history repeats itself, many of the bottom billion countries will crash as a result of these resource bonanzas, unless they rapidly improve their standards of governance.

During the last big bonanzas of the 1970s, almost all the resource-rich countries were autocracies. Now, thanks to the wave of democratisation described above, many of them are democracies. The next question is therefore whether the move from autocracy to democracy represents the required improvement in governance to harness these windfalls for sustained growth. It turns out, unfortunately, that democracy actually seems to make things worse in resource-rich countries. Outside the context of resource riches, democracy improves economic performance, but if there are big enough revenues from resources it actually undermines performance. Thus, instead of democracy regulating how the resources are used, the resources undermine democracy. In line with the processes described above, money flowing into the public coffers is very helpful in undermining a democracy and stealing an election. One reason why it is very helpful is that money from natural resources does not involve taxing the population. Around the world, however, taxation is the instrument that has provoked citizens into scrutiny of government. A resource-rich environment with big revenues for the government and very low taxation, and hence very low levels of scrutiny of government, allows the government to misappropriate these huge 'honey pots'. In addition, this misappropriated money is not wasted but is used to keep rotten governments in power by stealing elections.

A mature democracy has two central features. One is elections, which tell you how a government acquires power. The other is checks and balances, which tell you how a government uses power. Elections and checks and balances are very different. Elections can take place in any society, they are events. In Afghanistan and Iraq, for example, it was possible to hold elections in the midst of chaos. Checks and balances, on the other hand, are not events but processes. In economic terms, they are what are known as public goods. This means that nobody has a very strong incentive to supply them, because everybody benefits from them. The instant democracies are strong in electoral competition but very weak in checks and balances, which implies that the democracies of the bottom billion are very unbalanced democracies. Lots of elections; but no checks and balances.

Statistically, this matters. Uniquely, in resource-rich countries, electoral competition is very dysfunctional, whereas checks and balances are very functional. It is the checks and balances that these societies need. Unfortunately, however, the final statistical result is that resource riches systematically and gradually undermine even such checks and balances that are there to begin with. An obvious reason is that governments in resource-rich countries have an incentive to dismantle such checks and balances because they threaten, inhibit and constrain their ability to misappropriate. Thus, the agenda for the resource-rich democracies should be to strengthen checks and balances – that is the battle front.

In terms of what the international community can do, there are three policy instruments that need to be considered. The first instrument is aid, which is not very important in this environment. First of all, in the context of resource booms, aid is clearly irrelevant, because huge financial inflows are coming from the natural resource exports. Secondly, there is growing evidence that aid retards democratic accountability for the simple reason described above: it frees the government from the need for tax revenue, and this means that citizens are not 'provoked' through taxation. A third reason is that aid inadvertently leaks into military spending. A statistical analysis at the global level shows that about 11% of aid leaks into military spending. In post-conflict societies, in particular, big military spending by the government is provocative: far from keeping the peace, it provokes a reversion to violence. On the whole, I believe that aid is beneficial and should be increased despite these comments. H, as regards these particular problems – the violence in resource-rich countries and new democracies – I do not think aid is the solution at all.

Another solution is to provide more effective international security. This relates in particular to UN peacekeeping and offers of peacekeeping. Statistically, money spent on post-conflict peacekeeping is very effective in reducing the risks of reversion to violence and is therefore very cost effective. Our mistake is usually that we do not provide enough of it and we do not keep the peacekeepers in position for long enough. An over-the-horizon guarantee is a good exit strategy for peacekeeping and a supplement to peacekeeping on the ground. This is what the British government is experimenting with in Sierra

Leone. The French did it for many years, less formally, in francophone Africa, which unofficially enjoyed a sort of French security guarantee from the mid-1960s until the mid-1990s. It worked and it was credible because it was supported by military bases. In fact, the risk of large-scale violence in francophone Africa during those thirty years was only a third of what we would actually have expected it to be, given the characteristics of the countries. The most likely explanation for this is French peacekeeping.

Finally, the option that has the most potential involves international governance instruments, such as international standards and codes for the management of natural resource revenues. At the moment, there are virtually no standards or codes in this area, and yet they are a key issue in the countries of the bottom billion. They would guide the forces of reform, change and good governance within these societies. The one example we have is the Extracting Industries Transparency Initiative, which is a voluntary code that encourages governments to inform their own citizens of the revenues they were receiving. As soon as it was introduced by Tony Blair in 2002 as a British government initiative, reformers in Nigeria adopted it. It has now spread around West Africa and has made a big difference to the transparency of revenues. The transparency of revenues was the right place to start, but it is the wrong place to stop, because there are many other decision points that determine whether those revenues are actually used for sustained growth or whether they are just wasted by the government, which has so far been the norm.

International governance instruments can also be useful in connection with conditionality. The international community tried donor conditionality in the 1980s and 1990s and it was a disaster, because policy conditionality muddied up who was actually responsible for running the country. However, there is big difference between policy conditionality and governance conditionality. Governance conditionality is about insisting that a government is accountable not to donors but to its own citizens. This is not only entirely legitimate but also consistent with the whole historical process by which governments have gradually become more accountable to their own citizens. Usually, there was a lot of external pressure in one form or another that encouraged the move towards accountability. One of the very simple pieces of conditionality that would improve accountability is budgetary transparency. Budgets are where the money is and are central to what happens. Achieving budgetary transparency, so that citizens can see and track just how money is used, is a minimum form of governance conditionality.

International governance instruments are also a good starting point in post-conflict situations. Post-conflict situations get a lot of aid, and on average 11% of aid leaks into military spending. Military spending by the government in standard post-conflict situations is not just a waste of money but is also dangerous. It is inadvertently a signal to other groups that the government means to rule by repression. In fact, statistically, big military spending increases the risk of further conflict. The international community is inadvertently financing this high domestic military spending in post-conflict situations and should not be doing so. It is entirely legitimate to set conditions that prevent this money from being used to finance large-scale government spending on the military. This should be reinforced by a commitment to maintain international peacekeeping, so that the governments do not feel the need for big domestic military spending in post-conflict situations.

Some may claim that this is a step back to colonialism, but there are three reasons why this is not the case. The first is that the whole basis for national sovereignty in the countries of the bottom billion is much weaker than the historic roots of sovereignty. The historic roots of sovereignty are in the seventeenth century religious wars in Europe, where it was eventually realised that whatever a government did to its own population did not affect its neighbours. However, this basis for national sovereignty is simply no longer true, especially in the countries of the bottom billion. The costs of large-scale violence are not only enormous but more than half of them spill over to neighbouring countries, which are very badly affected. It is problematic for the neighbours themselves to have a share of sovereignty, because neighbours are usually in a very ambiguous position. They have legitimate interests, but they also have illegitimate interests. It is therefore perfectly reasonable to shift shared sovereignty up to a higher international level than that of the neighbouring countries, whose legitimate interests would thus in effect be protected by the international community, whether at the regional level (e.g., by the African Union) or at global level (e.g., by the United Nations). This is the fundamental case for shared sovereignty: it is not a return to colonialism but a dilution of national sovereignty, and I think it is legitimate.

In conclusion, the body that I would particularly like to see as the custodian of shared sovereignty is the United Nations Peacebuilding Commission, which was set up in 2005. At the moment, the Peacebuilding Commission is not performing this role; it is not rising to the challenge. It is trying to be yet another agency implementing change in a couple of countries, in this case Burundi and Sierra Leone. However, we do not need another implementing agency for aid in post-conflict situations. What we need is a body that takes upon itself the legitimate role of setting minimum standards of governance in these post-conflict environments.

What Development Does Africa Want?

Richard Dowden*

What development does Africa want? If you want a very simple answer, you can look at the most recent survey by Globescan. It asks Africans what issues affect them and their villages, and the answer, overwhelmingly, is: jobs. Now this tells us two things: firstly, that Africans are the same as everyone else in their concerns; and, secondly, that our image of Africa – an image of poverty, wars and disease – is not how Africans see themselves. All these issues were actually listed alongside jobs in the survey questions, but apparently what we think of as the most desperate concerns for Africans are not the ones they think of. For them it is jobs.

So what sort of development does Africa want? I would ask the question: Africa or Africans? Because, again, outsiders do not often distinguish between the two and they are quite distinct, particularly when you look at the past engagement of outsiders with Africa, where the needs of the people have sometimes come very much second to what lies on or under the soil, which is what outsiders see as valuable.

Whenever I hear: 'What Africa needs is' or 'African solutions to African problems', I reply: 'Which Africans? Are you talking about Egyptians or South Africans? Are you talking about Somalia, Malawi or Morocco?' Africa is a very big and varied place, it is very differentiated, and it has never been more so than now. So it is very difficult ever to state something like: 'Africa is ...'. There is always an exception. Africa is not just divided by nationalities, ethnicity and languages, it is also deeply divided by class: the ruling elite and everyone else. The image of Africa that still strikes me most forcibly is one that was written in the middle of the independence period, or just after, when there was immense international and African optimism about the future of the continent. Except among African novelists. If you read the novels of that

* Richard Dowden, Director, Royal African Society.

time, they are deeply pessimistic, especially those of Chinua Achebe, the Nigerian writer. His book, *A Man of the People*, contains a description of a house. He writes: 'We were all out in the rain; and there was the house, the colonial house, that the white man had left behind. And the lucky, the brightest, but not always the best' – if I can quote from memory – 'ran towards that house, and ran into it, and then slammed the door, and then broadcast to the rest of us, still outside in the rain, that all agitation must cease, that we had won.' That was his vision of the way Africa had been captured by African elites who have kept everyone else out. And I think they have remained in that house to this day.

It is very hard not to want to respond to the images of hunger on television or, if you actually go to Africa, to actually confront people who are poor, hungry and have diseases that are curable. But I would say that, in most of Africa, starvation is almost always the result of war. There are very few countries where it is simply the case that God has not provided enough food. Such cases are very, very rare indeed. In almost every situation where there is hunger, there has been displacement, and this displacement has been the result of war. It is important to tell the truth in this regard. The wars themselves may not be very dramatic, with major battles, but the victims are always the people who run, who leave their homes and their livelihoods, and then suffer and die. When British journalists Jonathan Dimbleby and Michael Buerk covered famines in Ethiopia – Dimbleby in Ethiopia in 1973 and Michael Buerk ten years later in 1984 – they did not mention the war. Their reason was that if they had said the famine was caused by war, people would not be sympathetic to the plight of the victims and would not send money. They presented the famine as a cataclysmic event of biblical proportions and the people as pure victims. In fact, they were victims of their own government and the rebel movement that together had caught them in the middle and forced them to leave their homes. Some were being forcibly removed by the government.

Although the prime causes of Africa's worst famines are not natural, there is a lack of development in Africa. There is a sense that things do not have to be this way, because Africa is a very rich continent, and that it is a mystery why Africa has not developed. Maybe now things are changing. Maybe this is a conversation that we will not need to have in five years' time. The economy of the whole continent has been growing at a rate of approximately 5% a year since 2000, which is above the global average. In fact, some people believe that it has reached take-off point. The Evening Standard of 17 October 2007 featured a full-page advert with a picture of a lion, and the title was: 'Africa – Get Ahead of the Investment Pack!' This was an advertisement for the new

'Star Heart of Africa Fund'. It said: 'After decades of unrest and economic instability, there are signs that Africa is changing, driven by increased democracy, debt reduction and the demand for natural resources...' and so on. So now Africa is the place to make money. This is where to put your pension. Only a few years ago, the chairman of a large multinational, with very large estates in Africa that were making good money, personally insisted that the word 'Africa' be removed from the company's annual report for fear of what it might do to the share price. Suddenly Africa has become not something that is just associated with failure, poverty and hopelessness but a place where you can make money.

On the Saturday after this advert appeared, *The Guardian* launched an appeal for a village called Katine in north-western Uganda, which was selected as the place where the funds raised in the newspaper's Christmas appeal would be spent that year. The headline was: 'Can we together lift one village out of the Middle Ages?' It compared Katine with fourteenth-century Europe. I have a problem with that image – that metaphor – because I think it implies that Africa is somehow where we were a century or two centuries or twenty centuries ago and now has to catch up. Our job therefore is to teach them or show them how to be like us. It implies a sort of backwardness. *The Guardian* chose to use this image, but buried deep in that article was the real reason why this particular area is poor. Katine is in the Teso area of Uganda, and in the chaos of the post-Amin years, the neighbouring Karimojong walked into a barracks and took all the guns and a large amount of ammunition. This militarised the Karimojong, who live in an area frequently affected by drought, so they started attacking the Teso and stealing their cattle.

I felt like writing a letter to *The Guardian* saying that maybe the appeal should be for AK-47s, so that the Teso could protect themselves, rather than an appeal to save these people and bring them into the twentieth century. In 1987 or 1988, I went to Ethiopia because a British aid agency there had launched a programme of 'integrated development' in a village. They claimed that this was going to be the start of something that would spread all over that country, transforming Ethiopia and then all of Africa. They were going to do development in a new way – not just a well here and a school there – they were going to do everything in that one village – a well, a school, a clinic, all the latest ideas about agriculture – and the whole area would take off. Then everybody would see how to do it, and the programme would be replicated all over the Third World. So I went there, and it was very impressive. They had – quite rare at that time – solar-powered computers, and the aid workers were documenting the whole area and putting in a lot of money: building clinics and schools, getting kids into school, all sorts of new agricultural techniques, providing water and so on. It was a terrific plan, and I wrote a long article about it. I never heard anything about it again A couple of years ago, I happened to be in Ethiopia and wondered what had happened to the project. I telephoned the aid agency and asked them. I spelled out the name of the place. But there was complete silence. No memory of it whatsoever. I called two or three times. I said: 'You must have a record of your great project there.' They had found my article but they had no record of their own. Aid agencies do not seem to keep records. The project was completely forgotten: no institutional memory, no lessons learned – nothing.

I decided to go and find out what had happened. I took a car and set off down a brand new road to the valley – but a valley, like many in Ethiopia, that suffers from failed rains. As I came over the ridge of the valley, I saw something that I had never seen before in Ethiopia – a woman on a horse. Men ride horses; women walk with a band around their heads and a great pile of wood or something on their backs. To see a woman on this nicely caparisoned horse was quite amazing. I thought: 'Something has happened here.' I drove on and met the local committee – there is always a committee in an Ethiopian village – and when I told them my story they laughed. They said: 'Yes, the aid agency left.' 'Why did they leave?' 'Well, I don't know: it may have been the war.' One thing that did survive, however, was the water project. It had cost a million dollars, but they had actually created a water system that pumped water from a spring at the bottom of the hill into a tank on the hillside. This system provided approximately twenty villages in the area with water. There was such pessimism after the aid agency left that nobody was interested in running it, but the women's groups said: 'We will run it. We know about water. Water is our business. We have to walk and fetch it. We wash, we cook. Water is for us.' According to the women, the men said: 'Well, you couldn't run anything, so we'll let you do that, and no doubt it will all collapse.'

The profit they had made from charging for the water amounted to something like $2,000. They were just meeting that week to decide what to spend it on. I asked them what had brought about the change in the valley, because it was definitely better off than it had been when I visited before. They replied: 'It's very simple. It was the road.' The nice new road down from Addis Ababa. That is what had changed the valley. 'Well, what about all these nice new agricultural ideas and schemes?' I asked. That produced a great burst of laughter. They said: 'What they told us to grow was red peppers, and red peppers do grow quite nicely here, but there is a limit to the amount of red peppers that Addis Ababa needs. However, what we did find extremely profitable is *qat*, and we sell that, and it goes off to Somalia.' So they were actually making their money from drugs. Actually, *qat* is a very weak drug, a mild amphetamine, but that is what had really brought some prosperity to this area.

This says a lot about the way outsiders come to Africa with big development ideas without really consulting the local people. By chance, some smart women had picked up the one thing in the project that could work and had done it well. Stories of failed development projects in Africa go on and on.

However, one group that has delivered development but is completely ignored is the churches. They have educated more people, built more clinics and delivered more medicines than anyone else. In bad times, they become like the monasteries in medieval Europe that held society together during terrible wars and disasters. I remember visiting Kisangani in the Congo just after one of the *péages*, when President Mobutu, worried about his army feeling poor, told them: 'Help yourselves, pay yourselves.' The soldiers looted the country, smashed into all the shops and took whatever they wanted. It was amazing to see a whole city devastated like that. The one place they did not touch, however, was the *Procure*, the diocesan headquarters. I spent a few days there and listed all the things that it did: it was a church, a school, a community centre, a clinic, a hospital, a repair workshop, a post office, a bank, an airline and a feeding centre. It served the city and the surrounding area and was the main link with the outside world. I think the churches have been successful because they do not follow fashions. They stay put, build up their local knowledge and experience and have a very strong institutional memory. They are the best proof that Africa actually works perfectly well at a local level.

That being said, Africa ought to do a great deal better at national level and be able to compete internationally. My feeling is that the reasons that it has not been successful are cultural. For example, in a village, age matters. Older people have authority; younger people cannot take big decisions. They are held back in that way. The elders also control the land. In most of Africa, there are still no title deeds for land, so trend analysis person cannot raise a mortgage on his property. Now this may be a perfectly good community way of running things – it is not as individualistic as the West – but there nevertheless has to be some way for a small farmer to leverage what he owns. In Africa, this is impossible due to the traditional systems in the villages.

In addition, in many parts of Africa, multi-party democracy may not be the best way of choosing a government. I know this is not a popular thing to say, but multi-party democracy tends to divide Western society horizontally, along class lines, although this appears to be softening. In Africa, first-past-the-post, winner-takes-all, multi-party democracy divides people vertically, along ethnic lines. Imagine if Europe actually became a single state and the French were all Muslims, all the wealth of Europe consisted of oil that was owned by the Germans, and the British only had so many votes. Now imagine what it would be like if there was a single multi-party system in the United States of Europe. This is what a lot of African countries are like. Europe has only twenty-three language groups. Nigeria has 400. Uganda has about forty. The multiplicity of ethnic groups, squeezed into states that they had no part in creating, creates problems for Africa. To misquote Bill Clinton: 'It's the politics, stupid!'

People say: 'Africa is like this, Africa is like that', but what has really damaged Africa in my experience is its politics. That has been the cause of the violence and the failure to develop. In particular, I am referring to those people who ran into Chinua Achebe's house, slammed the door and sat inside keeping all the wealth to themselves. In my view, it has not always been in their interests for their countries to develop.

Outsiders have tried different policies, but when you look at the policies that are being advocated for Africa now they are in fact much the same policies that were being advocated in 1980. It also needs to be acknowledged that other countries in what was known as the Third World, especially in Asia, used those policies and have done well. So what is it that has actually held Africa back? It certainly is not a lack of money. Would a Marshall Plan save Africa? My answer is: absolutely not. Africa has already had one several times over, but it has not produced much in terms of results. The whole project of giving Africa more aid – as advocated by Bob Geldof, Tony Blair and Gordon Brown – has completely missed the cause of Africa's failure. There seems to be a belief that all Africa needs is money, and then it will just develop and take off. The reason why this did not work in the first place – although, as we have seen, it often works perfectly well at a local level – the reason why these nation states have not taken off has been their politics. This goes back to the creation of these states and the trust – or lack of it – between the people within these states. Many of them simply do not work: there is no law, no national identity, no common purpose and no nationally accepted leadership.

Congo has to be the ultimate example of what is called 'a vampire state'. A lot of Africans now refer to it as such. It was just sucking the blood out of its population. However, this is not untypical in Africa. It is clear from the figures: 40% of privately owned capital is held outside the continent. This capital flight amounts to something like $60-100 billion, leaving at a rate of about $15 billion a year. This is slightly less than what is currently supposed to be flowing in in the form of aid. This reminds me of a proverb that the Kenyans used about the Moi government: 'If you are the only one on the teat, it does not matter how thin the cow gets.' In other words, as long as you are in power and you are doing well, it does not matter if your country is destroyed, as in the case of Zimbabwe. This is the logical result of the African political system, but it is not understood by the whole aid business and those who believe outsiders can change Africa.

Even if the problem of corruption – the problem of the elite sitting in the house, keeping everyone else out – were solved, there would still be a lack of capacity. The one issue that I believe we should concentrate on is, ironically, the one that Tony Blair actually advocated early on: education, education, education. You can see it if you can travel down any road in Africa at the beginning of the day: the thousands of school uniforms, a river of them flowing along – red ones, green ones, blue ones – thousands of children walking to school. The enthusiasm for education and schooling in Africa must be second to none in the world. African kids going to school look as if they are heading towards the future.

Tony Blair developed his grand plan, based on aid, trade and debt relief, and called for the doubling of aid to Africa. In fact, the Commission for Africa focused on a lot of other areas, and it has raised some very interesting issues. In the end, however, I believe that Mr Blair insisted that the Commission's report focus on those three issues, which could be sold to the electorate and the other members of the G8. When Sir Nicholas Stern, the economist who wrote it, did all the sums, adding up what it would cost to bring development – education, health, roads and everything else – to Africa, by an amazing coincidence, he ended up with exactly the same figure that the politicians had been calling for: a doubling of aid to Africa. Not a penny more or less. Instead of producing an objective report, the Commission was forced to conclude that money was going to solve the problem.

As in the case of the aid agency that tried to develop that valley in Ethiopia, however, things do not always work out quite as planned. That is why I personally believe that the most important thing is to understand Africa. In fact, this is the Royal African Society's mission. Listen and try to learn and understand how it works. Only then can you work with it and help it.

As Paul Collier notes in his paper, Africa is beginning to change fast. However, my views on the drivers of this change differ slightly from his. He talks about more democracy and the ending of wars, but I believe that the rise of China is the key driver. First of all, China drives commodity prices, so the amount of money already received by the oil states of West Africa from the increase in the price of oil is more than Africa will receive in aid. This, in turn, has led to the Star of Africa Fund's advertisement in the Evening Standard: 'Bring us your money!' It is not only oil producers who getting wealthy. Even countries that just sell sorghum and other basic crops are benefiting from the rise in prices. At a basic level, Africa is a primary commodity producer. Thanks to the Chinese demand for primary commodities, the price has risen again after falling from the early 1970s right through until the late 1990s. In contrast, the prices of manufactured goods rose during the same period, which created many problems for Africa. Now, thanks to China and other Asian countries, the prices of manufactured goods are falling again.

The second way in which China affects Africa is by its policy of government-to-government relations and non-interference. Paul Collier is very sceptical about this, but I am still neutral. African governments are tired of being told what to do, tired of the conditionalities, tired of the relationship with the West. China is a new partner for them – a partner that does not press things on them and does not interfere. It has also offered them vast amounts of money: $5 billion in loans and credits. This promise to double development assistance by 2009 was made at the November 2006 Africa summit in Beijing. In addition, $1.9 billion worth of trade deals were set up. At the previous summit, China had written off all of Africa's debt. It has also promised to provide skills training and education in everything from medicine to Mandarin. Many African schools now teach Mandarin.

The Centre for Chinese Studies at Stellenbosch University in South Africa publishes a weekly report on China and Africa. One of the reports for October 2007 contained the following information: China lends $5 billion to Congo for mining and infrastructure projects; Mauritania, China's newest oil supplier, gets a $61 million debt write-off; China National Oil Corporation buys a $2.3 billion stake in an offshore Nigerian oil and gas field; China will build a new dam on the Zambezi River in Mozambique which will cost them $2 billion; Minmitel, a Chinese metals company, buys a ferrochrome mine in South Africa and agrees to build a soccer stadium in Zambia for $70 million. This is all in one week. If you read the Centre's website, you cannot help but think that this is going to change Africa more than anything in the last fifty years.

The second driver, in my view, is mobile phones. Like everyone else, including the suppliers, I thought that mobile phones in Africa were probably unnecessary. No one except a few very rich people would buy them. Instead, the opposite occurred. The number of subscribers was four times higher than estimated in Nigeria. This showed one thing: Africa is not that poor. Mobile phones were not just being bought by flashy middle class bankers and lawyers. Market women, taxi-drivers, ordinary people like that – even nomads. In Somalia, I actually saw a nomad with his hands over his herding stick, using his phone to check the price of lamb in Jeddah with the traders in Berbera. For the nomads, it is crucial to know when to come down from the hills with their herds. If there is no boat ready, and the price is not right, they have to hang around the port and buy food for their animals. Market women in Lagos check the prices in the region so they know when to buy and how much to pay, and no taxi-driver in Africa will let you out of his car until he has given you his mobile number. It is said that one of the problems of Africa is time-keeping, but with mobile phones this problem disappears. 'Where are you? OK – I'll wait.' These kinds of changes make life much easier. Mobile phones have also had a huge political impact. In the 2000 elections in Ghana, I saw how radio stations said to people: 'Tell us what is going on at your polling station.' Suddenly, there were calls live on air – ballot-stuffing going on here, violence here, and all those things that Paul Collier mentions in his paper. Fixing elections becomes much more difficult when mobile phone usage is widespread, and mobile phones and radio stations allow the voices of ordinary people to be heard. The mobile phone is a great leveller. Suddenly people can talk to each other and find out they all think the same thing. Combined with radio, they are really transforming Africa.

The third driver is the return of exiles, especially professionals. In West Africa, I have recently come across several bankers, lawyers and doctors who have said: 'Well, I think I can make a living here now. I am coming back because the quality of life for my children will be so much better in Africa than it will be in east London.' A lot of people are now going back, and I believe that anything the government can do to help this process will be good. For example, to allow people to have a foot in both camps and not force them to make a choice, so that Africans here can go back for six months and try it out without losing their position here.

This is a moment of great opportunity for Africa: the wars have died down, and income has gone up. The question is how this money is going to be invested. Are the African states going to blow it all on a party? That is what a lot of them did in the early 1970s, the last time there was a commodities boom, and they ended up with nothing to show for it when it ended except for a terrible hangover and huge debts. Or is it going to be invested in the populations so they can reap the benefits in the future?

DfID's Transition from Aid Agency to Development Ministry: What Does Policy Coherence Imply?

Patrick Watt*

1. Introduction

Since mid-2007, when Gordon Brown became prime minister, there has been much discussion in the Department for International Development (DfID) about its ambitions to transform itself from an aid agency, responsible mainly for spending the UK overseas aid budget, into a development ministry capable of pushing a coherent and consistent approach to development across the whole of the UK government.

There are two aspects to the challenge of creating a coherent development policy across Whitehall. For rich countries like the United Kingdom to play an enabling role in the development process, they need both to positively assist the poorest countries and to stop doing those things that undermine development (a kind of 'Hippocratic oath' for development). At the moment, discussions about development policy tend to focus on the positive agenda, and in the United Kingdom especially on the role of DfID in giving aid. However, the UK aid programme is only one part, and often a minor part, of how the United Kingdom impacts on the development prospects of the world's poorest countries: a majority of developing countries, and even of low-income countries, receive only small sums of UK aid or none at all.

The government recognises this 'beyond aid' agenda in principle and, to some extent, in practice. At least two important changes have occurred since Douglas Alexander became secretary of state for international development. First, responsibility for trade has been moved out of the Department for Trade

* Patrick Watt, Policy Coordinator, Action Aid.

and Industry (now Business, Enterprise and Regulatory Reform, or DBERR) into DfID, with the secretary of state now chairing a Cabinet Committee on trade. Second, the Comprehensive Spending Review in the autumn of 2007 – which set public expenditure priorities for the next three years – placed a substantial portion of UK Overseas Development Assistance (ODA) under the control of other Whitehall departments, notably the Foreign and Commonwealth Office (FCO), the Ministry of Defence (MoD) and the Department of the Environment (DoE).

The second change – that of increasing the stake of other Whitehall departments in the aid budget – partly reflects the pressure created by a rising budget to do more than just give aid (which is projected to reach £9 billion by 2010-2011, or about one-third of current defence spending). However, it is also motivated by a recognition that a whole range of issues with a major bearing on development – migration, conflict, financial sector regulation and climate change, to name but a few – fall under the remit of other government departments. Given that the United Kingdom is one of the few countries with a genuine global reach, through its role in global governance structures such as the United Nations, the International Monetary Fund and G8, and through its economic, military and cultural power, getting the government as a whole to align with the development priorities articulated in recent DfID White Papers offers potentially large benefits for developing countries themselves.

2. A CHANGING UK DEVELOPMENT POLICY LANDSCAPE

DfID emerged from the Labour election victory in 1997, and was an abrupt departure from development policy under the previous Conservative government. Tony Blair's government fulfilled longstanding pledges to give international development a cabinet seat and full departmental status. The Overseas Development Agency was hived off from the Foreign Office, where it had been an implementing agency, and morphed into DfID. The creation of the new department was followed by substantial increases in the size of the aid budget and significant changes in how it is delivered. Aid increased from 0.24% of national income to 0.52% in 2006, and the United Kingdom has committed itself to meeting the UN target of giving 0.7% of national income in ODA by 2013 – something currently only managed by Sweden, Norway, Denmark, the Netherlands and Luxembourg.

In 2001, DfID aid was completely untied from the requirement that it be spent on UK goods and services – a practice that persists in many donor agencies and one that substantially reduces the value of aid to recipients.

There was also a big shift in geographical and sectoral focus, so that approaching 90% of all UK aid now goes to low-income countries, with more of it spent on basic services that benefit the poor, and less of it on major infrastructure projects. Perhaps most significantly, the organising framework for UK aid has changed, with the eight UN Millennium Development Goals (MDGs) for halving poverty and improving outcomes in health, education and other areas becoming the overarching objectives of UK development policy. This commitment to focusing aid on poverty reduction and insulating it from potentially competing commercial and geopolitical objectives was cemented by the International Development Act of 2002, which stipulated that aid must be given solely for the purpose of promoting poverty reduction.

Beyond aid volume and effectiveness, some foreign policy roles were ceded to DfID after 1997, especially in Africa: it was Hilary Benn rather than Margaret Beckett who negotiated on behalf of the UK government in the Darfur talks, and Clare Short rather than Robin Cook who led UK foreign policy on the Great Lakes region after the Rwandan genocide (more recently, this has been partly reversed with Africa and the United Nations falling to FCO minister Mark Malloch Brown).

The Conservatives have in recent years supported these changes and promised to retain DfID's cabinet status, the 0.7% target and the International Development Act if they return to government. David Cameron's announcement in 2006 of a Conservative Commission on Global Poverty – one of six new policy reports produced for the party – heralded an emerging consensus on aid in the United Kingdom. It is still a long way from the shared support for high aid levels among Christian Democrats and Social Democrats in some other Northern European countries, but it nonetheless signals a real political shift.

3. What does policy coherence imply?

In some senses, these changes in UK development policy since 1997 beg the question: 'What next?' Since 1997, UK development policy has shifted towards a Nordic-style approach – on aid-related issues, DfID keeps company with the Swedes, Dutch and others in the 'like-minded' group. Yet on wider international policy, notwithstanding the brief experiment in an 'ethical foreign policy' after 1997, a similar transformation has not taken place.

This should be a cause for concern at a time when the issues with which development, foreign and security policy are grappling are often closely entwined. Paul Collier's recent influential book, *The Bottom Billion*, draws on a growing body of evidence in highlighting the importance of peace and the rule of law to poverty reduction. It is also the case that, in many contexts, from Afghanistan to Haiti, and from Liberia to East Timor, the operational distinction between development, foreign and security policy is not clear-cut: development interventions overlap with military interventions and are often tied up with 'rich country interests' from drugs control to migration and energy security.

Unfortunately for DfID, the MDGs do not provide much practical guidance on how to link development, foreign and security policy. The first seven goals are concerned with progress on income, poverty, hunger, health, education, environment and gender equality. The eighth goal, on 'partnership', is concerned with how to achieve the preceding goals through aid, domestic spending by developing country governments, changes to the trade and investment system and other instruments for poverty reduction. In principle, MDG 8 should guide donor thinking on a coherent approach to development, but, unlike the other goals, it has never distilled into clear targets and commitments.

Despite the growing recognition of the links between development, foreign and security policy, several key questions thus remain unresolved. In particular, is foreign policy a sub-set of development policy, with poverty reduction the overriding purpose of the United Kingdom's external actions? (In short, does policy coherence mean coherence *for development*?) Or is development subordinate to wider geopolitical concerns? Or are they related, yet separate? There is no agreement within government, nor even in the 'development industry', about the answers to these questions, which, unsurprisingly, tend to reflect institutional interests.

4. DfID's Response and Questions for UK Policy

DfID has started to forge its own response to these questions during the past two years. Three significant changes are identified here. First, in 2006, the Department published its third White Paper since 1997. In it, policy coherence for development was identified as the next challenge, with a particular focus on governance and climate change as areas where DfID should be playing a stronger cross-Whitehall role to ensure that a development perspective was incorporated into government policy. Second, as already mentioned, other government departments were given parts of the aid budget to spend under the Comprehensive Spending Review of late 2007. One notable example is the Environmental Transformation Fund, which has committed £800 million over a three-year period to helping countries adapt to the effects of climate change and to environmentally sustainable development. Half of this money will be spent by the Department of the Environment rather than DfID, partly in a bid to get DEFRA (Department for Environment, Food and Rural Affairs) more actively involved in formulating development policy. Third, DfID ministers are carrying new cross-departmental remits. Among the posts created in mid-2007, an under-secretary of state now carries the trade brief with one foot each in DfID and DBERR (formerly the Department for Trade and Industry).

These changes raise some important questions for UK international policy. Assuming that DfID will be able to do what it wants to do and play a fuller cross-Whitehall role, we could expect significant changes to key areas of UK public policy. Take migration, which is an issue that has so far been dominated by debates about its impact on UK society and the economy. Relatively little attention has been devoted, outside the specific issue of health workers in the NHS, to the (positive and negative) impacts of migration on the developing countries from which many non-EU migrants come. It is conceivable that a migration policy driven at least in part by the potential of migration as a development tool would look very different from the system currently under consideration.

There are also questions about how greater coherence for development would play out at country level. Afghanistan is a case in point. The United Kingdom belongs to a military coalition, parts of which are committed to eradicating the opium crop that supplies the European market for heroin. Arguably, this strategy is immiserating many small-scale Afghan farmers and undermining many of the poverty reduction efforts being pursued by donor agencies from the NATO countries. There are no easy answers to the question of how to tackle these twin challenges of drugs control and development in a coherent way, but it at least needs to be recognised that, in Afghanistan, objectives in these two areas are, at best, in tension with each other and, at worst, in outright contradiction of each other.

In the case of Ethiopia, trade-offs have been made between the donors' concerns about the Ethiopian government's record, especially after the 2005 elections, and the fact that a sudden withdrawal of aid could substantially damage the government's ability to provide basic services. US and European interest in Ethiopia's role in Somalia further have complicated the policy mix. The point in these and other cases is that working out what policy coherence for development means operationally in developing countries requires difficult judgements about how to balance widely differing objectives. It is a moot point whether there is sufficient consensus across government to avoid these decisions being mainly about trade-offs between different departmental interests. Are other departments really brought into a vision of policy coherence *for development*?

Developing countries themselves may also be sceptical about aspects of this agenda. First, what looks sensible from a Whitehall perspective – such as the decision in the last spending round for lots of government departments to get a slice of ODA – may make less sense from the perspective of a finance or planning ministry in a low-income country that is wrestling with the transaction costs of a huge number of different donor instruments, initiatives and projects. Equally, developing countries may be wary of more coherence depending on the direction it takes. For example, a more coherent approach to aid and trade policy could involve donors deciding to make aid conditional on liberalisation of key markets and on providing technical assistance to this end. Unless a policy coherence agenda respects and responds to the policy priorities of the recipient country, there is a risk that it will undermine the 'ownership' principles that the United Kingdom and other donors have advertised through the OECD Paris aid effectiveness agenda.

For DfID, current efforts to build policy coherence across Whitehall also raise questions about the poverty focus of UK aid. Aid that is not part of DfID's budget – of which there is a growing amount – is not legally covered by the International Development Act requirement that it be used for poverty reduction. So while it may qualify as ODA under OECD Development Assistance Committee rules, it cannot be assumed that aid spending is necessarily poverty-reducing. Given that this is the case, there may be an argument for strengthening the provisions in the International Development Act to cover all UK ODA.

5. Conclusions

Current efforts to extend DfID's policy role beyond aid and into other areas of international policy are happening in the context of competing objectives between Whitehall departments. The FCO, MoD, DEFRA, DfID and other departments with an international remit have very different institutional interests, and it is unclear whether DfID currently has the political clout and sufficient media and public backing to pursue this course. The wider UK development sector and the members of the public who campaign with non-governmental organisations will be crucial in strengthening DfID's hand *vis-à-vis* other parts of government.

Complete policy coherence for development, or for any other objective, may be unrealistic, but there are steps that could be taken to reduce the current lack of coordination between development and other areas of UK public policy. First, a 'good for development' test could be applied – learning from experiences in Sweden and the Netherlands – to all areas of UK policy to ensure, at a minimum, that policies that undermine the effectiveness of DfID aid are not adopted. Government leadership, especially from No. 10 Downing Street and the Cabinet Office, will be crucial in helping to drive this agenda.

Second, donor countries such as the United Kingdom need to do a much better job of articulating their priorities across all areas of international policy to developing countries, in order to facilitate a genuine policy dialogue about how to match donor and recipient expectations and interests. The real test of whether greater policy coherence has been achieved is not whether harmony has broken out between government departments in London but whether, from the perspective of a low-income country, UK interventions at least equal the sum of their parts. To gauge whether this is the case, DfID needs to move beyond the current and rather narrow preoccupation with aid effectiveness and start evaluating the UK government's development effectiveness.

Ashanti Development in Ghana

Penny David*

The charity I work for, Ashanti Development, is based on the friendship of three people: Martha Boadu, a Ghanaian living in central London; David Williamson, a volunteer WaterAid engineer; and me, Martha's friend and neighbour.

Martha came to the United Kingdom in 1982. She married, had children and now works as a night cleaner and child-minder for the London Borough of Camden. But she never ceased to worry about the terrible lives of the people of her home village, Gyetiase (pronounced Jay-tee-ahser), and in particular the women who, she said, had to walk for four or five, or even six, hours a day to fetch water. From time to time, she would present me with requests for donations for a project for the village, but I was busy and never paid much attention.

Then, in 2002, Martha asked me to look at an estimate for £32,000 she had been sent by the Ghana Water Company for laying three kilometres of water pipes from the mains supply to Gyetiase. She wanted to know whether the amount was reasonable and whether I had any suggestions on how to raise the money. I rang WaterAid, and one of their water engineers, David Williamson, helped me conduct long-range bargaining with the Ghana Water Company, which brought the estimate down by several thousands of pounds. He was still not satisfied and volunteered to visit the village if we could find his fare. We did this, and he brought the total down to £18,000, picking up a grant of £10,000 from the UK High Commission in Accra in the process. We managed to raise the rest of the money in grants and donations, and the taps were finally turned on in Gyetiase amid general rejoicing in April 2005.

At that point, David and I were inclined to consider the job done and to move on. However, one of our corporate donors informed us that they had difficulty spending money well in Africa, that they had been pleased with the

* Penny David, Chief Executive, Ashanti Development.

way we had spent it and that they had therefore decided to give us £10,000 a year indefinitely to continue the work. We were taken aback by this unsolicited gift, which was not entirely welcome, but realised that £10,000 a year would enable us to do a great deal in Africa, and finally decided we should not refuse. In December 2005, the three of us registered Ashanti Development as a charity.

At this time, I knew little about Ghana, much less than is shown in the table below. I knew it was peaceful and prosperous compared with its near neighbours and that, with oil recently discovered offshore, its prospects looked good. I quickly discovered that inflation was high and often stimulated by shortages of hydro-electricity as a result of drought, and that prices and price rises varied widely in different parts of the country. I also came to doubt some of the official statistics. For example, Ghanaians are eligible for free anti-retroviral drugs, but obtaining a test for HIV/Aids can be difficult or even impossible, raising questions about the low official figure for HIV/Aids.

Development Indicators for Ghana in 2006	
Population, mid-year (millions)	22.5
Life expectancy at birth (years)	57
Infant mortality rate (per 1,000 live births)	68
Child malnutrition (% children under 5)	22
Literacy rate, youth female (% of females ages 15-24)	65.5
GNI (current US$ billions)	11.7
GNI per capita (Atlas method, US$)	520
Prevalence of HIV, total (% of population ages 15-49)	2.3
GDP (US$ billions)	12.9

Source: World Development Indicators

Gyetiase is in the Ashanti Region, which, by virtue of its gold and cocoa production, is the most prosperous region in the country. Unfortunately, the money does not seem to benefit local people, and, to make matters worse, NGOs bypass Ashanti, concentrating on the poorer regions in the north. As a result, the villages we work with are among the poorest that David, who has spent his working life in developing countries and disaster areas, has ever seen.

Gyetiase is on a hilltop and has 1,200 inhabitants, of whom 46% are under eighteen years old.[1] As I have already mentioned, until recently, the women

[1] ProNet, *Baseline Survey Conducted at Gyetiase in the Sekyere West District in Ashanti Region* (Ashanti Development, June 2006).

spent many hours a day fetching water and consequently had lost their traditional skills, like basket weaving or beadwork. At some point in their lives, most were forced to go abroad to work as prostitutes, so HIV/Aids is probably very widespread. The doctors we take to Gyetiase report seeing indications, such as a type of skin rash, at their surgeries.

As for the men, they farm on the hillsides, producing crops such as cassava, ground nuts, maize, yam, cocoa yam, okra and tomatoes. The grow enough to feed themselves and their families and make an annual surplus that we estimate at under £70 a year for the whole village. They use this money to buy clothes and shoes. In past years, they also grew cocoa, but it no longer thrives, perhaps because the soil is exhausted.

If you were anything of a strategic thinker living in Gyetiase, until recently you must have judged the outlook to be grim. For all sorts of reasons, it is difficult to move house in Africa, particularly in Ghana, which is densely populated and where much of the land is privately owned. Gyetiase must have seemed like a prison, stuck on top of a hill. The village was producing more and more children and the soil was producing less and less food. You must have thought that things could only get worse. Of course, you could try your luck finding work in one of the cities but, being illiterate and untrained, your prospects would have been poor.

There was, however, at least one other exit available. You could ask the head of your extended family to lend you the family gold, which had been collected in small lumps from the surface of the earth over several centuries. You could raise a bank loan against the gold and use it to buy a ticket to the United Kingdom. Then you could borrow or rent a friend's passport, get yourself a holiday visa and come to London, where you would post back the passport and look for work as an unlicensed taxi-driver or hotel worker. If you followed this route, your first duty would be to repay the bank loan and redeem the family gold. Soon after, you would be able to send money home to feed your wife and children – but you would very likely never see them again. The lives of illegal immigrants are typically miserable and lonely, and are lived in constant fear of discovery. Many miss their families terribly, while their families in Ghana long to see their husbands or fathers again.

Of course, a few illegals ultimately come home to Gyetiase. There are two or three large houses on the outskirts of the village that some of them have built. A few other houses, in a permanently half-finished condition, were built by illegals who were discovered and sent home and now have no money to finish the work.

The presence of these well-travelled people serves to add an unexpected street-wisdom to the local culture. The traditional village chief, for example, worked for twenty-six years for London Underground, and has a good line in Cockney jokes; while in 2006 the village elders responded to consultation about a new school building with the excellent and unexpected suggestion that we apply for a local authority grant.

There is no electricity in Gyetiase. Typical family size is about ten to seventeen, while one or two other children will have probably died in infancy of convulsions, usually due to drinking polluted water.[2] Families live in one- or two-roomed huts, using a rusty, roofless outhouse with a bucket as a washhouse and cooking on wood fires in the open air. Until recently, knowing that liquid seeps down from the hilltop to pollute the stream, these 1,200 people shared a ten-seater communal latrine. Long queues formed each morning in front of it and the smell travelled across the village.

Gyetiase has a primary and a junior secondary school where children receive nine years of free compulsory education in line with state rules.[3] In the past, pre-school children were left to fend for themselves while their parents worked, and some suffered serious accidents as a result. During the 1990s, Martha saved £13,000 from her wages to build a pre-school for the village and later gave this to the state. It is now attached to the primary school.

Everyone in Ashanti is desperate to own a mobile phone, and the connection between London and Gyetiase is usually better than between London and parts of Cornwall. Recharging a mobile phone may mean a long walk to the nearest electricity supply, but mobiles provide access to key information. They inform farmers, for example, of comparative selling prices for farm produce in several market towns, enabling them to know where they may get the best prices. They also enable villagers to summon help or keep in touch with relations who have moved perhaps to Kumasi – only forty kilometres distance but a long journey by bus.

As for health, the most widespread complaint is among women who suffer from severe muscular-skeletal problems from carrying water and other weights on their heads. The older they get, the worse this becomes, and some of the elderly are in constant pain, incontinent and unable to lean forward without falling. We are taking a physiotherapist to Ashanti in the hope that she can suggest a mass exercise programme that might be adopted in schools as well as among adults, with a view to prevention or cure.

---

[2] Much of the information in this section comes from structured interviews carried out in 2004-2007 with village residents chosen mainly for their ability to speak English.

[3] The Republic of Ghana, *The Educational System in Ghana,* available at: <http://www.ghanaembassy.or.jp/educational.html>.

The next most prevalent complaint is eye disease, including cataracts and a virulent form of conjunctivitis. Ashanti is on a trade route from North Africa to West Africa, via the old desert caravan routes, and the traders brought conjunctivitis from North Africa long ago.[4] They also account for the caftans some people wear and the Islamic religion.

Then, of course, there are the water-related sicknesses, diarrhoea and dysentery, and fevers including malaria. There are worms, which everyone has, and malnutrition – or at least lack of vitamins. The diet in Ghana is often said to be the worst in Africa.[5] Owing to poverty, Ghanaians eat very little meat, and little fruit or green vegetables through choice. They supplement the lack of protein in their diets with beans and ground nuts, but argue that fruit is worthless and not even proper food.

Report by Dr Claire Walford
Gyetiase Clinic, November 2006

Most patients had more than one presenting problem. The commonest presenting complaints in the general clinics were:

- *neck, waist (mid-back) or lower back pain;*
- *leg pain;*
- *conjunctivitis;*
- *poor vision/blindness due to cataract, corneal scarring, short- and long-sightedness; and*
- *fever often diagnosed as malaria, acute respiratory infection or diarrhoeal disease of varying origin.*

Less frequent presentations were:

- *high blood pressure either known or just identified;*
- *diabetes;*
- *abdominal pain, including chronic malaria presenting as enlarged spleen, jaundice and urinary tract infection;*
- *surgical conditions such as keloids, hernias;*
- *skin infections and injuries (cuts, burns, ulcers);*
- *cerebral palsy and delayed child development;*
- *congenital abnormalities, e.g., clubbed feet;*
- *malnutrition in adults and children;*
- *infestation, e.g., roundworm, ringworm, presumed threadworm;*
- *HIV – known or presumed; and*
- *gynaecological problems, e.g., heavy or painful periods, infertility.*

4 Interview with eye specialists at Kumasi Komfo Anokye Hospital, November 2006.
5 Interview with the London School of Hygiene and Tropical Medicine, June 2006.

In 2005, we took a GP to Gyetiase to obtain information about health. The villagers asked very strongly that the clinic he ran should be repeated, at least until some more sustainable healthcare became available to them, and we therefore brought other doctors in the following two years. One of our doctor-trustee's reports of the clinic she ran in 2006 appears on the previous page.

There are many churches in Gyetiase. Most, including the Pentecostal Church, Divine Grace International, Deeper Life Bible Church, Saviour Church, Seventh Day Adventists, Methodists, Church of Christ and Salvation Army, are based on Christian, particularly Methodist, teaching. There is also a Muslim congregation and two Kwatra churches, traditional religions worshipping the gods of wood, stones, sun and moon, run by witchdoctors who make libations of whisky and sacrifice animals.[6] The witchdoctors initially worked in opposition to us, particularly to Martha, who is the leader of the Divine Grace International Church. However, the principal witchdoctor has recently been negotiating with her on his possible conversion.

It would be hard to overstate the importance of religion to the village. Life is incredibly difficult, and the people consider God to be their only hope of a better life. They pray for up to half an hour on waking and again before sleeping. Many attend church every morning while it is still dark and spend hours at services on Sundays. Church is also a social event, and people typically meet their husbands and wives among church congregations.

The work that Ashanti Development undertakes in villages like Gyetiase can be divided into three main parts: water, health and general development. We always start by providing clean water and follow this with training in health and hygiene. This is a complex subject, and the training would probably be impossible to deliver for someone of a different culture, so we use a Ghanaian NGO called ProNet, founded and trained by WaterAid, for this purpose. They are remarkably successful and certainly, without their training, the villagers might well revert to drinking water from the stream. It is, after all, free – except in terms of time and effort, and these are contributed by the women – and many apparently think it preferable to the 'tasteless' liquid that comes from water pipes.

Finally, ProNet teaches the villagers how to make a latrine for each household. Villagers provide their labour and all locally available materials, while Ashanti Development pays for the rest.

We face two serious problems during this work. The first is the result of climate change, which often means that water supplies that were safe a few years

[6] Interviews, see *supra* n. 2.

ago now need large-scale investment, of the type only the government can provide, to remain so. The second is the geological structure of the ground, which makes it difficult to identify where best to drill boreholes. Only one in three of those drilled by the District (the equivalent of a UK local authority)[7] yields enough water to be worth the effort, and drilling is expensive.

In 2007, in line with their mission statement to 'shape a better world',[8] consulting engineers Ove Arup seconded a hydro-geologist and a geochemist free of charge to Ashanti Development to advise on this problem.[9] The two of them first carried out lengthy desk research, and made a site visit in September 2007. Their report[10] found that few groundwater exploration projects had been carried out in the region and that there was a high failure rate, but they were unable to identify a clear pattern of yields in relation to rock type. In other words, fewer than one in two boreholes was likely to be successful.

They therefore recommended that alternative surface water sources should be considered, including rainwater harvesting, infiltration galleries, mini-dams and borehole drilling, the latter on the basis of a more informed selection of site than had previously been available. They recommended that the work should be carried out in consultation with local water agencies, and that it should be documented with a view to informing future projects in similar terrain.[11]

At about the same time, we were fortunate in obtaining annual grants of £100,000 for the years 2008 and 2009 to provide water to outlying villages. There are 220 communities in the Sekyere West District, and Ashanti Development intends to provide clean water to as many as possible.

The second stage of our work is to provide primary healthcare. In Gyetiase, we have recently completed the ground floor of a ten-room, two-storey

---

[7] M. Meredith, *The State of Africa* (London, Simon & Schuster 2005). The current constitution is based on the one introduced by the British before independence in 1957.

[8] O. Arup, *The Key Speech* (Ove Arup & Partners 1970), available at: <http//www.arup.com/_assets/_download/download5.pdf>.

[9] See M. Tindale, N. Swain, V. Coy and S. Parry-Jones, *Global Strategic Partnerships to Share International and Local Expertise Between Private Sector and NGOs*, paper submitted to the 33rd WEDC International Conference, Accra, Ghana, 2008.

[10] Ove Arup & Partners, Ltd., *Water Resources Survey Report for Ashanti Development, Ghana* (Ashanti Development, October 2007).

[11] Ove Arup also organised a survey of waste disposal in several villages and will use this information to recommend ways of tackling the growing problem of waste. In one market town, an enormous rubbish tip is located next to the principal water supply, constituting a serious threat of cholera.

clinic to serve the village and surrounding communities. It will be staffed by a full-time nurse or midwife and equipped with some of the second-hand medical equipment that will become available when the Elizabeth Garrett Anderson Hospital in London closes in 2008. We hope it will also serve as a centre for other healthcare workers, who will be trained to work in outlying villages, and for a mobile clinic/ambulance.

Because we are not satisfied with the quality of local training available for healthcare workers, we are also planning as often as possible to bring over medical staff from University College London Hospital (UCLH), asking them to pay their own fares, board and lodging. We hope they will run clinics, including occasional clinics in specialist health areas, while boosting the training of the Ghanaians we recruit. There will also be an initial large build-up of patients, most of whom have never received any form of medical care before, for them to work through.

Forty doctors, a nutritionist, a physiotherapist and a couple of nurses responded to the first advertisement we ran on UCLH's internal website for medical staff to spend two weeks in Gyetiase at their own expense. In our experience, medical staff not only want to help developing countries but, like the Ove Arup specialists mentioned above, also see this as an important means of gaining experience. We recognise that it is not a sustainable exercise but hope that it will fill a short-term gap.

The clinic will have a second function. One of its rooms will be equipped as an operating theatre and used for cataract surgery under the provisions of Vision 2020. We are currently paying for two local women to receive training at Kumasi Komfo Anokye Hospital, so that they will be able to identify operable cataracts. They will then be employed at the clinic at Gyetiase with the aim of summoning the Kumasi surgeons when they have enough patients for one or two days' worth of operations.

Surgery will be part-funded by the Ghanaian National Insurance Scheme, though at about £10 a year it is too expensive for most villagers. We are therefore extremely grateful to SpecSavers, the London opticians, for agreeing to finance the first 1,000 operations. SpecSavers are also collecting second-hand spectacles for Gyetiase in their London shops.

Operating space in Kumasi Hospital is at a premium, and the eye surgeons are considering using Gyetiase for more of their operations, possibly even making it a centre of eye health for the District.

Our third objective is to pump a little money into the local economy. Thus, for example, we buy local farm produce to provide free school meals for children between the ages of three and five. We do this in the knowledge that if a malnourished child survives to age three, he or she will probably live to be an adult. A spin-off benefit is that, as soon as we announce we are going to provide free meals, registrations typically double. However, we still spend time arranging for local hospitals to admit starving one- and two-year-olds, in the hope they survive long enough to qualify for free school meals.

At the villagers' request, we have also set up a wood-carving school. They found a carving teacher for the school and persuaded him and his family to move to Gyetiase for a year. We now sell carvings in UCLH's reception hall, along with strips of the traditional *kente* cloth, and clothing or greetings cards made from local material in this country. Our hope is that we may be able to train Gyetiase women to take over the sewing, thereby giving them a regular income.

In 2006, Ashanti Development was given thirty-five acres of farmland by a local chief in gratitude for the water we had brought to his village. As stated above, the men of Gyetiase are short of farmland, and we are now on the verge of concluding an agreement about how they will use it. Lending money to men in the developing world is high-risk, but we cannot see how the villagers can manage without loans for seed, tubers, tools and a tractor to clear the land. In mid-2007, we therefore asked the men to work out a safe system on the understanding that, when the money was fully repaid, they or other people from Gyetiase might borrow it again and that this would continue indefinitely.

The men suggested they divide themselves into three groups, growing cassava (of which they say there is a national shortage), cow pea (which will hopefully boost their protein consumption) and yam, respectively, on a rotating basis. We have arranged for them to receive training in setting up this system, including selecting officers, and opening and using one bank account for each group. In the planting season, in March, we will provide money to hire a tractor to clear the land and to buy seed or tubers and tools. After each harvest, the men will pay back as much as they can afford, with the aim of repaying the total, plus 23% interest (the standard local agricultural interest rate) before the end of the year. If any man fails to repay his share, the rest of the group have undertaken to pay it back for him.

The men added all sorts of embellishments – providing, for example, that each man signs a copy of the agreement, possibly by means of a thumbprint, and attaches a passport photograph. They also asked that the loans should be extended to cover the cost of Wellington boots, to protect them from snake-bites. We have told them that if all goes well, they may borrow the money again for a second year so that they can extend the land, and that after the cassava harvest we will buy the women a cassava-milling machine to enable them to market *gari* locally and also provide technical and organisational training for this purpose.

Thereafter, the village will redistribute the money in the form of new loans. We doubt there will be a shortage of applicants, as we regularly receive requests for money, often based on carefully thought-out plans. People in particular want to breed grasscutters – a hamster-like animal that is a good source of protein – and keep bees.

In the second half of 2008, two British women have agreed to go out to Ashanti for several months to set up a micro-finance system for the women. This is a system of small loans, repayable over a long period with a high rate of interest.[12] It has been hugely successful in many parts of the world, though less so in Central and West Africa for reasons we do not know, though possibly some form of local adaptation is required.

We have also financed the construction of a clinic and one household latrine per family, as well as public latrines for the schools. We intended to pay for labouring work for the construction of the clinic as a means of putting money into the local economy, but the villagers decided to do the work themselves, free of charge. We were told that in June 2007 there were sometimes over 200 men working on site. This gives us confidence that they have acquired a sort of 'ownership', which will encourage them to maintain and manage it well in our absence – but leaves us to find other means of putting money into their pockets.

Finally, we would like to improve education, particularly among primary school children. The local language is Twi, and the children need to learn English before they can progress to reading and writing. Many currently leave school illiterate, so in 2006 we invited the District Director of Education to come to London and visit some of our primary schools, in the hope she would pick up new teaching methods. As a direct result of this, she is transforming the Gyetiase primary school into a model school for the District and encouraging teachers from other schools to come and observe. Some of the schools she visited have collected and shipped books and teaching aids to Ghana, and several teachers have volunteered to teach for a few weeks in the summer. We hope this will be the start of a series of visits by volunteer teachers, whether or not they have teacher training.

Our aim for the next five years is to work for the benefit of all 143,000 people living in the 220 communities of Sekyere West District. Many consist of

---

[12] M. Yunus and A. Jolis, *Banker to the Poor: Micro-Lending and the Battle Against World Poverty* (Aurum Press Ltd. 1998).

refugees from eighteenth and nineteenth century tribal wars that took place all over Ghana and further afield.[13] The local chiefs allowed them to settle on hilltops in Sekyere West, and because of the bad roads and absence of bicycles or donkeys we suspect that many may still retain their particular tribal characteristics. We are therefore beginning to document their histories and cultures before they disappear.

For the future, we are confident that, with the help of Ove Arup and the grants we receive, we will succeed in taking many of these villages through the first two stages of our work – water and health. However, to help them develop further will take money, time and planning well above our current capacity. We are therefore seeking to network with community groups including Rotary Clubs, women's organisations, schools and churches that are willing to adopt a village or a school. We hope to take representatives of such groups out to Ashanti to introduce them to suitable villages and to interpret and facilitate their discussions with community representatives with the aim of drawing up agreed strategies for village development. Groups and villages will be free to choose the methods they prefer, and hopefully valuable lessons will be learned in the process. Ashanti Development will try to record and disseminate these, always remaining available for help and advice.

Ashanti Development has itself developed over the years. Two doctors, a banker and a lawyer have now joined our original three trustees and our annual income has risen from £25,000 in 2006 to £91,000 in 2007, with new grants of £100,000 promised for 2008 and 2009. We work to five key principles:

1. Our work must be sustainable – no village shall be allowed to become dependent on us. *Some of our work is clearly not sustainable except in the short term, but where necessary we include provision for its continuation by others. For example, we have a written commitment that the District will take responsibility for providing free school meals after five years; the village woodcarvers understand they must find outlets for their carvings over the next few months; and the UCLH doctors are invited to Gyetiase to clear a backlog of patients and boost training, but not indefinitely.*

[13] Martha describes how the people of Gyetiase left their homeland in southern Ghana following a dispute over high taxes. They walked for many weeks inland, gathering members of a different tribe en route, and finally settled in the town of Nusuta. However, because they were quarrelsome, the Nusuta chief eventually told them to leave but allowed them to settle in Gyetiase. She does not know when this took place.

2. Villagers must contribute to every project, usually by giving their labour free of charge. *As described above, they now carry out labouring work free of charge for us, whether we ask for it or not.*
3. Whenever we give a village clean water, we will follow it up with training in health and hygiene and the construction of latrines.
4. We will always consult the villagers and take account of their views at a formative stage in our programme planning. *Our methods vary according to the message involved and the circumstances and include public meetings, with or without giving the interpreter a written transcript to study in advance, and smaller meetings with the chief, assemblyman (the equivalent of a UK local authority councillor), village unit committee or other specific groups. We try to walk round the villages at least once a day, so that individuals can speak to us. We also consult through Martha, who often telephones several times a week; directly by letter; through ProNet; and, via a complicated route, by email. We judge our success by the feedback we receive. None of these methods is completely satisfactory, but we are improving with practice.*
5. Our trustees and helpers in the United Kingdom are 100% volunteers so that every penny we raise goes towards funding our programmes. *We have never run short of volunteers.*

We have recently developed an informal link with the Development Planning Unit of University College London, which is particularly valuable because none of our trustees is expert in general development. In the framework of this link, a group of students, known as Friends of Ashanti, makes a study of the Ashanti Region and responds to occasional requests from us for advice; they are also welcomed to carry out research in the area.

Ashanti Development's principal asset has always been the close friendship between Martha Boadu, David and me. At first, the object of our work was no more than to help Martha's friends obtain the clean water that they desperately needed. This meant that we were careful to check whether we were doing exactly what people wanted, and, since we were ignorant of local customs and language, we did this through Martha. Only later, as our reach extended, did more formal consultation become necessary.

Our work in Ashanti has so far been almost wholly with two villages because, until Ove Arup came to our rescue, we could not see how to provide others with clean water. Though at first this seemed disappointing, we now see it as a benefit: it enabled us to follow a steep learning curve without becoming overextended and forced us to consolidate relationships before moving on.

As a consequence, we now confidently entrust the villagers with supervision, procurement and overall management of all our building projects, and with the job of buying provisions and delivering free school meals to the children. At first we did this with trepidation, particularly since government and company officials were not slow in asking for a little ink for their pens. However, projects run by villagers recommended by the chief, assemblyman and Martha are invariably finished on or before time, and on or below budget, and the District Engineer comments that the buildings are of very high quality.

The villagers thank us constantly for our help, and show their gratitude with gifts of food and *kente* cloth. We were particularly pleased when, in September 2007, the sum of £250, which had been misappropriated during my first visit to Ashanti, was returned by the Unit Committee.

Gyetiase shows only small signs of economic upturn so far. These include the opening of at least ten small shops, some no more than table-top, while four people have bought bicycles. We cannot claim to have banished malnutrition but feel that free school meals must be making a contribution. Our hopes are that, with the help of the various micro-credit schemes we plan for 2008, which will for the first time put extra money into the hands of a substantial number of people, the villagers' finances will start to improve more rapidly.

As to the future of Ashanti Development, as time passes, we aim to put more work into the hands of volunteers,[14] either in this country or in Ghana. Meanwhile, each of our seven trustees now has responsibility for a specific area of interest, and Martha, David and I continue to coordinate from the centre.

We estimate that, at least in the short term, we shall continue to expand, and that the work will get easier as we learn more about the villages. The unknown for 2008 is whether we shall be able to network successfully with other community groups under our Adopt a Village scheme. If so, our rate of progress could become much faster.

---

[14] To find a new administrator to help me in the United Kingdom, I recently sent advertisements to all those in my email address book whose names began with A, B, C or D. I received nine applications.

The European Union in Africa

Niagalé Bagayoko*

1. Introduction

Through the so-called 'multi-functional approach' outlined in the European Security Strategy[1] – the so-called 'Solana Document' adopted in December 2003 – the European Union is promoting a holistic approach, whereby security, economic development and democracy are seen as essential ingredients in order to generate political stability in the European Union's international environment. The European Union insists on its added value as a multi-institutional organisation likely to provide all types of crisis management tools – civilian and military as well as humanitarian – within a unique framework. Because of the multiplicity of the problems it is facing – war, poverty, humanitarian catastrophes and so forth – the African continent is a suitable target for this multi-functional approach.

A case study of EU security policy in Africa shows that the linkage between security, governance and development relies for a large part on institutional dynamics. EU security policies in Africa are at least as much determined by African realities as by the bureaucratic affiliations of the concerned EU actors. African security can be seen as a field where EU actors are improving their institutional capacities. In fact, EU African security policy is often driven by internal power relations. Beyond this, and more importantly, the European Union's policy in Africa is an interesting case study for demonstrating how new international relations concepts – in this case the linkage between security, governance and development – can in reality be largely

* Dr Niagalé Bagayoko, Research Fellow in Security and Development, Institute of Development Studies.

[1] Council of the European Union, *A Secure Europe in a Better World: European Security Strategy*, drafted under the authority of EU High Representative Javier Solana, 12 December 2003.

driven by institutional issues. Indeed, the linkage between security, governance and development, which informs the European Union's current security policies in Africa, largely relies on institutional dynamics within the European Union. The importance of these institutional dynamics can be seen in three areas.

First, African security is a field of experimentation for the institutional actors responsible for the definition and implementation of the Common Foreign and Security Policy (CFSP) – the so-called second pillar. Second, African security is a field likely to provide a new legitimacy for the development policies led by the European Community (EC), which is responsible for the management of first pillar activities. Third, African security is a field of Europeanisation for traditionally bilateral member-state security policies.

These dynamics, however, also suggest far-reaching institutional ambitions and interests. African security triggers competition between the different European institutions, which are all eager to be the driving force of a policy that can offer some additional resources and autonomy. Meanwhile, the triangle formed by security, governance and development presupposes coordination and cooperation between these institutions, which are little used to working together.

2. African security: a field of experimentation for the European Security and Defence Policy?

Most of the CFSP proposals still lack a practical translation. The CFSP remains highly inconsistent in Africa. In fact, the European Union has rather invested in the development of the European Security and Defence Policy (ESDP), which is perceived as a more straightforward policy field.

The field of conflict prevention and management in Africa constitutes an ideal field of experimentation and validation,[2] especially for the Petersberg tasks, which consist of humanitarian and rescue tasks, peacekeeping tasks and tasks of combat forces in crisis management, including peacemaking.[3]

[2] N. Bagayoko, 'Les politiques européennes de prévention et de gestion des conflits en Afrique subsaharienne', 16 *Les Champs de Mars* (2004) pp. 93-110.

[3] The Petersberg tasks were defined in the Petersberg Declaration, adopted by the Western European Union (WEU) Council of Ministers on 19 June 1992, as the role of the organisation was redefined. The part of this Declaration where the Petersberg tasks are defined was then integrated word for word into Article 17(2) of the Treaty of Amsterdam in 1997.

Operation Artemis,[4] which was launched within the ESDP framework and took place from June to September 2003 in the Democratic Republic of the Congo (DRC), was clearly a founding act in the mobilisation of the second pillar instruments in Africa.[5] The ESDP's field of experimentation had until then not extended beyond the Balkans. Beyond this geographic expansion of the potential field of intervention, Operation Artemis also inaugurated a new form of partnership between the European Union and the United Nations.

More importantly, however, the new EU military structures gained legitimacy from both an external and an internal perspective.

Firstly, Artemis proved that the European Union was able to plan military operations autonomously, without resorting to NATO means and instruments.[6] The operation was planned entirely within the European Union's military structures – the EU Military Committee (EUMC) and EU Military Staff (EUMS) – which worked in close coordination with France, the 'framework nation' in charge of operational planning. An alternative to the resort to NATO's Supreme Headquarters of Allied Powers in Europe (SHAPE) was thus successfully tested. Africa is now often seen by ESDP actors as a field of European influence that can evade the strict implementation of the 'Berlin Plus' option[7] and where the ESDP can gain increasing international credibility.

Secondly, Artemis also provided the ESDP with increased legitimacy within the EU institutional architecture. Operation Artemis established that the decision-making procedures at the politico-military level – which depend on the relations between the Political and Security Committee (PSC) and the EUMC – could lead to rapid decisions, contrary to what had been suggested

---

4 Launched on 12 June 2003, Operation Artemis aimed to prevent a humanitarian catastrophe in Ituri, in the north-east of the Democratic Republic of Congo. The operation was thus explicitly mandated by the UN Security Council (Resolution 1484). The aim was to control the situation while the mandate of the UN mission in the DRC (MONUC) was reinforced and its strength increased.

5 C.R. Olsen, 'The EU and Conflict Management in African Emergencies', 9(3) *International Peacekeeping* (2002) pp. 87-102.; F. Faria, *Crisis Management in sub-Saharan Africa: The Role of The European Union*, Occasional Paper No. 54 (Paris, EUISS 2002).

6 However, as shown by its ongoing support to the AU mission in Darfur (AMIS), NATO has since stepped up its interest and expertise in Africa, which tends to qualify the idea that Africa could constitute an ideal environment for experimentation with an autonomous European defence.

7 Berlin Plus is a strategic partnership agreement between NATO and the EU. It allows the EU to make use of NATO's logistical and planning resources in its crisis management activities.

by the long planning delays for Operation Concordia.[8] The PSC, which is composed of the member states' PSC ambassadors, plays a central role in the definition and follow-up of European crisis responses. It provides the political control and strategic direction for the ESDP operations, basing its decisions on the recommendations expressed by the EUMC and the Committee for Civilian Aspects of Crisis Management (CIVCOM). The EUMC is composed of the member states' military commands. It follows the progress of military operations, makes recommendations to the PSC on all military aspects of the ESDP and gives instructions to the EUMS. CIVCOM was created in 2002 to define and supervise civilian operations. It is also in charge of the inter-pillar coordination of the European Union's civilian actions.

To these Council institutions must be added the General Secretariat of the Council (GSC), led by the Secretary-General of the Council of the European Union and High Representative for the CFSP (SG/HR), with its directorates general. DGE, the directorate general in charge of external relations, is divided into geographical and functional directorates.

Finally, Operation Artemis gave way to other ESDP operations that consolidated the European Union's contribution to peace and post-conflict reconstruction in the DRC. Two subsequent missions were launched in the DRC, this time focusing on Security Sector Reform (SSR): EUPOL Kinshasa, a police mission, and EUSEC DR Congo, which provides assistance and advice on the necessary reforms to the Congolese authorities in charge of security. Another military operation, finally, recently confirmed the European Union's capacity to lead an efficient, albeit short-term, mission with a clear objective. EUFOR DR Congo was deployed in Kinshasa from 12 June to 30 November 2006, during the period encompassing the elections in the DRC.[9] All three missions in the DRC have been carried out in very close coordination with the United Nations. EUFOR, like Artemis, was meant to support MONUC and the Congolese authorities. A fifth mission is being carried out in Darfur. The EU civilian-military supporting action to the mission of the African Union (AU) in Darfur, AMIS II, provides the African Union with political, military and technical assistance. In 2004, the PSC adopted the European Security and Defence Policy (ESDP) Action Plan for Africa, which sets out practical recommendations for the implementation of the European Union's contribution to Africa's security.

[8] Operation Concordia took place in the former Yugoslav Republic of Macedonia (FYROM) from 31 March to 15 December 2003.

[9] EUFOR consisted of 1,200 troops in Kinshasa and an equal number in neighbouring Gabon, ready to be deployed in the event of a crisis.

The recent EU operations in Africa illustrate a major trend in ESDP operations, namely the increasing development of civilian means, thus giving a practical dimension to the civilian side of the ESDP.[10] This 'civilianisation' of the ESDP in Africa has important implications for interinstitutional coordination. Firstly, it requires close coordination between the military and civilian dimensions of ESDP operations, which is complicated by their separate management by different institutions and funding instruments within the second pillar.[11] Secondly, while the military dimension of the ESDP is a second pillar exclusivity, its civilian dimension is necessarily linked to – and at times overlaps with – the Community pillar's civilian activities.

3. African Security: A Field of Relegitimisation for the European Commission?

For some years now, a discourse that emphasises the role of security as a precondition for development has emerged within the European Union's Community institutions. The first EU document focusing on African conflicts was proposed by the Commission[12] and promoted the notion of 'structural stability', which underlined the key role played by development in the pre-

---

[10] Although many tend to focus only on the military side of the ESDP, it also has an important civilian crisis management side. The EU has actually made faster operational progress in this so-called 'soft' dimension of crisis management than in the military one, which was initially was as a priority in the development of an EU crisis response. See A. Nowak, 'Civilian Crisis Management within ESDP', in A. Nowak (ed.), *Civilian Crisis Management: The EU Way*, Chaillot Paper No. 90 (Paris, EUISS 2006) pp. 15-37.

[11] While the military side of the ESDP is essentially conceptualised and implemented by the EUMC and the EUMS, its civilian side is managed by CIVCOM. A civilian-military cell was created within the EUMS in 2004 to enhance civilian-military coordination in crisis management operations. However, this cell is only responsible for coordination within the second pillar. The civilian and military aspects of the ESDP are also financed separately: the civilian aspects are covered by the CFSP budget or additional financial instruments such as the African Peace Facility, while military expenditure is managed by a special mechanism called 'Athena'. See Council Decision 2004/197/CFSP of 23 February 2004 establishing a mechanism to administer the financing of the common costs of the European Union operations having military or defence implications (ATHENA).

[12] European Commission, Communication from the Commission to the Council: The European Union and the Issue of Conflicts in Africa: Peace-Building, Conflict Prevention and Beyond, 6 March 1996.

vention and regulation of African conflicts. This increasing involvement in African conflict management issues constitutes a means for the Commission and its Directorate General for Development (DG DEV) to respond to the doubts expressed about the efficiency of its development strategies in Africa[13] and the general validity of development aid.[14] This explains the growing attention given to conflict prevention and management through military means.[15] This security angle in the approach to development is determined by the interests of some directorates general within the Commission – in particular DG DEV – in defending their privileged geographic area of intervention and investing a functional field in which they do not traditionally intervene.

Relations between the European Union and sub-Saharan Africa have long been reduced to the sole issue of trade and development cooperation through the Yaoundé and Lomé partnership agreements between the European Union and the Africa, Caribbean and Pacific (ACP) group of states.[16] EU-Africa relations are being increasingly politicised and securitised, however, as apparent from the last two Lomé Agreements and their successor, the Cotonou Agreement, signed in 2000.[17] The very first article of the Cotonou Agreement closes the development, good governance and security triangle by underlining that the agreement was concluded 'with a view to contributing to peace

---

[13] European Commission, Green Paper on relations between the European Union and the ACP countries on the eve of the 21st century: challenges and options for a new partnership, 20 November 1996; European Commission, Communication from the Commission to the Council and the European Parliament: Towards Improved Coherence between Community Development Policy and Other Community Policies, 26 April 2000.

[14] M. Lister, 'The European Union's Green Paper on Relations with ACP Countries', 26(3) *Oxford Development Studies* (1998) pp. 375-390.

[15] G.R. Olsen, 'The EU and Conflict Management in African Emergencies', 9(3) *International Peacekeeping* (2002) pp. 87-102.

[16] GEMDEV, *La convention de Lomé en question: les relations entre les pays d'Afrique, Caraïbes et du Pacifique (ACP) et l'Union européenne après 2000* (Paris, Karthala 2000). Some have even considered aid programmes to be a cornerstone of the European integration process. M. Lister, *The European Union and the South: Relations with Developing Countries* (London, Routledge 1998).

[17] It is important here to stress the European Union's institutional sharing of responsibility. While the Council is responsible for negotiating international treaties, the Commission is in charge of implementing the Community elements of these treaties. The Commission, however, also enjoys a power of initiative and often designs the treaties. This is especially true in the case of the EU-ACP agreements, which are managed and implemented by the Commission's DG DEV and, since the Cotonou Agreement, DG Trade.

and security and to promoting a stable and democratic political environment',[18] thus emphasising the third dimension – security. The assistance provided to partner countries is increasingly political rather than purely technical, and the concept of the rule of law clearly drives some of the reforms advocated in the Cotonou Agreement.

The principles laid down in the Cotonou Agreement are accompanied by more concrete policies and instruments. The European Commission divides its conflict prevention and peacebuilding efforts into two categories: direct and indirect initiatives. Direct initiatives range from humanitarian activities to support for conflict resolution initiatives and institutional reforms, while indirect initiatives refer to the mainstreaming of conflict prevention objectives into sector programmes in the areas of development and trade. Direct initiatives include the humanitarian actions led by the European Union's Humanitarian Aid Department (DG ECHO). Humanitarian action is a shared competence, but it is implemented by the Commission's institutions, and more precisely by DG ECHO, which enjoys an important latitude within the Commission, while its impartiality is established in Article 7 of the Humanitarian Aid Regulation.[19] Direct initiatives also include early warning and action mechanisms. The Crisis Management and Conflict Prevention Unit, within the Commission's Directorate General for External Relations (DG RELEX), played an instrumental role in the introduction of conflict assessments and in the integration of risk factors in the Country Strategy Papers. More importantly, however, the Crisis Management and Conflict Prevention Unit is in charge of coordinating and mainstreaming the Commission's conflict prevention and management activities. As part of DG RELEX, it also provides the necessary link between the Commission's institutions in charge of conflict prevention and management and their Council counterparts. The Commission at times seems to suggest, in its policy documents, that any development programme can contribute to conflict prevention.[20] The Com-

---

18 Cotonou Agreement, Article 1.

19 In fact, the policies managed by DG ECHO are far from politicised. DG ECHO strictly defines humanitarian assistance as an apolitical, neutral and impartial activity. DG ECHO is not part of the 'crisis management' system and is therefore not a crisis management instrument, as the humanitarian policy does not aim to stabilise a political situation nor to prevent a crisis, and can therefore not be considered a political instrument.

20 European Commission, IQSG Programming Fiche on Conflict Prevention (Conflict Prevention Guidelines), available at: <http://ec.europa.eu/comm/external_relations/cfsp/cpcm/cp/doc/cp_guide.pdf>.

mission has issued indirect initiatives in the form of more targeted policies that aim to link trade and security concerns in a practical manner. Of particular significance in this context are the efforts to regulate the trade of particular goods that fuel violent conflicts. The Kimberley Process Certification Scheme, which aims to prevent the trade in so-called 'blood diamonds', and the EU Action Plan for Forest Law Enforcement, Governance and Trade (FLEGT), which regulates the trade of timber, are two cases in point.

4. African security: a field of Europeanisation for member states' security policies?

The launch of a dynamic ESDP in Africa is also a symptom of the Europeanisation of the former colonial powers' traditional African policies and of their capacity to be the driving force behind a collective policy on the continent.

Rather than being a driving force, France has long been an obstacle to the European Union's further involvement in African security issues. France's unilateralist policy in Africa acted as a deterrent to other European states, which were reluctant to associate their image and the image of the European Union with a policy often considered neo-colonial. The integration of French interventions within the ESDP framework could allow it to remain involved on the African continent – still considered a central asset for France's position on the international scene – while rendering groundless the accusations of paternalism and neo-colonialism. Operation Artemis offered an interesting illustration of the progressive Europeanisation of France's involvement in African crises[21] and proved that European member states could decide collectively to

[21] Operation Artemis was not, strictly speaking, the result of a European initiative; it was in fact initially a French intervention that was subsequently Europeanised. At the beginning of May 2003, in response to the UN Secretary-General's call, France considered intervening in the DRC at the head of an international coalition. The initial operation, known as 'Mamba', was eventually proposed by French diplomats to the European partners and took place within the ESDP framework. In accordance with the Council Decision of 12 June 2003, the operation's command was entrusted to France, which took on the role of 'framework nation'. In fact, the operational headquarters of Operation Artemis were set up in the courtyard of the French army's high command in Paris and benefited from the work that had previously been achieved by the Centre of Planning and Operational Command (CPCO – *Centre de planification et de conduite opérationnelle*) for Operation Mamba. Consisting a small core of CPCO officers, the operation's high command was joined by officers from other member states as well as by liaison officers from the EUMS. France also provided the high command on the

contribute to a crisis management operation that was initially supported by only one of them. It also enabled France to re-engage in the Great Lakes region and beyond, in Central Africa, from which it had progressively withdrawn since the much criticised Operation Turquoise in Rwanda. Finally, and beyond these central political issues, the Europeanisation of its Africa policy also enables France to share the costs of military and defence cooperation.

The Franco-British rapprochement in Saint-Malo led to both the creation of the ESDP and the Europeanisation of the two countries' African policies, even though the United Kingdom has since seemed less anxious than France to Europeanise its African policy. Since 2001, the United Kingdom's efforts to develop African peacekeeping capabilities – through British Peace Support Teams (BPST) that provide training in former British colonies – have become part of a much more ambitious conflict prevention project, known as the Africa Conflict Prevention Pool (ACPP).[22] The thematic focus of the ACPP, from enhancing peace support operations capabilities to addressing the economic and financial causes of conflict, underlines a holistic understanding of conflict prevention. The United Kingdom has placed a strong emphasis on African peacekeeping by setting up a special fund, the Africa Pool.[23] The United Kingdom highly values its bilateral activities in Africa. Unlike the French, the British are not worried when their activities do not have a European label: their approach is less institutional than the French one. At this stage, the British consider that their bilateral programmes in Africa are very efficient, particularly in the SSR field, and therefore do not need to be Europeanised.

Portugal is also an important European actor in Africa. Since the early 1990s, it has been developing technical and military cooperation with African

---

ground. See N. Bagayoko, 'L'Opération Artémis, un tournant pour la politique européenne de sécurité et de défense?', 209 *Afrique contemporaine* (2004) pp. 101-116.

22 The ACCP is an interdepartmental mechanism that draws together the conflict prevention resources of the Department for International Development (DfID), the Foreign and Commonwealth Office (FCO) and Ministry of Defence (MOD).

23 A key part of the United Kingdom's long-term strategy to build African conflict management capabilities consists of supporting security sector reform (SSR) projects. The largest British commitment in the field of SSR is in Sierra Leone, where the United Kingdom actively supports the reform of the army, the police and the judiciary, as well as *ad hoc* institutions such as the Anti-Corruption Commission, the Special Court and the Truth and Reconciliation Commission. In addition, it provides technical assistance to the government of Sierra Leone. See A. Leboeuf, 'La réforme britannique du secteur de la sécurité en Sierra Leone: vers un nouveau paradigme?', 98 *Politique africaine* (2005) pp. 63-78.

Portuguese-speaking countries (PALOP). Portugal also has its own African peacekeeping capabilities support programme, the Programme for the Support of Peace Missions in Africa (PAMPA – *Programa de Apoio às Missões de Paz em África*). Like France, Portugal would like the PAMPA programme to be integrated into the EU training policy framework. Portugal, however, does not wish the programme to be fully Europeanised.

EU member states seem increasingly convinced of the importance of Africa for European security. The rather impressive list of contributing nations to EUFOR DR Congo confirms this.[24] Moreover, some member states such as the Netherlands and Sweden have in effect recently stepped up their involvement in African security issues.[25] Alongside France and Portugal, Belgium, which recently resumed a more active Africa policy after having largely withdrawn from the African scene following the assassination of ten of its parachutists in Kigali in 1994,[26] is one of the most active supporters of a substantial European commitment in Africa. It is followed in this by Spain and Greece.

5. INTER-INSTITUTIONAL RELATIONS: COMPETITION OR COOPERATION?

Each and every new policy paper focusing on the European Union's security policy in Africa insists on the necessity of interinstitutional and inter-pillar coordination and mainstreaming. In fact, one of the conditions of success in the European approach to conflict prevention and management in Africa

---

24 The following EU member states contributed to EUFOR: Austria, Belgium, Cyprus, the Czech Republic, Finland, France, Germany, Greece, Hungary, Ireland, Italy, Lithuania, Luxembourg, the Netherlands, Poland, Portugal, Slovakia, Slovenia, Spain, Sweden and the United Kingdom. Turkey, although not an EU member, is also among the contributing nations. See Factsheet: List of contributing nations to EUFOR RD Congo, GSC website, available at: <http://consilium.europa.eu/uedocs/cmsUpload/ListofcontributingnationstoEUFORRDCongo.pdf>.

25 On the latter's involvement in Africa, see L. Wohlgemuth, 'Swedish relations and policies towards Africa', in L. Wohlgemuth (ed.), *The Nordic countries in Africa: old and new relations* (Uppsala, Nordic Africa Institute 2002).

26 Belgium is particularly active in the Democratic Republic of the Congo, which is a former Belgian colony. The Belgian defence ministry, in cooperation with South Africa, provides training support to Congolese troops. Belgium also provided logistical and operational training to the Beninese battalion about to be sent to the UN Mission to the DRC (MONUC). Belgian EU civil servants are important actors in the European Union's policy on Africa. Within European institutions, Belgians are often in charge of African affairs, both in the GSC and in the Commission, especially in DG DEV.

depends on the European Union's capacity to overcome the rivalries born out of the different institutions' desire to play the role of a 'lead agency' on these issues. It appears that competition rather than convergence remains the main trend in EU interinstitutional relations. Frequently, the linkage between security, governance and development is still at the core of EU interinstitutional competition.

First, a lot of agreement does exist both within the first and second pillar. The intermingling of fields in conflict prevention and management policies requires close coordination between the different branches of the Commission. In fact, unclear divisions of labour are problematic inside the Commission, between its different sectors and directorates general (DGs). It is obvious, however, that these DGs often pursue different, or even contradictory, objectives. DG Trade will want to defend the European Union's commercial interests, DG RELEX will be careful to increase the European Union's security, external relations and international visibility, while DG DEV should contribute to increased prosperity in the ACP states. On the other hand, the European security structures of the second pillar are very young[27] and are therefore all struggling for legitimacy. The responsibility for coordinating the management of African security issues is at the heart of a competition. If DGE VIII, which is in charge of defence issues, were tasked with coordinating the activities in Africa, it could gain renewed legitimacy. Indeed, DGE VIII is currently having some difficulty imposing its views on the Military Staff, also located within the GSC. Moreover, both DGE VIII and the Military Staff are competing with NATO. Because the ESDP consists of two closely interlinked fields – military and civilian crisis management – the recently established civilian-military cell could also seek the responsibility of trying to coordinate the civilian and military aspects of EU security policy in Africa. Nevertheless, DGE IX, which is in charge of the civilian aspects of crisis management[28] and has no rivalry with NATO, is perhaps in a better position at the moment. Indeed, DGE IX seems to be getting closer and closer to the Commission services – such as DG DEV and DG ECHO – in charge of implementing civilian programmes in the security field.

---

27 The ESDP was launched during the June 1999 European Council held in Cologne and was declared operational at the December 2001 European Council held in Laeken.

28 The following therefore report to DGE IX: the Police Unit, which plans and leads crisis management missions consisting of a police deployment; the Policy Planning and Early Warning Unit (Policy Unit), an instrument of strategic and geopolitical analysis at the service of the High Representative for the CFSP; and the Situation Centre (SITCEN), in charge of 24-hour intelligence, analysis and warning.

Moreover, cross-pillar rivalries are dividing first and second pillar actors. The Commission can have a decisive influence over the implementation of the ESDP. The African Peace Facility (APF) is a good example of the Commission's capacity to encroach on the Council's prerogative over the CFSP and ESDP. The APF is a funding instrument dedicated to financing peacekeeping operations led by African actors. Launched in 2004, the APF was funded from the resources of the ninth European Development Fund (EDF), which is drawn from member states' voluntary contributions. Although the EDF is not part of the Community budget, the Commission is in charge of managing it, which gives it a decisive influence. With regard to the APF itself, however, the member states have the last word. The APF was supposed to be a provisional instrument, and its perpetuation has given rise to heated debates between member states and the Commission. The use of the APF was therefore at the centre of competition between the Commission, which wanted the APF to focus on support to the African Union,[29] and the GSC and some member states, which wanted these funds also – or even exclusively – to be used to support sub-regional organisations.[30] This debate found a provisional conclusion when the African Union was called upon to intervene in Darfur. The European Union agreed, in April 2006, to provide an additional amount of €300 million under the tenth EDF to be able to continue the APF for another three-year period (2008-2010).[31]

---

[29] The Commission underlined that the African Union had achieved considerable progress at the institutional level, particularly through the creation of its Peace and Security Council. The African Union's Peace and Security Council could be regarded as the security organ of the New Economic Partnership for Africa's Development (NEPAD). The Commission's preference for the African Union is therefore consistent with the link it has been drawing between development, on the one hand, and conflict prevention and management policies, on the other.

[30] The GSC, spurred on by some member states, favoured sub-regional organisations and more particularly the Economic Community of West African States (ECOWAS), which actually possessed the necessary operational experience and had started developing the adequate institutional framework. See B. Nivet, *Security by proxy? The EU and (Sub-)Regional Organisations: The Case of ECOWAS*, Occasional Paper No. 63 (Paris, EUISS 2006).

[31] Nevertheless, the nature of the final mechanism will certainly depend on the interpretation of the Instrument for Stability, launched in November 2006 in order to improve consistency and coordination between the Community's short-term and long-term conflict prevention and management instruments. Regulation (EC) No. 1717/2006 of the European Parliament and of the Council of 15 November 2006 establishing an Instrument for Stability.

Another example of the European Union's institutional rivalries over African security is the recent case brought before the European Court of Justice, which also underlines the problems caused by the unclear division of labour between Council and Commission. In February 2005, the Commission, in an action against the Council, accused it of assuming the right to contribute to ECOWAS in the framework of the Moratorium on Small Arms and Light Weapons (SALW). For the Commission, the Council decision affects Community powers in the field of development aid, since actions against the spread of SALW are already covered by the Cotonou Agreement and the regional indicative programme for West Africa.[32]

6. DISAGREEMENTS BETWEEN MEMBER STATES

Germany's position has evolved considerably in recent years, from reluctance to a readiness to contribute to short-term ESDP missions, such as EUFOR, whose operational command was provided by Germany. Nevertheless, there is still a lot of reluctance, especially within the German ministry of defence, to engage more in Africa.[33] The new EU member states, which have no traditional African policy nor specific interest in this geographical area,[34] are generally in favour of reinforcing African capabilities in order to create an autonomous African security system and avoid increasing costs to the European Union.

Indeed, funding constitutes a central issue. Some member states, such as France and Portugal, thus share a strong desire to have access to the Community development cooperation funds, although they are not ready, in exchange for this access to Community funds, to hand over their management

32 ECJ, Case C-91/05 *Commission* v. *Council* [2008] *ECR* I-3651.

33 Germany is essentially interested in three aspects of African affairs: the migration of African populations to some neighbouring states, natural resources (oil and gas) and multinational operations on the continent. These operations can offer Germany the opportunity to improve its military skills in crisis management and provide it with a new legitimacy and credibility in the field, as was shown during the EUFOR operation in Kinshasa (DRC) last year.

34 Nevertheless, some of these new member states are becoming more active in Africa. For instance, Poland contributed 150 soldiers to EUFOR (this commitment is linked to the close relationship between Poland and Germany, which commanded the EUFOR mission on the ground and provided funding for the strategic transport of Polish troops and for their logistics). A Hungarian observer was also sent to Darfur and afterwards to the Mali Peacekeeping School.

of military cooperation to Community actors. Other European partners wish to avoid a situation in which some member states' African policies would be funded by the European Union, especially from the EC budget. This financial issue drives Germany, Austria and the Netherlands, which are particularly cautious when it comes to funding EU security activities in Africa. Most new member states share this financial concern. They wish to see a fair balance between the structural funds they receive and the development aid dedicated to non-EU states.

Moreover, countries such as Germany and the Nordic countries favour an ethical approach and consider that development funds should not be used to finance the ESDP, whose progress they do not consider as crucial as France. The United Kingdom, on the other hand, is already implementing a policy that clearly puts the stress on the linkage between security and development. The British position on the question is therefore driven not so much by ethical concerns as by a reluctance to 'Europeanise' a policy that is already considered efficient at the national level.

Finally, the issue of multilateral cooperation with other Western actors is another bone of contention. France's insistence on involving the European Union in Africa can be read as an attempt to avoid coordination with other actors, in particular NATO and the United States.[35] The United Kingdom, on the other hand, insists on the necessity of coordinating EU member states' activities with non-European actors such as the United States, Canada and Norway. The EU strategy for Africa and the G8 Gleneagles Plan for Africa are viewed as totally interconnected. The British, followed in this by Germany, also promote cooperation between NATO and the European Union.

7. TOWARDS INCREASED COOPERATION?

The current evolution towards longer missions with a growing civilian dimension – which are increasingly dedicated to promoting good governance and sustainable development over the long term – renders essential close cooperation between the civilian and military crisis management activities of the second pillar and the traditionally civilian activities of the first pillar.[36]

[35] For instance, the new 'maritime section' of the RECAMP concept, which is devoted to strengthening African states' sovereignty over their coastlines, is designed to counter American influence on offshore oil production in the Gulf of Guinea.

[36] On this issue of inter-pillar coordination in military and civilian crisis management, see C. Gourlay, 'Civil-Civil Coordination in EU crisis management', and R. Kohl,

One of the biggest challenges for EU policy in Africa will most probably be cross-pillar coordination, that is, the coordination of CFSP/ESDP activities and EC development programmes. The GSC, the Commission and the EU member states have recently engaged in common reflections on the European Union's policies in the field of African security. A first important document, the *EU Strategy for Africa*, was jointly drafted by the Commission and the GSC and was adopted in December 2005.[37]

In November 2005, following a French request,[38] the PSC asked the Commission and the GSC to draft a concept for strengthening African capabilities for the prevention, management and resolution of conflicts. The PSC took note of the concept on 29 September 2006[39] and stated that it should be seen as part of the implementation of the EU strategy for Africa. The GSC and the Commission were once again invited to explore and find practical ways of implementing the options proposed in the paper, in cooperation with African partners. Indeed, a number of financial and institutional issues remain unresolved, issues that underline the disagreements that still divide member states,[40] as well as the rivalries within and across pillars. As far as funding is concerned, there is an urgent need to address the absence of harmonisation of the existing financial tools. At the moment, financial resources from member states have to be mobilised to support African capabilities such as military training, which is not eligible for funding under the CFSP budget[41] or the

---

'Civil-Military Coordination in EU crisis management', in A. Nowak (ed.), *Civilian Crisis Management: The EU Way*, Chaillot Paper No. 90 (Paris, EUISS 2006) pp. 103-138.

37 Council of the European Union, *The EU and Africa: Towards a Strategic Partnership*, adopted by the European Council on 15-16 December 2005.

38 The French request stemmed directly from its will to Europeanise the RECAMP concept and involve the EU in the training of African forces. France actively lobbied for the definition of this concept throughout 2006.

39 From July to September 2006, the final version of the concept paper underwent a validation process, during which five working groups of the Council – the Politico-Military Group (PMG), the Africa-Caribbean-Pacific (ACP) group, the Africa Working Group (COAFR), the Military Committee (EUMC) and the Committee for Civilian Aspects of Crisis Management (CIVCOM) – were asked to prepare recommendations relating to the concept.

40 There is no obligation, in the concept paper, for member states to proceed with the implementation of the concept.

41 The CFSP budget cannot fund any expenditure of a military character. The Treaty on European Union states that military expenditure is jointly financed by the member states, but that they do so outside the Community budget and in accordance with the gross national product scale (Treaty on European Union (TEU), Article 28.3,

African Peace Facility (APF). Some progress has been made since the adoption, in November 2006, of the 'instrument for stability', which aims to ensure a better linkage between short-term crisis response and long-term development instruments. Its capacity to solve current funding issues, however, will largely depend on how the EU institutions choose to interpret it. While it clearly combines a number of formerly separate instruments, it does not as yet provide a clear perspective on the future of other instruments such as the APF.

Some of the inconsistencies observed in the field, where policies are actually implemented, can in turn be explained by this experimentation process and the inter-institutional dynamics to which it is linked.

second paragraph). A special mechanism called 'Athena' has been put in place to manage this expenditure. See Council Decision 2004/197/CFSP of 23 February 2004 establishing a mechanism to administer the financing of the common costs of the European Union operations having military or defence implications (ATHENA).

Abbreviations

ACP	Africa-Caribbean-Pacific Group
ACPP	Africa Conflict Prevention Pool (UK)
APF	African Peace Facility
ASF	African Standby Force
AU	African Union
BPST	British Peace Support Team
CFSP	Common Foreign and Security Policy
CIVCOM	Committee for Civilian Aspects of Crisis Management
CSP	Country Strategy Paper
DCMD	French Military and Defence Cooperation Directorate
DDR	Disarmament, Demobilisation and Reintegration
DfID	Department for International Development
DG	Directorate General
DG DEV	Directorate General for Development
DG ECHO	Directorate General for Humanitarian Aid
DG EuropeAid	Directorate General Europe Aid Cooperation Office
DG RELEX	Directorate General for External Relations
DG Trade	Directorate General for Trade
DRC	Democratic Republic of the Congo
EC	European Community
ECOWAS	Economic Community of West African States
EDF	European Development Fund
EIDHR	European Initiative for Democracy and Human Rights
EPA	Economic Partnership Agreement
ESDP	European Security and Defence Policy
EU	European Union
EUMC	European Union Military Committee
EUMS	European Union Military Staff
EUSR	European Union Special Representative
FCO	Foreign and Commonwealth Office (UK)
FLEGT	Forest Law Enforcement, Governance and Trade
GSC	General Secretariat of the Council
MOD	Ministry of Defence (UK)
MONUC	UN Mission in the Democratic Republic of the Congo
NATO	North Atlantic Treaty Organisation
PALOP	African Portuguese-speaking countries
PAMPA	Portuguese Programme for the Support of Peace Missions in Africa

PSC	Political and Security Committee
RECAMP	French programme for the strengthening of African peacekeeping capabilities
RIP	Regional Indicative Programme
RRM	Rapid Reaction Mechanism
SALW	Small Arms and Light Weapons
SG/HR	Secretary-General of the Council of the European Union and High Representative for the CFSP
SHAPE	NATO's Supreme Headquarters of Allied Powers in Europe
SHIRBRIG	UN Standby High Readiness Brigade
SITCEN	Situation Centre
UN	United Nations
WTO	World Trade Organisation

The Changing Face of Western Colonialism in Africa

Antoine Roger Lokongo*

In his paper, Professor Collier highlights the legacy bedevilling poor countries, a legacy characterised by poverty and stagnation, large scale violence and internal conflicts that are quite hard to stop. Nevertheless, he strikes a note of optimism when he observes that many poor countries now find themselves in a fragile post-conflict situation while embracing democracy. These countries, most of which are new democracies, he notes, could redress this legacy if they utilised the large revenues deriving from the current global boom in commodities and rocketing oil prices for their own development and growth. Even in these new democracies, however, the accountability factor is very weak, so much so that most governments capture these revenues for themselves, taking advantage of the lack of checks and balances therein. 'You can win an election without being a good government,' Collier observes.

As a way out of this vicious circle, Professor Collier advocates ditching the idea that aid policy is the only instrument capable of solving the problem. He argues that aid is not important in these situations because too much aid provides governments with room for manoeuvre. So, instead of channelling their countries' revenues from resources into development, they capture them for themselves and leak the aid money into military spending. Donors are therefore financing this militarisation. After aid money has covered their military budget, governments maximise their profits by selling their natural resources at a reduced price to multinationals and taxing them less and less in the process.

Professor Collier pleads for the reinforcement of an effective UN peacekeeping force in countries in post-conflict situations in order to prevent them from falling back into violence, despite the fact that the peacekeeping bodies

* Antoine Roger Lokongo, London-based Congolese independent journalist.

of the United Nations often turn out to be just another agency delivering aid instead of setting standards of good governance.

Instruments such as an international management code for natural resources (e.g., the Kimberley Process and the Transparency Initiative) should be put in place by international intergovernmental agencies, so that the money generated is used to sustain growth and is not spent on big parties.

Professor Collier states that aid money is very often unsupervised, despite the conditionality imposed by the donors. There is therefore a need to strengthen the forces that are fighting for good governance and accountability and for getting transparency into the budget. 'Governments,' he notes, 'should be accountable to the people, not to donors.'

Finally, Professor Collier worries that his thesis might be construed as undermining sovereignty and therefore advocating a return to colonialism. 'That is not the case,' he declares, explaining that that sovereignty was a seventeenth century Western concept that implied that what governments did to their people did not affect their neighbours, but that today violence in one country easily spills over into the neighbouring countries. He concludes that it is therefore logical for neighbours to share sovereignty, in order to have their interests protected (by regional, continental or international organisations).

Frankly speaking, I have a problem with some of Professor Collier's conclusions, especially regarding international instruments and international management of natural resources. Being a native of the Democratic Republic of the Congo, I know very well that no international initiative, let alone intervention, has really benefited the Congolese people. We have perceived UN interventions, in particular, as covert operations for the protection of Western interests.

In 1960, the UN Mission in the Congo (ONUC) was deployed not to avert the Katanga secession as, it should have been, but to neutralise Patrice Lumumba, the Congo's independence hero and first democratically elected leader. On 14 July 1960, following Lumumba's request, the UN Security Council swiftly passed a resolution calling for Belgian troops to withdraw from the Congo. A peace keeping force under a Swedish commander, General Karl von Horn, was deployed to the Congo. The first contingent, made up of Ghanaian troops under a British officer, General Alexander, who was still serving in the Ghanaian army, arrived in the Congo on 15 July 1960. UN soldiers did not go immediately to Katanga but occupied every other Congolese province and then proceeded to disarm Congolese troops loyal to Lumumba while arming those loyal to Mobutu. Mobutu carried out his first *coup d'état* on 14 September 1960 when he placed Lumumba under house arrest.

The rest is history. Mobutu would reign as a despotic ruler until the end of the Cold War.

The overthrow of Mobutu by Lumumba's disciple, Laurent Kabila, in 1997, was followed by a war of invasion carried out by proxy forces from Rwanda, Uganda and Burundi, with the complicity of 'Congolese Tutsi of Rwandan origin' and 'Congolese rebels', during which more than five million Congolese lost their lives and the Congo's natural and mineral resources were systematically looted.

This time, a UN peacekeeping force code named the UN Mission in the Congo, know by its French acronym as MONUC, was officially created by UN Security Council resolution 1291 of 24 February 2000. It now boasts more than 17,000 troops. However, the mission has been marred by controversies.

MONUC suffered a loss of confidence when it not only failed to stop Laurent Nkunda (a Tutsi dissident former general in the Congolese army and a war criminal wanted by the International Criminal Court) from seizing the City of Bukavu in June 2004 and his soldiers from committing innumerable rapes and murders, but also behaved as an accomplice of the insurgents, as the city fell right under its nose whilst MONUC was in constant communication with the insurgents.

Although Pakistan is the biggest contributor to the UN peacekeeping force in the Congo, Pakistani UN peacekeeping troops have traded in gold and sold weapons to the Congolese militia groups they were meant to disarm. These militia groups – such as Cobra Matata's 'Front des Nationalists de l'Ituri' (FNI) – were guilty of some of the worst human rights abuses during the war. The trading went on in 2005, but according to the BBC a UN investigative team sent to gather evidence was obstructed and threatened. The team's report was buried by the United Nations itself to 'avoid political fallout'.

Soon the Pakistani officers were doing deals directly with the FNI militia. The gold from mines run by militias went to Pakistani peacekeepers. As the trade developed, the Pakistani officers brought in the Congolese army and then Indian traders from Kenya.

The United Nations was alerted to the allegations of gold trading by Human Rights Watch in late 2005. In June 2005, Human Rights Watch published a report, entitled, 'The Curse of Gold: Gold fuels massive human rights atrocities in Ituri, the northeastern region of the Democratic Republic of Congo'. The report documented human rights abuses linked to efforts to control two key gold mining areas, Mongwalu (Ituri District) and Durba (Haut Uélé District), both bordering Uganda. Local warlords and international companies were among those who benefited from access to these gold rich areas, while local people suffered from ethnic slaughter, torture and rape. The report documented how a leading Swiss gold refining company, Metalor Technologies, had previously bought gold from Uganda. After discussions and correspondence with Human Rights Watch beginning in December 2004, and after the report had gone to press, the company announced on 20 May 2005 that it would suspend its purchase of gold from Uganda.

The United Nations subsequently launched a major investigation by the Office for Internal Oversight Services. What they uncovered was even more explosive. The battle for mining concessions has indeed cost countless lives. Worse still, the arms surrendered by ex-combatants were secretly returned to them. There were militias that had been disarmed one day but were rearmed the very next day. The Pakistani battalion was giving arms back to the militias under the 'arms for gold' scheme.

When the Congolese people say that MONUC has brought more harm than good, they are perfectly right. The Congo was ravaged for six years by an unjust war of aggression, in which extreme sexual violence against women and children not only played an integral part but was in fact a 'weapon of war'. Girls are terrified of all military, foreign and local officials. The people of the Congo relied on the United Nations for both military protection and humanitarian aid. Yet the protectors unexpectedly turned out to be violators, just like Tutsi troops in the Congo and the militia they were backing.

Kofi Annan, then UN Secretary-General, insisted on 'zero tolerance' of sexual exploitation by peacekeepers. However, after at least 150 charges of sexual exploitation and abuse of Congolese women, boys and girls were made against UN personnel who were sent to help and protect them, only a few 'peacekeepers' – let us call them predators – were deported (including Tunisians, French, South Africans and Uruguayans), and no UN staff were charged with criminal activity (UN rules apply only to UN employees; military personnel fall under the jurisdiction of their own governments). Moreover, it took the United Nations six months to release its own internal report on the Congo sexual abuse scandal after media reports began to surface. One French 'peacekeeper' was abusing young girls in exchange for food and filming it, thus enriching his paedophile network back home.

Professor Collier claims that in the 1970s there were autocratic rulers throughout Africa but that now almost the entire continent consists of democracies. However, this has not brought an increase in good governance. 'Democracy should increase economic performance. Yet it undermines it,' he notes.

We have indeed seen such a shift in the last two decades. One wonders, however, whether these changes have sprung from within or whether they have been imposed from outside. During the Cold War, the 'one party system' was the order of the day in Africa. We had 'presidents for life'. Now, under new democracies, we see the same democratic leaders standing for three, even four terms, and handpicking their successors in the end.

So what has really changed? For large and powerful Western democracies, term limits are relative, depending on whether they are happy with the leader of a certain country or wish for his departure. It follows that Britain and America would have no problem with Ugandan President Yoweri Museveni serving a third term, albeit unconstitutionally, but this is exactly the same scenario that they hate to see in Robert Mugabe's Zimbabwe (under the Zimbabwean constitution, you can stand as many times as you want), following the controversial land reforms that affected the descendants of British settlers in the former Rhodesia.

President Mugabe has always accused Britain, Zimbabwe's former colonial power, of turning a bilateral conflict into a multilateral one, after Tony Blair's government stopped funding the land reform in Zimbabwe in 1997 – previously agreed to by both the Thatcher and Major governments – thus trampling the principle of continuity of the state. It now seems that Zimbabwe has won the argument, because Britain did not attend the EU-Africa Summit in Portugal in December 2007, whereas Zimbabwe did.

The external factor of corruption and lack of good governance should also not be overlooked. We know for certain that Angola's embezzled oil revenues end up in banks on Jersey. The late Nigerian military dictator, Abacha, looted more than $8 billion from his country and brought the money to Britain. Mobutu did the same in Zaire and shifted about $14 billion to Swiss bank accounts. What is puzzling is the fact that, when Western countries see these thieves bringing stolen money to their immoral banks, they initially let them in and then cry wolf afterwards!

In 2002, the UN Panel of Experts on the Illegal Exploitation of Natural Resources and Other Forms of Wealth of the Democratic Republic of the Congo published the names of all the multinationals from every Western country involved in the looting of the Congo's mineral wealth during the invasion. The OECD proved to be a weak instrument, because even after the Panel had established that international rules and standards had been broken, no government in Europe or North America was willing to launch an internal investigation – right up to this day.

Where do all these thugs who are raping women in eastern Congo get their weapons from? Even the international NGOs operating there are obliged to cooperate with the militias, otherwise they cannot carry out their humanitarian relief. Yet after they have treated the raped women, including stitching their mutilated private parts, the latter return to their villages only to be raped again. We do not manufacture guns in Africa (except for South Africa). Gun runners from the West and private military companies are a big problem in conflict zones. A British mercenary by the name of Simon Mann was arrested in Zimbabwe, as his company was allegedly poised to stage a coup in Equatorial Guinea. The son of the former British Prime Minister Margaret Thatcher was also involved.

It is no secret that multinational companies employ 'dogs of war' to protect their mining or oil concessions in conflict-ridden countries in Africa, besides the establishment of Western military bases all over the continent as part of the 'fight against terror'. Western countries must clean up their own backyards before shouting 'corruption, corruption'. Instead, they do everything to preserve the sad status quo.

That is why China is gaining ground in Africa. China is bringing investments to Africa without attaching any conditionality, as well as trade, exchange of technological know-how and lending with no interest. At the end of the day, Africa will judge its true friends by their willingness to share new technological know-how with Africa. Africa should not continue providing raw materials to others and buying back finished goods from those to whom it provides those raw materials. It must manage to transform its own natural resources in Africa and thus create jobs.

There is a strong suspicion in the West that China is simply grabbing African natural resources to feed the 'rising dragon'. And what do Africans themselves say? I was struck by an opinion piece by Femi Akomolafe in the November 2007 issue of *New African* magazine, which is published in London. The piece epitomises the common thinking of Africans on Sino-African relations:

> The Chinese, as history records, were on the African shores long before Europeans could navigate outside their waters; yet the Chinese didn't think of conquest, slavery or colonisation. They engaged in honourable trade and went back home... Today, the children of those Europeans who came to Africa to rob, plunder and settle are telling me that I should be afraid of the Chinese. I ask: What the hell for?

It has been argued that African leaders made a terrible blunder in 1963 when, at the launch of the Organisation of African Unity (OAU), now the African Union (AU), they decided that the borders inherited from colonisation were to remain sacrosanct. It has also been claimed that this was a recipe for endless conflicts and that these boundaries must be re-examined.

This is true only to a certain extent, because most African leaders who took part in the launch of the OAU were puppets of foreign interests who came to power by staging bloody coups. African pioneers of independence were the first to recognise that these boundaries represented a 'ticking bomb' and should be discarded. However, when Kwame Nkrumah, the first leader of independent Ghana, and Patrice Lumumba, the Democratic Republic of the Congo's first elected leader after independence, advocated the idea of a 'United States of Africa', with one government, one army, one currency and so on, they so angered the West that Nkrumah was overthrown and died in exile and Patrice Lumumba was assassinated. Both tragedies bore the CIA's fingerprints according to now declassified secret documents!

Belgium still owns large unused chunks of land (old plantations) in the Democratic Republic of the Congo. In addition, France still literally owns the Ivory Coast. Any leader who dares to change such a status quo plays with fire. When Congolese President Laurent Kabila dared, his neighbours were used against him and now he is gone. Ivorian President Laurent Gbagbo knows this only too well. The Zimbabweans know it only too well, as land reform has only brought British and American-led sanctions. However, the time will come, if it is not already here, when Africa will deal with the rest of the world on its own terms.

African union is now being revived as an idea. African unity is initially being achieved at regional level, and it will slowly be achieved at continental level, despite the fact that some leaders are still puppets of foreign interests. One concrete example of this is that, within the Southern African Development Community (SADC), visa requirements will soon be a thing of the past. In fact, this has already come into effect between Zimbabwe and Mozambique, where citizens from both countries can freely move and trade without any visa requirements at the border. It is already happening in our lifetime. Africa will achieve full unity some day!

Part IV:
Public Lectures on Conflict

The Art of Prevention of Conflict

Rolf Ekéus*

Within the realm of international security policy, it should be easy to find consensus around the idea that prevention is better than the cure. However, translating such a statement into concrete preventive action as regards international violence, or indeed genocide, appears to be difficult.

Take for example the Security Council of the United Nations, an organisation that has been given the task of protecting coming generations from the scourge of war and which, in accordance with Article I of the UN Charter, should take effective measures for the prevention and removal of threats to the peace. Only a modest fraction of the Council's working time is devoted to actual prevention, while the agenda is dominated by crisis management, conflict resolution, post-conflict operations, peace enforcement and peacekeeping.

It is not a lack of will that makes prevention of violent conflict such a rare phenomenon in security policy around the globe. It is instead the complexity of the problem and the difficulty to define exactly what constitutes the actual threat. That is because serious security problems are rarely generated by a single cause, and such situations consequently need to be addressed by a set of preventive measures. If the threats in question constitute mass violence or even genocide, prevention must be a matter, not of random or improvised actions, but of systematic and structural measures.

In recent years, two types of threat have been highlighted as the most urgent ones – the proliferation of weapons of mass destruction and international terrorism. Both of them, especially in combination, carry the potential of mass destruction and even genocide. The European Security Strategy specifies a limited set of key threats, namely terrorism and proliferation of weapons of mass destruction, to which are added regional conflicts, state failure and organised crime.

---

* Ambassador Rolf Ekéus, former Director of the UN Special Commission on Iraq.

Professor Robert Jay Lifton, who has spent a lifetime studying the psychological dimensions of violence – with regard to the Holocaust, terrorism and the use of nuclear weapons and other WMDs – has defined what he calls the 'genocidal mentality', an expression of power generated by the control over nuclear weapons and the capability to use them without discrimination.

Even if we admit without hesitation the genocidal dimension of terrorism and nuclear weapons, it is disappointing and surprising that the issues of majority-minority conflict and ethnic tension are not mentioned in the European Security Strategy.

Until fifteen years ago, international conflicts, at least in Europe, were a matter of clashing state interests. This goes back to more than 360 years ago, when the Westphalian system of states was established. Once in almost every generation, there was a major war in Europe. However, contemporary conflicts are first and foremost generated by tensions between ethnic groups or majority-minority situations. A majority of the over 200 wars witnessed since World War II were not international wars but internal armed conflicts. There is no doubt that the international terrorism of today constitutes a clear and present danger, but this fact should not be allowed to overshadow the structural threat of ethnic conflict with its historically proven genocidal potential.

Three European empires – the Romanov, Ottoman and Habsburg empires – were destroyed during World War I, but another was rising from the ashes – the Union of Soviet Socialist Republics. The Soviet empire, having with great suffering withstood the tremendous assault of the German army, emerged from World War II with self-confidence and boundless ambitions. After 1945, the Soviet empire as a functional phenomenon extended beyond the already considerable stretches of land of the Soviet Union, deep into the Europe of the former Ottoman and Habsburg empires. The Warsaw Pact countries were not only militarily but, more importantly, also politically and ideologically part of the socialist empire of the Soviet Union. The socialist/communist parties of Poland, Hungary, Czechoslovakia, Romania, Bulgaria and East Germany were beholden to Moscow, with the Kremlin serving as a sort of secular Mecca for the socialist world. The Socialist Federation of Yugoslavia became something of an independent adjunct to the Soviet Union, competing on the socialist turf in a similar way to how the Serbian Orthodox Church related to its larger brother, the Orthodox Church of Russia.

The common denominator for all these states and republics was an identity rooted in socialist characteristics. Poland was thus not a state for Poles, but a state of socialist, political and economic structures. Like the other states in the Soviet sphere of power or within the Soviet empire, it was the People's Republic of Poland, not the Republic of Poland or the Polish Republic. East

Germany was named the German Democratic Republic, a code word for a socialist Germany. As regards the fifteen republics within the Soviet Union, they became double-hatted as both socialist and Soviet, like the Latvian Soviet Socialist Republic.

In sum, the communist party was the only source of political power in these states and republics, and in the end all these parties in turn had to obey the one and only ultimate source of power, the communist party in Moscow, its politburo and executive.

The collapse of the Soviet Union was accompanied by the breakdown of the communist/socialist order. In the ensuing chaos and confusion that engulfed the whole sphere of influence of the disintegrating Soviet empire, states and republics lost the socialist identity on which they had been built. Out of the ruins of the fallen empire emerged new states that defined themselves in various ways as market economies (liberal or democratic), but without exception as nation states. The ethnic and religious majority came to constitute the identity of each of the new states. These changes of identity did not happen without pain. The Red Army, all but dissolved, could do little or nothing to interfere in or halt the outbreak of violence all around the former Soviet Union.

The common denominator for the regional violence was the tension and hatred between the different majorities and minorities in the former Soviet republics now gaining independence as states. All this reflected the repercussions of the national ideology practiced by Josef Stalin. A major ingredient of the Stalinist national ideology was the idea of preventing the formation of nationally unified republics in the regions which might be tempted to challenge the dominance of the Kremlin, the Party and Russian ethnicity and culture. Thus, the borders of the republics had frequently been drawn to cut through the habitat and geographic ethnicity of the nations. For example, large portions of the areas populated by Tajiks, including the proud historical cities of Buchara and Samarkand, had been allotted to Uzbekistan, while territories inhabited by ethnic Uzbeks had come to belong to Turkmenistan and to the Ferghana Valley portion of Kirgizstan. Parts of Abkhazian, Armenian and Azeri populated areas were transferred to Georgia, while Nagorno Karabach, which geographically belonged to one and was populated by the other, became a perennial source of contention between Armenia and Azerbaijan. Moldova had to function with a Romanian-oriented and Slavic/Russian population in an uneasy and unstable cohabitation.

When the defining structures of the republics turned into nation states, the majority-minority situations, further influenced by the nationalistic and security interests of neighbouring kin-states, created ethnically driven tensions that developed into violent confrontations and serious atrocities in Central Asia, the Caucasus and Moldavia. This was a consequence of the manipulative and calculated way in which the Kremlin had used regional ethnic differences to control its vast territory.

In contrast, the Baltic states, especially Latvia, which during the Stalinist era had been subject to a strategy of ethnic cleansing, combining the transfer of its nationals to the Gulag with large-scale Russian immigration, managed to obtain independence without any bloodshed, despite resistance by a Russian minority that was loyal to Moscow.

The potential for violence when nationalistic sentiments are released has been amply illustrated by the tragic events in connection with the dissolution of Yugoslavia, including local wars and ethnic cleansing, especially against the Muslim population in Bosnia and both Muslims and Serbs in Kosovo.

The collapse of the Soviet system and the break-up of the monolithic Soviet Union proper and its equally monolithic supporting alliance system in Central and Eastern Europe meant that millions of individuals had to search for an identity other than being a communist subject striving for the realisation of the Marxist vision. That identity had to be found as members of resurrected nation states. Belonging to one specific nationality meant an opportunity to lay claim to territory, a country, provided history and size of nations coincided to make this possible. The alternative was to settle for a minority status within a state and adjust to the realities of minority life, which included challenges relating to language, education, history, participation in governance and self-realisation. Too frequently, the political reality for minorities has been that fundamental rights have been questioned and discrimination has become a reality, even in cases where discrimination is proscribed by law.

Like the Soviet Union, colonial Africa was politically divided without much consideration for ethnic, religious or tribal realities. Economic, geographic, military and security factors determined the division of the continent into colonial entities. When of the time to dismantle the colonial structures arrived, new African leaders, like Nkrumah, Kenyatta, Nyerere, Senghor and others, agreed that the colonial borders should be retained as the borders of the new independent states of Africa. In this way, border disputes between the emerging states on the continent would be minimised. Some fifty years later, however, respect for this order started to crack. Following the sorry pattern of Central Asia and the Balkans, majority-minority and tribal disputes descended into violent and bloody conflicts, civil war and even genocide.

Summing up, if we reflect upon the violent conflicts that have occurred since the end of the Cold War in South-East and Central Europe, the Caucasus and Central Asia, as well as in Africa and South-East Asia, we find that the vast majority of these events have been generated by ethnic tension and strife. Genocides have been the result of atrocities directed against minorities.

Returning to the starting point of this paper, namely that prevention is of the essence, it should be obvious that international efforts to prevent new conflicts that could potentially lead to genocide should focus on inter-ethnic problems and majority-minority relations.

The long-term structural prevention of conflicts depends on a number of factors, including economic stability, inter-ethnic integration, a society based on law and respect for human rights. The main onus for creating such conditions rests on individual states. They must foster an environment and political structure within their borders that is representative and pluralistic, allows for equal opportunities and protects and promotes the rights of all citizens and residents.

However, the international community must provide the appropriate normative framework and encourage states to address inter-ethnic and inter-religious tensions at local and national level. The repeated failure of the international community to act in prevention of mass violence, and indeed of genocide, in spite of universally recognised human rights makes it imperative to consider more radical steps in support of prevention. A most welcome development in dealing with communal conflicts has been the growing support for the concept of the 'responsibility to protect'. This responsibility rests first of all with the individual state, which is responsible for acting within its own borders. However, in extreme cases, such as the treat of a mass atrocity, the international community may justifiably assume the responsibility to protect and intervene in the conflict. However, we are all aware that the concept is looked upon with considerable scepticism and concern by developing countries and the majority of the members of the UN General Assembly, which are sensitive to any attempt to call into question the principle of national sovereignty. It should also be noted that protection can only be activated when a violent conflict has already broken out and may necessitate enforcement actions within the territory of a state. Prevention sounds more attractive, it does not necessary imply military intervention or the use of arms, and should definitely be more compatible with the principle of national sovereignty. What speaks against prevention is that it is arguably infinitely more difficult to realise than protection. One reason for this is that the need for action is generally not understood before actual violence has broken out. However, lessons learned from the post-Cold War era of ethnic conflicts should lead preventive action to focus on ethnic and religious tensions that could have major security implications and lead to the outbreak of war or large-scale military confrontation – tensions that involve the national majorities and minorities.

There are three major ways to deal with such situations: (1) separation or partition; (2) assimilation, either voluntary (the US model) or enforced; and (3) integration with respect for diversity.

The first option worked well in the case of Czechoslovakia, which underwent a harmonic partition, but had tragic consequences in Yugoslavia, including the most recent problems regarding the independence of Kosovo. The prospect of the separation from Georgia of Abkhazia and South Ossetia, as well as, possibly, the Armenian-speaking part of the country, could potentially lead to violent conflict and war. Likewise, the partition of Moldova or even Ukraine (including Crimea) would have far-reaching consequences for international peace and security. The complex situation in Central Asia, including the potential separation of traditional Tajik-populated areas from Uzbekistan or Uzbek-populated areas from Kirgizstan, or the considerable radicalisation of parts of the region's Muslim population, could have serious implications. A general rule as regards national minorities in many countries is that the mere suspicion of solidarity with a kin-state creates serious tensions with the majority population. Outside Europe, the examples in Africa of Biafra and Katanga demonstrate the possible fatal consequences of separatist policies.

The second option, assimilation in a voluntary fashion along the lines of the US model, may also not be completely problem-free. Professor Samuel Huntington, who famously wrote of the 'Clash of Civilisations', is fighting a rearguard struggle to save the United States as an Anglo-Protestant citadel against the onslaught of the waves of Hispanic/Mexican immigration. According to Professor Huntington, the centuries old policy/practice of assimilating mass immigration appears is being challenged by the unwillingness or inability of the new immigrants to assimilate. Thus, the notion of the United States as a united nation with one culture is being put at risk. Although Huntington's ideas about the Hispanic challenge have met with vigorous opposition in American academia, they are argued with force and cannot be ignored, as they may enjoy a wide appeal in the United States and, like so many other American intellectual and social innovations, be transported to Europe.

In any case, non-voluntary assimilation is a problem of more immediate concern in terms of conflict-driving policies. For example, Turkey's policy towards its national minorities does not recognise any groups other than the ones defined under the 1923 Lausanne Treaty. The atrocities committed against the Armenian national minority is still a recent memory. Today, the Turkish policy of forcing assimilation on the Kurdish population in Turkey's south-eastern region is a source of high tension and could lead to disastrous violence. The Kurdish population in Turkey, which numbers around fifteen million, is prohibited from using its language and culture. It is impossible for Kurdish children to receive education in their mother tongue, even at primary school level. The explosive situation in the Kurdish-speaking part of Turkey is further complicated by the unpredictable development of and the unsettled situation in the Kurdish region of Iraq. The Kurdish problem remains a major, even definitive, obstacle to Turkey's chances of joining the European Union as a member state in the foreseeable future.

Options one and two, separation and enforced assimilation, illustrate that the costs and risks of attempts to create ethnically pure states – by peaceful or violent means – have been unacceptably high. The logical choice of any society should therefore be to find ways to exist in a multi-ethnic context. Option three, the integration of minorities with respect for identity, thus remains the only possibility.

Europe's complex ethnic background has produced an immense wealth of linguistic and cultural diversity. Multi-ethnicity is a source of strength and an asset but requires policies and tools that develop pleasant human habitats, where different cultures and religions are appreciated and equal opportunities and rights are guaranteed for all. These norms and tools would be largely ineffective without a mechanism to promote their implementation. Since multi-ethnicity is a national phenomenon, moreover, these mechanisms have to function within societies, which is a major problem considering the fact that governments generally dislike instruments for involvement in internal affairs of state. With the creation in 1992 of the office of the High Commissioner on National Minorities (HCNM), the OSCE (then CSCE) acquired a mechanism that was designed to operate inside states on issues relating to majority-minority relations, with the specific task of preventing the outbreak of violent conflict. As a way to make this tolerable to governments, the HCNM was mandated to work confidentially. Since its creation, the HCNM has operated all over the OSCE area without any drop in the confidence of the participating states in the institution.

The solution to problems relating to inter-ethnicity should be sought, as far as possible, within the framework of the state itself. The most vital contribution to the elimination of minority problems as destabilising elements is the promotion of a more harmonious relationship between the majority and minorities in the state itself. In Europe, the post-totalitarian transition societies placed national identity high on the agenda. This is equally applicable to both the majority population and minorities. Under these circumstances, minorities strive to return to their long-suppressed ethnic and religious identities and frequently demand self-determination. This often leads to conflicts between the majority and minority populations regarding what constitutes the collective identity. The consequence of such a process of identity formation is a struggle between the minorities' efforts at self-assertion and the majorities' determination to forge a national identity based on its own ethnic, religious and cultural traditions and to prevent any further loss of territory and power.

Self-assertion as a minority can be achieved within the framework of the state. It does not necessarily require a territorial expression, but may be achieved through legislation promoting the development of the identity of the minority in fields such as culture, education and public affairs. It is the responsibility of the government to provide for the security and protection of everyone inside its jurisdiction, including minorities, and to promote an inclusive national identity. In practical terms, to achieve this end is to integrate different ethnic communities within the state. The minorities must be given the means to build their society, together with the majority, in such a way that the state is the common home for all, where no one is treated as a second-class citizen.

Integration involves a balance of rights and responsibilities on both sides. On the one hand, the state respects the right of the minorities to maintain their identity, for example by facilitating education and broadcasting in the language of the minority and by encouraging their participation in public life. On the other hand, members of the minority give their allegiance to the state, pursue their objectives by means of their participation in the public life of the state and refrain from challenging its territorial integrity.

Over the years, with the assistance of international experts, the HCNM has produced written guidelines in key areas, such as education, language, political participation, minority language broadcasting and policing, which are then used as recommendations adapted to the parties concerned in a particular case or dispute. These issues usually reflect the core concern of persons belonging to national minorities and require particular attention and resources from governments.

It goes without saying that integration is doomed to fail without complementary steps in the socio-economic sphere. Where minorities are faced with economic marginalisation, strict non-discrimination must be applied with regard to access to jobs and professions, including in the public service. There is also a strong link between integration and education and training, for example access to higher and technical or vocational training.

Prevention of conflict in our times must focus on matters relating to inter-ethnic tension. In order to answer the question of how to implement the task of prevention, we have to address the choice between assimilation, integration and separation or partition. The answer should be simple: to search for the middle ground between the two extremes – forced assimilation and partition – namely integration with respect for diversity. That is the best way.

A sceptic might say that this is easier said than done, and I would agree. However, we have not found a better solution.

Leslie Prince Memorial Lecture of the Anglo-Jewish Association

General Sir Rupert Smith*

This paper falls into three sections. First, I will argue that there has been a change in the face or paradigm of war and that our institutions are unsuited to conduct the new form of war because they all developed to manage the previous one. Then, I will illustrate some of the characteristics of this new form of war with examples from the conflict between Israel and Hezbollah in 2006. Finally, I will make some brief suggestions of where we need to look not so much for the answers but for the changes we must make.

It is my contention, argued in *The Utility of Force*,[1] that the nature of operations today and in the future is fundamentally different from that of the past, which our institutions were developed to conduct successfully. I call this form or model of war 'war amongst the people', in contrast to the industrial war of the past. The essential difference between the two is that military force is no longer used to decide the matter. It is used to create a condition in which the strategic result is achieved by other means, the strategic object being to alter the opponent's intentions, rather than to destroy him. As a result, we do not move in a nice linear way – as described in the Old Testament – of peace, crisis, war, resolution, peace. That is what our institutions have grown up to manage. Now, we live in a world of continuous confrontations and conflicts in which military actions in the conflict support the achievement of the desired outcome of the confrontation by other means.

When I talk of institutions, I am referring to the institutions of governance, whether they be those of Whitehall or Tel Aviv, whether they be parliamentary or administrative, and whether they be national or intergovernmental. I

* General Sir Rupert Smith, KCB, DSO & Bar, OBE, QGM.

[1] Rupert Smith, *The Utility of Force: The Art of War in the Modern World* (London, Allen Lane 2005).

am referring to the executive institutions: the diplomatic service, the intelligence services, the armed forces, the development services and the multinational organisations that we form from elements of these. Finally, I am referring to the defence industries. Linking all of these institutions are processes, relationships and authorities that bring them into a whole. I am not, except in general terms, referring to particular weapons or equipments or organisations. If we are to change, to recognise this change in the face of war, then we must understand the complexity of what we are about and the fact that the institutions are functioning and in many cases engaged. In any event, what is required is not changing the tools, but changing the way we think about using them, and the outcome that we wish to achieve with them. In other words, we need to change our method of using the tools and thus, when and where necessary, to change the organisation and the practice.

As an example, consider the world of art. The Impressionists were trained as realists. They had the same paint brushes, the same palette, the same canvas – and they looked at the same view – but the Impressionists had a completely different idea of the outcome. In information theory, one might say that they ordered the data differently. And they produced a compellingly different result. If we are to triumph in the wars of today, we have to learn to perform the trick the Impressionists did in the world of art. As you will see, I have not chosen Impressionism by mistake. What I am arguing for is a similar shift in our institutions.

The second reason that we must have this profound change in our understanding of the use of military force, rather than in the first instance considering the tools and the equipment, also results from the shift from industrial war to war amongst the people. In industrial war, we set out to achieve advantage by having superior equipment in superior numbers. We knew, or had decided on, the worst case opponent, and we matched our inventories accordingly. Tactically, the way these means were used was always important, as it was occasionally at theatre level. But in war amongst the people, where the opponent is formless, operating deliberately below the threshold of the utility of our equipments as we want to use them, and using them amongst the people and with objectives to do with altering intentions rather than destruction, the way we use our equipment is a strategic act as well as a tactical one. Clausewitz said that a triumph in a fight was the product of the trial of strength and the clash of wills – the product of those two characteristics. Consider a football match or a boxing bout or anything like that. There are two more or less equally matched sides. It becomes a trial of strength and a clash of wills. If either one of those comes to zero, you have lost.

Instead of industrial war, in which the opponents set out with the primary objective of winning the trial of strength, devoting all their forces and resources to destroying the opponent's capability to resist and thereby winning the clash of wills, we now have war amongst the people, in which the primary objective is to win the clash of wills. In industrial war, the opponents seek to resolve the political confrontation that was its cause directly, by force of arms. The objectives for the use of military force are hard and simple. Words like 'take', 'hold', 'destroy', 'defeat' and 'annihilate' are used. They all describe the desirable outcome of a trial of strength. In war amongst the people, the objectives are malleable and complex. They describe a condition that enables intentions to be changed or formed by other means. To take a current example, in both Afghanistan and Iraq the words 'to create a safe and secure environment' are used. In war amongst the people, military force does not resolve the confrontation directly. The conflicts or forceful acts contribute to the efforts of one side or the other to win the clash of wills – to capture the will of the people or, at the very least, to neutralise it and thus work towards deciding the confrontation to advantage. I have said that we are in this world of confrontations and conflicts, and I will try to explain what I mean by these words. I do not use them as synonyms, although much of our press does.

A confrontation occurs when two or more bodies, in broadly the same circumstances, are pursuing different outcomes. Political affairs of all stripes, national and international, are about resolving confrontations. However, when one or both sides cannot have their way and will not accept the alternative outcome, they sometimes seek to use military force to achieve their goals. In other words, they turn to conflict. In the case of industrial war, we sought to resolve certain matters by means conflict. War was strategically decisive. This is no longer the case.

In adopting conflict as its course of action, the weaker side – if it is wise – does not play to the opponent's strength, but rather follows the path of the guerrilla or the terrorist, avoiding set battles except on its own terms and avoiding the operationally or strategically decisive engagement so as not to present the stronger opponent with the chance to deliver the mortal blow. It follows a generic strategy composed of three strands: the propaganda of the deed, provocation and the erosion of the will. It does this so as to advance its position in the overall confrontation. Alternatively, it seeks to replicate that strength – like Iran or North Korea and possibly others – and develops nuclear weapons while following that same generic strategy. This leads to the consequence that we see all about us: that conflict occurs but that its effects are usually only tactical. Very occasionally, you get a theatre-level effect, but in some instances force, however forceful it looks, achieves only sub-strategic goals.

If you are very strong and have nuclear weapons, you have too much to lose in using them. But whether you have them or not, you have to find a way to exert your power, to use your strength, which is more than just your military forces. For, as the philosopher Michel Foucault said, power is a relationship, not a possession. Finding the way to establish that relationship to advantage is the strategic question of our time. How, and to what end, do we apply force sub-strategically, in the conflict, so as to gain our strategic and political position in the overall confrontation and prevent our opponent from doing likewise? Or, put another way, how do we avoid the observable phenomenon of being able to win every fight but losing the war? How, in what way and with what means do we translate these tactical successes into a strategic success? I believe that our institutions of governance have failed to find the answer.

This form of war – war amongst the people – has six defining characteristics. Although they are presented in the form of a list, they should be understood as being written in a circle with each one playing on the other five. In addition, they are all dependent upon the circumstances of the particular confrontation in terms of the weight that must be attached to each characteristic. Nevertheless, they define war amongst the people.

The first trend has already been discussed above. The ends for which we employ or deploy military force are changing from the hard objectives of industrial war to those malleable objectives of changing intentions. This means that the objectives are to establish a condition in which other measures can achieve the desired outcome of forming or changing the opponent's intentions. For example, the Korean War started in 1948 when we changed our intentions, when China intervened, because to do otherwise was to use the atomic bomb. We settled on a divided career along almost the same lines on which the war had started, which, incidentally, is where the Second World War in that part of the world had finished. And we are still there in confrontation with the conflict unresolved. It just looks as though it is nuclear at the moment, and with a bit of luck and hope is about to de-nuclearise. We referred to the Cold War as a war, and we thought we might have to go to war, but we did not. We changed the intentions of the people. We did not change the intentions of their leaders. First, the peoples of the western satellites of the Soviet empire changed their minds and changed their leaders, and then the people of Russia did. It was a confrontation, not a conflict. It is all about deterrence, namely to change someone's intentions, not to destroy him. In the Yom Kippur War, President Sadat's objective was to create a condition by military force in which the confrontation between Egypt and Israel over the Sinai could be resolved to his advantage. That is as good an explanation as any for the intelligence failure. Bosnia, Kosovo and now Afghanistan and Iraq all provide examples – regardless of the rhetoric used at the time – of the military being used to establish a condition usually expressed, as already noted, as something like 'a safe and secure environment', rather than to resolve the confrontation.

I will now turn to the conflict between Israel and Lebanon in 2006.

What were the ends or objectives of Hezbollah and Israel? Hezbollah is said to have initiated the conflict, either separately or in sum, to take prisoners for bargaining purposes, a tactical act to improve one's position in a conflict. Indeed, Hassan Nasrallah, the Hezbollah leader, had been saying that he would do this for about a year so as to recover some of the men taken and convicted by Israel. He is quoted as saying, after they had taken the two prisoners: 'No military operation will return the captured Israeli soldiers. The prisoners will not be returned, except through one way – indirect negotiations and a trade of prisoners.' He is also – or Hezbollah is also – said to have done this to draw Israel into an attack on Lebanon, a condition to enhance Hezbollah's position in Lebanon by showing they could defend it successfully against Israel and/or to improve their position *vis-à-vis* Hamas, who were doing the same thing down in Gaza, and/or to further the Iranian and Syrian objectives in their confrontations with Israel and the United States.

In all cases, Hezbollah is using military force to establish a condition to advantage, not to achieve a direct strategic result. Israel, on the other hand, declared the attack by Hezbollah's military wing as an act of war and promised Lebanon a very painful and far-reaching response. In short, they saw themselves not at war with the state of Lebanon itself but with a non-state actor, Hezbollah, in Lebanon. However, they wanted the Lebanese government to take responsibility for Hezbollah and to control what went on in Lebanon. The Israeli government authorised severe and harsh retaliation on Lebanon, and the Chief of Staff said: 'If the soldiers are not returned, we will turn Lebanon's clock back twenty years.'

A former commander said: 'Israel is attempting to create a rift between the Lebanese population and Hezbollah's supporters by exacting a heavy price from the elite in Beirut.' The message is: 'If you want your air conditioning to work, and if you want to be able to fly to Paris for shopping, you must pull your head out of the sand and take action towards shutting down Hezbollah.'

In all of this, we can see that Israel was also setting conditional objectives, namely to get the Lebanese to deal with Hezbollah. However, these pronouncements were accompanied by others that were couched in the hard terms of industrial war, namely that the objective was to destroy Hezbollah and defeat the rocket attacks, which gave an early hint that there might be divided counsel in Tel Aviv. However, as events unfolded, the Lebanese were seen by Tel Aviv to be powerless. The rockets still fell on Israel's towns and Hezbollah fought on. These objectives were adjusted to the conditional objectives of gaining a viable internationally guaranteed buffer zone, obtaining a better position in the bargaining for prisoners and re-establishing the deterrent effect of the IDF. This explains why I have called the objectives of 'war amongst the people' malleable.

I have provided this range of examples to show that this trend has existed for a long time, and in most cases forces may be deployed strategically but are used or employed sub-strategically. The next trend is that we tend to carry out these actions in multinational or non-state groupings. The good guys tend to be in the former and the bad guys tend to be in the latter. These current issues need not be the formal ones, like the NATO alliance, the United Nations or the Coalition in Iraq today, but are often, and particularly in the theatre of operations, informal and include, in effect, other agencies, such as the OSCE or non-governmental organisations like UNHCR, Oxfam or *Médecins Sans Frontières*. Then, of course, you can have local actors, such as the Iraqi or Afghan security forces, as part of your informal alliance. Alternatively, and more dangerously, you find yourself dining with the devil for short-term gain, like when we made alliances with the Northern Alliance in Afghanistan as we bombed and bribed our way into Kabul, because we needed somebody on the ground to take advantage of our bombs. The same occurred with the Kosovo Liberation Army in the bombing of Kosovo at the turn of the century.

Then, of course, we have the non-state actors: Hezbollah, Hamas, ETA, IRA, the Taliban, al-Qaeda and so forth. The obvious example from Lebanon is that Hezbollah is a non-state actor, and that Israel was attacking Hezbollah in and on Lebanese territory, and killing Lebanese people and destroying Lebanese property, because Lebanon was not acting as a state. Israel is clearly a state and was in large measure acting like one. However, as will become clear when we examine the other trends, it too was limited by this characteristic of engaging with a non-state actor. I will not go into great detail regarding the tangle of relationships that reached all the way to the United Nations and the Security Council and to the meetings of the G8 during the months of July and August 2006. The United States, the United Kingdom and Israel were opposing terror organisations generally and Iran in particular. Other actors include Hezbollah, Iran and Syria, the European allies and, subsequently, UNIFIL, a multinational force with contingents, each answering to different capitals. All of them, to one degree or another and at one stage or another, were actors and in some cases still are actors in that theatre of operations.

The third and most obvious trend is that war takes place amongst the people. First, the objective is the will of the people. Secondly, the opponent, often operating according to the tenets of the guerrilla and the terrorist, depends on the people for concealment, moral and physical support and information. Thirdly, the strategy of provocation and propaganda of the deed requires the people to be there for these strategies to work. However, these conflicts also take place amongst the people in another sense – in the media. Whoever coined the phrase 'the theatre of operations' was very prescient. I say this as somebody who has served as a theatre commander. In these modern wars, these wars amongst the people, you now stand there as the commander like a producer of some gladiatorial contest in a Roman circus. Only, down there in the pit with you and your gladiators is at least one other producer and his gladiators, and you have different scripts. Mixed up with you are all the people who are late for their seats, the fools who cannot find their car parking places, the ice-cream sellers and the ticket touts. They are all milling around where you are. All around you in the stands is a highly factional audience that pays attention to what is going on in the pit by looking at the noisiest section through the drinking straw of their Coca Cola cans.

Your business as the theatre commander, the producer, is to wait and act and tell the most compelling story to the people in the stands. And if you can, you have won.

The conflict between Hezbollah and Israel in 2006, an event in a much longer and unresolved confrontation, took place amongst the people in both the senses I have described. In Israel, the people in their houses, in the towns and cities, were manifestly the targets of Hezbollah's rocket attacks. Israel, in attacking Hezbollah, operating amongst the people and seeking to coerce the Lebanese people, hit Lebanese people and property, killing some 1,200 Lebanese and causing great damage to infrastructure and the displacement of over a million people. In that theatre or circus, who had the most compelling narrative?

On balance, and judging by the majority view, it was probably Hezbollah, which, with disciplined silence and an uncommon lack of organisational ego, played to the generic strategy of the propaganda of the deed. With the strategy of provocation – particularly within the context of the greater confrontation over the existence of Israel – they were able to cast themselves as the victims, or at least as the representatives of the victims.

A few weeks after the ceasefire, *The Economist* declared on its front cover: 'Nasrallah Rules. The war'. In a poll conducted at the same time, 65% of

Israelis wanted their prime minister to resign because of his handling of the war. Israel had not achieved its stated objectives, and Hezbollah had maintained its attacks from southern Lebanon in the face of the mighty idea. In the view of the Arab street, Hezbollah had done what should be done. Under the UN ceasefire, however, the Lebanese Army and UNIFIL were to operate on the border with Israel and prevent attacks across it. Hezbollah had thus lost its freedom of action in the south.

Criminal law, treaty law or international humanitarian law – how do we show that our actions are legitimate and those of our opponents are not?

The fourth trend is that war amongst the people is timeless. We set out to win industrial wars quickly because the whole of society was involved, and we wanted to get back to peace and have a normal life just as the Old Testament said. In our new circumstances, it is more important to do things at the right time rather than twice. In the theatre, it is all about timing, not about sticking to some staff officer's railway timetable. The basic tactic is only to engage on one's own terms – not today or on Tuesday, not when your opponent wants to, but when it is to your advantage to do so safely. When our military objectives are to seek set conditions in which other instruments of power are to resolve the matter, to resolve the confrontation, then we must maintain those conditions until they have succeeded.

We are still in Korea, Cyprus, Kosovo and Lebanon. The rhetoric at the time of the initial engagement, based on the concept of industrial war, said otherwise, but the reality is that we are still there. These confrontations are timeless because we have to maintain the condition until other means can be found to resolve them. As already noted, the conflict in Lebanon in 2006 is one event in a long-running confrontation. People are already forgetting how long forces under the UN flag have been deployed in Lebanon, let alone the region. The first 'I' in UNIFIL stands for 'interim'. They were deployed in 1978. How long is interim?

The fifth trend is that we fight to preserve the force. No commander wants to suffer any more casualties to his men and equipment than he has to. However, in industrial war, it was, in the main, possible to replace your losses. We developed the production lines to do this: conscription, on the one hand, and defence industries, on the other. We had depots of kit and reserves in place. These hardly exist anymore, and where they do it is extremely difficult to call upon them – particularly the manpower resources. We fight to preserve our forces for other reasons. We have to sustain the operations because they are timeless, because they are not strategically decisive and we have to maintain the condition. As an officer responsible for handling this side of life towards the end of my career, I developed what I call 'Smith's Underpants Rule'. You have one on, one off and one in the wash, as an absolute minimum. So to any bright spark who suggested to me: 'Oh, we only need a battalion to do that', I would say: 'You need three battalions as a minimum!' And you very quickly run out of British Army if you do that. The factor is actually rather higher than three. In fact, it is closer to five, and ideally you want to push it even higher than that. We fight not to lose the force for the same reason that the guerrilla fights that way. It is expensive to acquire more forces, move them and prepare new men and equipment. Finally, politicians at home, uncertain of the popularity of the venture, wish to keep the cost of men and materials within what they judge, in the circumstances, to be politically sustainable boundaries. We can see this trend in the course of the conflict between Hezbollah and Israel.

The cause of the conflict was the taking of prisoners; the reaction was to preserve the force. In industrial war, we all took prisoners. No one had a fight to recapture prisoners. There is a whole genre of literature about prisoner-of-war camps and about escaping from them. Now, we actually go to war for two men. However, it is important to understand that this is a different thing from what we used to do. Two men were the small change of industrial war. While I do not know enough about the internal workings of Hezbollah, Israel was extremely cautious when it came to conducting land operations, particularly after it lost a tank, its crew and a number of other soldiers during the initial follow-up to the raid that took the prisoners.

We can also see that fighting to preserve the forces is not the same as avoiding casualties. People were killed in large numbers where the fighting took place. The figures are far from reliable, but something in the order of 1,000 Lebanese civilians and somewhere between 250 and 500 Hezbollah fighters were killed. In Israel, 120 soldiers and police and some forty-four civilians were killed, showing the value of a well-prepared civil defence and the relative inefficiency of the unguided rocket as a weapon.

The sixth and final trend is that new uses are being found for weapons and organisations acquired and developed for different purposes. I am not arguing for one minute that a commander should not adapt his force to the circumstances; he should. That is what he is paid for. If we look at the use of some of our weapons, however, they are not being used for the purpose or in the way they were intended to be used. If we are not using our weapons in this way, then something must have changed.

What is happening is that our opponents are operating below the threshold of the utility of our forces as we would wish to use them. They are deliberately doing this. It is a deliberate decision by a thinking enemy. He will not give us the opportunity to use our potential strength. When we try to use our strength in the way of industrial war, we play to his position, his generic strategy of provocation and propaganda of the deed. The conflict of 2006 provides examples of this.

Israel's use of its reserves is another case in point. The main weight of the initial response was in the air and artillery strikes. Ground operations of any size, a company or two, were not mounted for about ten days. These operations were directed towards Hezbollah strongholds and were intended to prevent rockets from being fired from these areas. Hezbollah were in well-prepared positions and ready for a fight. By this stage, reserve units were being called up, and these units were trained, organised and equipped for armoured manoeuvre. However, they were receiving orders to achieve objectives to do with stopping the rocket attacks, while avoiding civilian casualties. It seems that the commanders and their staffs lacked the language to explain what was required in terms that the reservists could understand and for which they were trained. Eventually and slowly, because the call-up process was found to be inefficient, Israel built up a sufficient force to conduct a general advance to the Litani river, which got under way some three days before the ceasefire was called.

Hezbollah's use of the Katyusha rocket is another example of using weapons for a different purpose than the one for which they were intended and of operating below the threshold of the utility of Israel's weapon systems. This aerial weapon was originally designed by Russia to provide general support to an attacking ground force by thickening up its artillery barrage from a distance with an easily transportable system suitable for movement with bulk logistic handling systems so as to be fired in large numbers in a short period. This is an evident requirement if you are conducting industrial war.

In 2006, we saw it being used undefeated as a surrogate air force against a population. Hezbollah fired a few rockets at a time, from concealed storage sites, on a 'shoot and scoot' basis. For all its inaccuracy, its small warhead and its inefficiency, it was an effective weapon in the circumstances.

It is important to note that, in spelling out these characteristics, I have not said that there will be no more big fights. Indeed, the examples I mentioned at the beginning of the is paper provide plenty of examples of big battles. Nor have I said that these fights will not be in support of the achievement of objectives to do with state sovereignty. I am saying, however, that force will not achieve this directly or strategically. It may, if used well, establish conditions in which the objective is achieved by other means. I am also not suggesting that battle is in any way less awful than it ever was.

Finally, what is to be done?

The single most important thing is to change the way we think about the use of military force, to recognise the change in paradigm and to acknowledge that our institutional mindsets, developed and honed during years of industrial war, need to change. Force has utility. If it does not, why are we so concerned about terrorist groups, the spread of nuclear weapons and so forth? Why is it that our opponents appear to understand the utility of force rather better than we do? How do we bring our military forces to bear, with advantage?

We need to understand the outcome desired in the overall confrontation as being one of imposing one's will and changing intentions, and then we need to choose the objectives that support the achievement of that confrontational goal. In addition, we need to establish which of these objectives are to be achieved by military force and with what priority. Based on this understanding of the relationship between the confrontation and the conflict, we need to form the driving logic to direct the operation as a whole, so that all the leaders of power, such as diplomacy, the economy and so forth, can be brought to bear coherently and be *supported* by the use of military force.

It is important to respect one's opponent as a thinking pro-active enemy who is bent on imposing his will. You do not have to agree with him, you do not have to like him, but it pays to respect him. It is also important to understand that while, in the context of the conflict, the currency of the fight remains fire power, that of the confrontation is information. It is in that theatre, it is with information, that you change people's minds. We must learn to act in the view and the hearing of the parties to the confrontation and to those observing it, so that our narrative is the one they believe to be correct and the one that they follow. We must dictate the narrative. We must learn to operate so as to dislocate the opponent's military actions in the conflict from his measures to achieve his confrontational objectives, while maintaining that essential linkage in our own.

Bearing this in mind, here are my master questions for those engaged in confrontations on Israel's northern border. This might be one way of interpreting the events of 2006 and looking into the future. It might explain some of the assassinations, fighting, bombings and political and diplomatic squabbles that took place in the aftermath of the conflict as people search for the answers to these questions.

Can Israel convert its apparent loss into a win? After all, it has an internationally guaranteed buffer zone. Hezbollah cannot operate as it did before in the south of Lebanon, and the government of Lebanon is now sovereign in its territory. In addition, Hezbollah lost a lot of men and material. How is this best presented so as to enhance Israel's position in its other confrontations, on its other borders?

Can Hezbollah avoid becoming the loser? Can it avoid being blamed by the rest of Lebanon? Will Syria and Iran continue to back it, and to the same degree? Can the government of Lebanon establish a dominant relationship with Hezbollah?

Can UNIFIL collaborate with Lebanon to secure the border? If the relationship between Hezbollah and Lebanon breaks down or is dominated by Hezbollah, can UNIFIL swing the balance in Lebanon's favour? If it breaks down, what is UNIFIL's role? Depending on the party in question, what is the role of military force, and in combination with what other measures can it be used to achieve the objectives that best serve its purpose in these confrontations? As suggested above, you can see this being played out in the period since the conflict, and it still has a long way to go.

Until the shift from the model of industrial war to that of war amongst the people is recognised at these political and strategic levels, and until we start to think about the use of military force accordingly, we will not change our institutions so as to be able to achieve our purpose in our world of continual confrontations in which these conflicts nest. And, more importantly, Israel will not rest in peace.